D1595539

BACH & GOD

BACH & GOD

Michael Marissen

OXFORD
UNIVERSITY PRESS

OXFORD
UNIVERSITY PRESS

Oxford University Press is a department of the University of Oxford. It furthers
the University's objective of excellence in research, scholarship, and education
by publishing worldwide. Oxford is a registered trade mark of Oxford University
Press in the UK and certain other countries.

Published in the United States of America by Oxford University Press
198 Madison Avenue, New York, NY 10016, United States of America.

Library of Congress Cataloging-in-Publication Data
Names: Marissen, Michael, author.
Title: Bach & God / Michael Marissen.
Description: New York : Oxford University Press, [2016] | © 2016 |
Includes bibliographical references and index.
Identifiers: LCCN 2015041101 | ISBN 978-0-19-060695-4 (hardcover : alk. paper)
Subjects: LCSH: Bach, Johann Sebastian, 1685–1750. Cantatas. | Bach, Johann
Sebastian, 1685–1750. Passions. | Bach, Johann Sebastian, 1685–1750.
Musikalisches Opfer. | Bach, Johann Sebastian, 1685–1750.—Criticism and
interpretation. | Bach, Johann Sebastian, 1685–1750.—Religion. | Church
music—Lutheran Church—18th century.
Classification: LCC ML410.B13 M267 2016 | DDC 780.92—dc23
LC record available at http://lccn.loc.gov/2015041101

1 3 5 7 9 8 6 4 2
Printed by Sheridan, USA

for Lauren

CONTENTS

PART IV Religious Expression in Secular
   Chamber Music

PREFACE

As a scholar and lecturer who studies the religious import of Bach's music, I am often chided—or praised—for being a young German Lutheran proselytizer. The fact is, however, that I am neither young nor German, I have never been and most likely never will be Lutheran, and I am wholly uninterested in trying to convert anyone to any particular religious viewpoint. (Not that there is necessarily anything wrong with being young, German, Lutheran, or proselytical.)

What gives me the "right," then, to expound upon Bach and Lutheranism? How did I come to study these subjects?

I grew up in Canada in an immigrant community of poor, uneducated, extremely conservative Dutch Calvinists who fervently sought to practice a separation from the world. They looked upon Lutherans as theological slackers and, just like Roman Catholics, far too interested in worldly pleasures such as art and music.

Thankfully, not all was aesthetically grim. The elderly grandfather of a friend of mine from our small Dutch Calvinist elementary school happened one day to play for us several excerpts from his LP set of Bach's complete organ works, performed by the great German organist Helmut Walcha. We were transfixed. Henceforth, I carefully saved up my farmhand and newspaper route money to buy an old upright piano, and at the age of twelve I started music lessons, likewise at my own expense. Within the year, I applied for and received—they were evidently rather desperate—the job of organist at the town's Lutheran church, a place an entire universe away from our Dutch Calvinist church, even though the two were literally across the street from each other.

Through a miraculous set of circumstances, the extraordinary musician Jan Overduin was a teacher in my Dutch Calvinist high school for a few pivotal years. Pivotal for *me*, that is, because he introduced music—choir only, since bands and orchestras were too expensive and secularistic—into the curriculum. Overduin happened to be a virtuoso organist, and he had recently won several international competitions in Europe. I became a page turner for his concerts, where I had the unspeakable thrill of watching him up close playing the preludes and fugues, trio sonatas, and Lutheran chorale prelude settings by Johann Sebastian Bach that I had first heard in Walcha's magnificent recordings. Overduin also lent me his LPs of Bach church cantatas performed by the Munich Bach Choir and Orchestra under the direction of Karl Richter and by the King's College Choir with the Leonhardt Consort under the direction of Gustav Leonhardt. Who knew, for instance, that the first stanza of the chorale "Wie schön leuchtet der Morgenstern," a hymn I had led the Lutheran congregation many times in singing, could be dressed up into more than *eight minutes* of sublime fourteen-staff polyphony for chorus and an orchestra of strings, horns, and oboes (BWV 1)?

Unusually for my background, I planned to go to college. I wanted to continue studying music. I had intended to venture out completely from my Dutch Calvinist milieu and attend a secular Canadian university, but because of a lark trip to Grand Rapids, Michigan, where I heard a spectacular concert of medieval music performed by faculty and students at Calvin College, I decided to go there instead. I was undeterred by the skepticism of the folks in my congregation back home, one of whom told me, in a heavy Dutch accent, "There is no need to go past high school, and anyway you should not go to that Calvin College, for it is a den of liberal iniquity."

Settled at the college, I was exhilarated to be around so many people interested in music and in books. I was especially influenced by my classes in philosophical aesthetics with Nicholas Wolterstorff and in music history (particularly a whole course on Bach's *Mass in B minor*) with Calvin Stapert. Both professors worked hard and well to instill a seriousness of purpose in their students.

I wanted to study further after those four years, and I went on to graduate school at Washington University in St. Louis, where I was first exposed to the hard-core rigors of traditional Bach research, mostly in German, in a proseminar with Professor Laurence Dreyfus. At the end of that year, Dreyfus and many of the rest of the music history faculty left for other positions, and I was fortunate to be able to switch quickly, with the crucial help of Dreyfus (as my worldly wherewithal was then rather underdeveloped), to Brandeis University. That same year, the relatively junior Bach scholar Eric Chafe had been hired at Brandeis, and he was joined the next year by the internationally renowned senior Bach scholar Robert Lewis Marshall. Chafe introduced me to Luther's writings in a seminar on Bach's church cantatas and Passion settings, and he later hired me as a research assistant to trace tonality patterns and their possible theological relevance in the complete vocal works of Bach. Marshall was the main adviser for my doctoral thesis, on the social significance of the instrumental combinations and of the formal experimentation in Bach's *Brandenburg Concertos*. For one year of its research, I lived in West Berlin, where on account of the terrific music, often including Bach's cantatas, I attended the services at the *Kaiser-Wilhelm-Gedächtnis-Kirche*.

Through my entire education, however, I had remained more or less indifferent to religion in my study of music. It was only after having settled into a teaching job at Swarthmore College (1989–2014) that I became truly interested in Lutheran theology and its relation to Bach. Concerned that my academic music journal articles were being deemed Marxist (for exploring social implications, per se, it seems) by some of my colleagues in the Bach guild, I decided that in order to make proper sense of what I was up to in studying Bach's music, I ought to expand my dissertation into a book that would include a chapter on biblical Lutheran notions of social hierarchies. I was invited to teach a graduate seminar for the fall semester of 1992 in the Music Department at Princeton University, and the subject we settled on was the religious import of Bach's secular instrumental music for the Berlin courts, namely, the *Brandenburg Concertos* and the *Musical Offering*.

After my monograph on the social and religious designs of the *Brandenburg Concertos* and my article on anti-Enlightenment Lutheran sentiment in the *Musical Offering* (the essay that forms chapter 7 in this book) were published a few years later, I came to the attention of the *Internationale Arbeitsgemeinschaft für theologische Bachforschung* (International Working Group for Theological Bach Research), a consortium whose leadership consisted predominantly of orthodox German Lutheran theologians studying Bach's librettos for their theological content. They were highly excited by what I was up to, as it seemed to show, in an easily understandable way, that Bach's *music itself* was Lutheran in character—welcome proof, indeed, for them that "God's Word" need not be logocentric. For this group, I wrote the essay on Bach's church cantatas that forms chapter 1 here, where I argue that Bach's music can make a contribution to a work's plausible meanings that goes beyond setting the words in an aesthetically satisfying manner; the music sometimes puts a *spin* on the text in a way that is readily explainable as orthodox Lutheran in its orientation.

As far as the *Arbeitsgemeinschaft* was concerned, this was terrific. They were further delighted when I published an article in the *New York Times* (chapter 5 in this book) and a monograph on Bach's *St. John Passion* arguing that Bach and his librettist had steered away from theological anti-Judaism in the commentary sections of the oratorio. Now I was their golden boy, and they declared that, thanks to me, they could *at last* "safely" pursue the idea of organizing a conference on the question of religious polemic in Bach.

Many in the *Arbeitsgemeinschaft* were sorely disappointed, and indeed violently angry, then, when I went on to write a detailed conference paper on theological anti-Judaism in Bach's cantata *Schauet doch und sehet* (BWV 46) (chapter 3 here) and a subsequent conference paper on Bach's *St. Matthew Passion* that included a detailed exposé of Luther's heightening in his translation whatever degree of anti-Judaic tendencies there might be in the Greek source text of the Gospel of Matthew (chapter 6 here). What struck my *Arbeitsgemeinschaft* colleagues as further scandal was the fact that my research for these projects had been supported by an *Alexander von Humboldt Stiftung* research fellowship at the (large and overwhelmingly Lutheran) Theological Faculty of the University of Leipzig. It happened that senior theologians at the university during my year in Leipzig had likewise strongly disapproved of the research, repeatedly telling me, several times via purple-faced screaming, that it was absolutely impossible for Luther or for Bach's Lutheran liturgy to have said such and such a thing about Jews. They were utterly unmoved by the historical texts I showed them that obviously did say precisely those very things that they had declared impossible. It was a frustrating year, but on the other hand, I will always remember with great appreciation the excellent renderings of the *Thomanerchor* and the remarkably sensitive sermons delivered by Pastor Christian Wolff at the weekly services of that most venerable of *evangelisch-Lutherische* institutions, the St. Thomas Church.

A few years later, when I was again on sabbatical, I was asked by Oxford University Press to vet the translations of the more than two hundred librettos included within the draft of Richard Jones's revision and translation of Alfred Dürr's classic two-volume survey of the Bach cantatas. This involved, among other things, close consideration of allusions to the wordings of the Luther Bibles in Bach's day and how to capture them properly in English translation.

I collected especially interesting or difficult examples along the way and then wrote up my findings as an essay for a volume in honor of Robin A. Leaver, a much-admired friend and a great scholar of many subjects, not least among them Bach and religion (this is the essay that forms chapter 2 in this book). That work inspired me to go on to produce a book of annotated translations of the Bach oratorio librettos, a project that brought me very much deeper into the arcana of Luther's Bible and his voluminous exegetical writings.

For the spring semester of 2010, I was invited to teach a graduate seminar in the Music Department at the University of Pennsylvania, and the subject we settled on was religious polemic in baroque music. This was mostly devoted to study of Handel's *Messiah*, but we also considered Bach's church cantatas, and some of this material eventually worked its way into the essay that forms chapter 4 here, a study of Luther and Bach's reception of the "synagogue ban" in the Gospel of John.

For the fall semester of 2012, I was invited to be visiting fellow in the *Centre for the Study of Jewish-Christian Relations* at the Woolf Institute in Cambridge, United Kingdom. My duties included delivering a lecture to the graduate students in their program affiliated with the Theology Faculty at the University of Cambridge, and the material addressed in this lecture formed the basis for chapter 4 of this book.

Over the past several decades, I have delivered hundreds of general-public lectures on Bach and Lutheranism, mostly in pre-concert talks for various European and American early-music groups and Bach festivals but also in preservice talks for Lutheran churches blessed with the ability to render Bach's choral music within their liturgies. This has proved an excellent way to test out ideas and interpretations.

The upshot is that although I am not Lutheran and do not have training in biblical or religious studies, I have very much made it my business to inform myself as best as I could in these subject areas.

There is a different but related and possibly somewhat sensitive matter I would like to discuss here in closing.

To those Bach-loving readers who might be concerned that this book will be overly theological, I should spell out that I am presenting merely what I gather is the projected religious import of Bach's vocal and instrumental music. That is to say, I am not weighing religious truth claims. This book is scholarly but not also devotional.

I am interested in religion principally for its explanatory power in understanding Bach's music. I am not at all interested in discussing the theological or spiritual usefulness of Bach's music. I left the Dutch Calvinist fold several decades ago before turning to Methodism, then flirting with Reconstructionist Judaism and more recently becoming an agnostic. Thanks to Bach (and Handel, Haydn, Josquin, Mozart, Schütz, and Zelenka), though, I will probably never be a *comfortable* agnostic. I am well aware that many Christian believers are profoundly wary of potential anti-Christian bias among nonbelievers. I am also well aware that many secular humanists are profoundly wary of religious discussion, since *any* such discussion (even by an agnostic) is by definition, they often say, not "objective."

In this book, I have aimed not so much to be dispassionate as to be thorough and honest. I hope secularists will find the results interesting and illuminating. And if Christian believers happen to find devotional sustenance in the "positive" aspects of the religious discussion, that would be splendid, I should think. But I do hope both sorts of readers, and others, will not gloss over the "negative" aspects.

What many Christian believers and so-called pure aesthetes have in common, I have found over many years of writing and lecturing, is an arguably oversanguine take on what I have presented as the "negative" aspects in Bach and his Lutheranism.

Aesthetes often celebrate the beauty or magnificence of Bach's musical settings and ignore or trivialize his attendant texts. The problem with this, as I see it, is that in Bach, the texts and their musical settings are inextricably linked. Meaning is not exhausted in, or shut out by, musical beauty and magnificence. The words matter.

Christian believers, especially in America and Germany, often celebrate the central truths of the Christianity found in Bach and deny or ignore or sweep under the rug any darker content and contexts of Bach's life and music.

Many devotionally minded writers consider Bach's music for the Lutheran liturgy effectively to be ecumenically compatible with Roman Catholicism, evidently unaware, for example, that Bach's cantata *Gleichwie der Regen und Schnee vom Himmel fällt* (BWV 18) delivers a rather febrile musical setting of the following radically jaundiced text: *Und uns für des Türcken und des Pabsts grausamen Mord und Lästerungen, Wüten und Toben, väterlich behüten. Erhör uns, lieber HErre GOtt!* ("And in the face of the Turk's [that is, of the Muslim's] and the Pope's fierce murderousness and blasphemies, outrages, and rantings, protect us [that is, 'us Lutherans'] in a fatherly manner. Hear us, dear Lord God!").

Other such writers consider Bach's music for the Lutheran liturgy essentially to be friendly to Calvinism, evidently unaware, for example, that as a condition of his employment as a Thomas School teacher and an ordained church musician in Leipzig, Bach on May 13, 1723, signed a document not only affirming the "pure and true doctrines of our [Lutheran] churches" as they are listed in *The Saxon Visitation Articles of 1592–93* to be "*in all aspects* in accordance with Holy Scripture" but also gainsaying the doctrines of "the Calvinists" as "false and unjust," with the further promise that he "would never endorse, or *in any way* defend them." Signing this pledge was not a pro forma matter; all pastors and schoolteachers in Saxony were required to take the oath, and the authorities in Leipzig certainly meant business. Consider, for example, that in 1728, just a few years after Bach took up his post, the pastor of the St. Peter's Church in Leipzig, Adam Bernd, was defrocked for suggesting that Calvinists and Roman

Catholics could receive salvation (that is, without converting to Lutheranism); consider, too, that the Leipzig authorities, in order to discourage Lutheran attendance, barred the city's small Calvinist community (most of whom were French Huguenots) from holding services in German.

The topic of Bach and his Lutheranism's God is nuanced and intricate, and I have sought to explore it in its far-ranging complexity.

CREDITS

The essays included in this volume, all lightly edited and updated, are reprinted here with permission.

A version of chapter 1 originally appeared as "On the Musically Theological in J. S. Bach's Church Cantatas," *Lutheran Quarterly* 16 (2002): 48–64.

A version of chapter 2 originally appeared as "Historically Informed Rendering of the Librettos from Bach's Church Cantatas," in *Music and Theology: Essays in Honor of Robin A. Leaver on His Sixty-Fifth Birthday*, edited by Daniel Zager (Lanham: Scarecrow, 2007), 103–120.

A version of chapter 3 originally appeared as "The Character and Sources of the Anti-Judaism in Bach's Cantata 46," *Harvard Theological Review* 96 (2003): 63–99.

A version of chapter 4 was first written for the volume of essays *Constructions of Judaism and Jewishness in Baroque Music*, edited by Lars Fischer (forthcoming).

A version of chapter 5 originally appeared as "Perspectives on the 'St. John Passion' and the Jews," *New York Times*, Sunday Arts & Leisure section, April 2, 2000; another version appeared as "Bach's St. John Passion and the Jews,"

Yale Institute of Sacred Music—Colloquium Journal: Music, Worship, Arts 4 (2007): 141–143.

A version of chapter 6 originally appeared as "Blood, People, and Crowds in Matthew, Luther, and Bach," *Lutheran Quarterly* 19 (2005): 1–22; an abridgment of this article appeared in *Luther Digest* 16 (2008): 43–45.

A version of chapter 7 originally appeared as "The Theological Character of J. S. Bach's *Musical Offering*," in *Bach-Studies* 2, edited by Daniel R. Melamed (Cambridge: Cambridge University Press, 1995), 85–106.

ACKNOWLEDGMENTS

For providing vital support in my working on these materials, I am grateful for fellowships from the National Endowment for the Humanities, the American Council of Learned Societies, the *Alexander von Humboldt Stiftung*, and the Woolf Institute.

Friends and colleagues who vetted individual chapters are thanked at the start of the notes for those essays.

Many thanks to Suzanne Ryan, editor extraordinaire at Oxford University Press, for her staggering professional acumen. Likewise to her editorial assistant, Andrew Maillet.

For eagle-eyed copyediting, I thank Wendy Keebler; and for marvelous production editing, I thank Rob Wilkinson of Newgen and Louise Karam of Oxford University Press.

For steadfast help and support over many years, I would like to thank my great colleague and great friend Daniel Melamed.

And once again, above all, I thank Lauren Belfer. Once again, she knows the reasons why.

BACH & GOD

Introduction

Bach & God may strike some readers as a rather outré book title.

I had originally planned to call this project *Essaying Bach and Religion*, but the good folks at Oxford University Press, understandably, asked me instead to consider something simple and direct that would be likelier to grab the attention of the more general reader while still resonating with the more academic reader.

So I ought to say up front that this volume is not about Bach the person in some sort of literal partnership with God the biblical deity. Several books have, in fact, been written on this subject, including a recent extended survey by Rick Marschall (who bizarrely—indeed, I should have thought, blasphemously—put forward the claim that "the Creator God allowed His humble servant Johann Sebastian Bach the privilege of transcribing *His music* for a brief season," adding that "*many people* behold Bach's vast lifetime accomplishments as those of a man who took musical *dictation* from the Lord" [my emphasis]).[1]

In my title, the words "Bach" and "God" are used metonymically. By "Bach" I mostly mean "Bach's music," and by "God" I mostly mean "the religious content of Bach's music." Surely no one would

---

1. Rick Marschall, *Johann Sebastian Bach* (Nashville: Thomas Nelson, 2011), 120–121. Nearly every page of this book contains serious factual errors and interpretive lapses. For a recent religiously oriented life-and-works of Bach that is musicologically responsible, see Calvin R. Stapert, *J. S. Bach* (Oxford: Lion Hudson, 2009).

look upon *Bach's Music and the Religious Content of Bach's Music* as a good name for a book. Hence the metonymy.

Even if many might see Bach as some sort of direct collaborator with God, my extensive experience is that most people in their thinking about Bach—laypersons and scholars alike—go to the opposite side of the spectrum and see him as a Great Artist with no truly meaningful ties to religion at all. Yes, Bach did write a lot of liturgical music, but that was only to pay the rent, they say, and in his heart of hearts, all Bach really wanted to do was compose and perform "pure" instrumental music, like the *Brandenburg Concertos*, the *Well-Tempered Clavier*, the *Goldberg Variations*, and the *Art of Fugue*.[2]

Bach's liturgical music, according to that view, was intended only in a trivial sense for the religious edification of its original church audiences. In a properly authentic sense, such repertory was meant—that is to say, such music is just in and of itself designed—ideally for the "purely aesthetic" pleasure of Bach's modern record-collecting and concert-attending audiences. Today we can and should ignore the words in Bach's vocal music, and only in doing so will we be able to approach a True Understanding of the Essential Bach.

My view, though, is that this triumphal-supersessionist-secularist view of Bach's music may well be just another form of interpretive slander and just as likely to be misguided as the extreme view of Bach as amanuensis of God.

In any event, as I indicated in the preface, my interest in writing about Bach and God is not, as some readers may fear or hope, to promote Christianity in general or Lutheranism in particular. (As likewise explained in the preface, I am an agnostic.) What I am interested in is investigating the explanatory power that

---

2. On the possible religious import, for example, of Bach's concertos, however, see Michael Marissen, *The Social and Religious Designs of J. S. Bach's Brandenburg Concertos* (Princeton: Princeton University Press, 1995).

religion does seem to have, after all, for eliciting a greater understanding of Bach's compositions. And so, again, I want to stress that I am principally focused not on Bach's life but on his music. Although I see no reason to doubt that Bach's personal beliefs corresponded more or less to the religious content of his compositions, it is not logically necessary to demonstrate a connection, and so this book does not address biographical questions to any great extent.[3]

If Bach's musical settings of religious poetry bore no relation to its verbal content, one might perhaps rightly claim to essentially understand the repertory by ignoring the words and focusing exclusively on Bach's pitches, rhythms, and tone colors.

But the words do seem to matter. (If they truly did not matter, we might habitually see concert-hall performances of the *St. Matthew Passion* also in December.)

Now, even if all Bach's musical settings ever did was heighten the emotional expression of their texts, one might, to the purpose of better understanding "the music," reasonably feel obligated to study the words and their various contexts.

I suggest in several chapters of this book that there are, however and moreover, vocal works of Bach's in which his musical setting puts a religious spin on its religious text. That is to say, in these especially nuanced and interpretively noteworthy cases, "pure" aesthetic appreciation of Bach's pitches, rhythms, and tone colors would lead to serious *misunderstanding* of the repertory.

---

3. For this reason, incidentally, I will strive to use past-tense verbs whenever Bach the person is the subject of a sentence and present-tense verbs whenever the music of Bach is the subject of a sentence. Thus, I would say, for example, "Bach often employed chromaticism" but that "the *Musical Offering* (BWV 1079) often employs chromaticism." (Compare this with traditional religious discourse, which customarily gives quasi-timeless formulations such as "Paul teaches that Christians should not divorce spouses who are unbelievers" and "the book of Corinthians teaches that Christians should not divorce spouses who are unbelievers," when the former, to be precise, ought to have been given as "Paul taught that Christians should not divorce spouses who are unbelievers.")

Then, as a special category, there are also works of Bach's, as I suggest in several chapters of this book, in which Bach's musical settings may, in fact, more or less only reflect their texts but in which the words have become increasingly difficult to ignore on account of their now generally unwelcome polemical character. I have participated, for example, in many public discussions before concert performances of Bach's *St. John Passion*, and one is often struck at these gatherings by the hollowness of statements from those aesthetes, typically knowing next to nothing about the Bible or Luther and very little about Bach, who say things like "Well, yes, Bach, you know, was a *great* composer, and, ahem, we can, and indeed *should*, simply ignore all that unpleasant talk in the text—which, to be sure, *Bach* didn't write—about 'the Jews' and their shouting for the death of Jesus. . . . Bach's *music*, you know, is *so* magnificent!"

Vocal works are one matter, however prominent they may be among Bach's output. Perhaps most important, methodologically, at least, for the argument of this book, is his repertory often said by aesthetes to be the only music he really wanted to write, the so-called pure instrumental works. It has become standard to speak of Bach's "sacred" as opposed to "secular" repertories, by which is usually meant his (superficially) religious works versus his (evidently) nonreligious works. Strictly speaking, though, the distinction should be between "liturgical" and "secular," as all indications are that both types of music would, justifiably, have been deemed "sacred" or "religious," the one type lodged "in the church" and the other "in the world" (which is what, from its Latin etymology, the word "secular" means). Both the churchly and the worldly realms were wholly God's, and thus both were sacred, according to the orthodox Lutheranism of Bach's day. This is why I thought it crucial to include in this book, deliberately placed at the end, a detailed essaying of the theological nature of Bach's *Musical Offering* (BWV 1079). This is repertory that is widely accepted as representing some of the composer's most sophisticated, rarefied, and "abstract" art for art's sake. My assessment, however, will be that this awe-inspiring collection of secular instrumental music represents Bach & God at its very peak.

To give a quick overview of the specific contents of this volume might be useful. Its seven essays are lightly edited versions of articles that appeared earlier in academic religion journals and elsewhere. The idea in bringing the essays together was to make them more readily available to interested readers, both academic and general. The collection shares the goal of exploring the religious character of "the music itself" in Bach, but each chapter is also meant to be able to work as a stand-alone essay.

Part I concerns basic Lutheran ideas in Bach's cantatas, how they are expressed both textually and musically.

Chapter 1 explores via several detailed examples the notion that Bach's musical settings of church cantata poetry can project significant Lutheran theological meanings that are not identical to those arrived at by simply reading the librettos; that is to say, Bach's music can *interpret*, not only reflect, the words.

Chapter 2 shows via several detailed examples how Bach's cantata librettos and even their musical settings are often seriously misunderstood, including in the "historically informed performance" world, on account of unacquaintance with the specific phraseology and import of the Luther Bibles of Bach's day.

Part II concerns the taking up of Lutheran and biblical anti-Judaism in Bach's church cantatas. This large subject is still understudied and controversial. In my experience, though, the controversy is more of an emotional than an intellectual matter. I argue that religious polemic cannot be attributed simply to interpretation or misinterpretation of the Bible and of Bach; in the New Testament and in Bach's cantatas, traditional theological anti-Judaism is found right there in the plain sense of the texts.

Chapter 3 maintains that Bach's great church cantata *Schauet doch und sehet* (BWV 46) expresses a marked contempt for Judaism,

as it reflects irremediably damningly upon God's purported punishment of Jews for rejecting Jesus as God's Son and Messiah, something explicitly reinforced in the accompanying liturgical prayers
and also in the readings from the first-century historian Josephus's
Jewish War that were rendered within the Leipzig church services
of Bach's day.

Chapter 4 demonstrates via detailed consideration of biblical-
studies literature that Luther was right to translate the Gospel of
John's now controversial *hoi Ioudaioi* as "the Jews" and not as "the
Judeans" or "the Jewish leaders." It goes on to show that some of
Bach's church cantatas straightforwardly share John's and Luther's
severe views of Jews and Judaism, despite vehemently expressed
recent scholarly and devotional claims to the contrary.

Part III is about anti-Judaism *not* being taken up in the commentary sections from Bach's *St. John* and *St. Matthew Passions*.
One might well expect to find the commentary poetry in these
oratorios engaging in traditional anti-Judaism. I suggest that their
reasons for not doing so are essentially liturgical: both of Bach's
Passion settings respect Luther's frequently unheeded advice that
there are welcome times and places in the church year for engaging
such polemic but that the Passion season is not one of them.

Chapter 5 shows that in Bach's *St. John Passion* (unlike in the
church cantatas), all interest in Jewish guilt for the crucifixion
of Jesus is laid aside so that during the Passion season, Bach's
intended Lutheran listeners can be encouraged to focus on their
own sinfulness.

Chapter 6 first argues, via my own original research on the
New Testament, that the Greek text of the Gospel of Matthew
made a meaningful distinction in its Passion narrative between
laos ("the people," that is, historical Israel, the Jews) and *ochloi* ("the crowds," that is, the gatherings of Jews *and* Gentiles
together). Second, it argues, via my own original research on the
character and sources of Luther's Bible translation, that Luther's
rendering of the New Testament obliterated in an anti-Jewish

manner Matthew's distinction between "the people" and "the crowds." And third, it argues, via my own new research on the relevance of Bach's own theological library, that the *St. Matthew Passion*, especially in its commentary on Matthew 27:25, mitigates the anti-Jewish sentiments amplified by Luther's translation of the gospel.

Finally, Part IV aims to show that even Bach's so-called pure instrumental music can share a great deal with his liturgical vocal music in projecting religiosity. Questions of meaning in his secular chamber music need not be deemed somehow fundamentally different from those in his church music. Both types of music warrant being viewed as religious, as opposed to the one being religious and the other secularistic (or, for that matter, to *both* types being at base no more than aesthetically oriented).

Chapter 7 puts forward the view, then, that Bach's *Musical Offering* (BWV 1079) was not, as is often argued, a pro-Enlightenment homage of "abstract" chamber music (that is, of art for art's sake), designed to honor its dedicatee, King Frederick the Great of Prussia, but was a carefully scored defense of anti-Enlightenment Lutheranism, designed primarily, as was all of Bach's music, to honor God.

PART I

Basic Lutheranism
in Cantatas

Chapter 1

On the Musically Theological
in Bach's Cantatas

From informal Internet discussion groups to specialized academic conferences and publications, an ongoing debate has raged on whether J. S. Bach ought to be considered a purely artistic or also a religious figure.[1] A recently formed but now disbanded group of scholars, the *Internationale Arbeitsgemeinschaft für theologische Bachforschung*, made up mostly of German theologians, has made significant contributions toward understanding the religious contexts of Bach's liturgical music.[2] These writers have not entirely captured the attention or respect of the wider world of Bach

---

1. For the academic side, the most influential has been Friedrich Blume, "Umrisse eines neuen Bach-Bildes," *Musica* 16 (1962): 169–176, translated as "Outlines of a New Picture of Bach," *Music and Letters* 44 (1963): 214–227. The most important responses include Alfred Dürr, "Zum Wandel des Bach-Bildes: Zu Friedrich Blumes Mainzer Vortrag," *Musik und Kirche* 32 (1962): 145–152; see also Friedrich Blume, "Antwort von Friedrich Blume," *Musik und Kirche* 32 (1962): 153–156; Friedrich Smend, "Was bleibt? Zu Friedrich Blumes Bach-Bild," *Der Kirchenmusiker* 13 (1962): 178–188; and Gerhard Herz, "Toward a New Image of Bach," *Bach* 1, no. 4 (1970): 9–27, and *Bach* 2, no. 1 (1971): 7–28 (reprinted in *Essays on J. S. Bach* [Ann Arbor: UMI Reseach Press, 1985], 149–184).

2. For a convenient list of the group's main publications, see Daniel R. Melamed and Michael Marissen, *An Introduction to Bach Studies* (New York: Oxford University Press, 1998), 15. For a full bibliography to 1996, see Renate Steiger, ed., *Theologische Bachforschung heute: Dokumentation und Bibliographie der Internationalen Arbeitsgemeinschaft für theologische Bachforschung 1976–1996* (Glienicke and Berlin: Galda and Walch, 1998), 353–445.

scholarship, however, probably at least in part because, with a few exceptions,[3] their work has focused much more on Bach's librettos than on his musical settings of them.[4] Although Canadian musicologist Eric Chafe published a major study that does integrate extensive theological and musical analysis of Bach's liturgical vocal works,[5] advocates of so-called purely aesthetic contemplation have often continued to be quick to criticize any form of theological Bach research. They argue that Bach's role consisted only in giving musical expression to assigned texts;[6] and since it is Bach's first-rate musical settings, not his artistically second-rate cantata librettos, that typically excite modern interest, the verbal content of his vocal works, theological or otherwise, becomes of no real import. Arguments against an exclusively aesthetic approach have occasionally been advanced by appealing to the explanatory power of

3. These exceptions include, for example, Meinrad Walter, *Musik—Sprache des Glaubens: Studien zum geistlichen Vokalwerk Johann Sebastian Bachs* (Frankfurt: Verlag Josef Knecht, 1994); and Renate Steiger, "Methode und Ziel einer musikalischen Hermeneutik im Werke Bachs," *Musik und Kirche* 47 (1977): 209–224.

4. For an example of a remarkably insightful study of Bach's librettos that does not engage his musical settings, see Elke Axmacher, *"Aus Liebe will mein Heiland sterben": Untersuchungen zum Wandel des Passionsverständnisses im frühen 18. Jahrhundert* (Neuhausen-Stuttgart: Hänssler-Verlag, 1984).

5. Eric Chafe, *Tonal Allegory in the Vocal Music of J. S. Bach* (Berkeley and Los Angeles: University of California Press, 1991). For a simpler approach that remains sensitive to theological concerns, see Alfred Dürr, *Die Kantaten von Johann Sebastian Bach* (Munich and Kassel: Deutscher Taschenbuch Verlag and Bärenreiter, 1985); translated and revised by Richard D. P. Jones as *The Cantatas of J. S. Bach: With Their Librettos in German-English Parallel Text* (Oxford and New York: Oxford University Press, 2005).

6. See, for example, David Schulenberg, "'Musical Allegory' Reconsidered: Representation and Imagination in the Baroque," *Journal of Musicology* 12 (1995), 203–239; see also Paul Brainard, "Bach as Theologian?" in *Reflections on the Sacred: A Musicological Perspective*, edited by Paul Brainard (New Haven: Yale Institute of Sacred Music, 1994), 1–7; and Joyce L. Irwin, "Johann Sebastian Bach: A Musician, Not a Theologian," in *Neither Voice nor Heart Alone: German Lutheran Theology of Music in the Age of the Baroque* (New York: Peter Lang, 1993), 141–152.

Lutheran theology for interpreting Bach's secular instrumental music (that is, a repertory in which it is not a matter of text setting).[7] In this chapter, I would like to put forward the notion that Bach's musical settings of church cantata poetry can project theological meanings that are purposefully different from those arrived at by simply reading his librettos.

In so picturing Bach as a sort of musical-religious interpreter, my goal is only to gain a deeper understanding of Bach's compositions. The biographical question of whether Bach himself sincerely held whatever religious views might be projected in his works is a related but somewhat different matter, and it will not be pursued here. My method will deliberately be more suggestive than exhaustive. Rather than seeking a full-blown, unified theory of the theological aspects of Bach's music, I will illustrate a few ways in which theology and composition might be read as interacting, mutually productive forces.

Theological approaches admittedly run the risk of leaving some readers with the feeling that virtually anything could be "demonstrated." For interdisciplinary work, one might prefer philosophy to theology. John Butt, for example, has declared that "God who was central to Bach's life as an active and devout Lutheran is not always the same as the God of his compositional mind. . . . Bach's compositional mind can be illuminated—if it cannot directly be explained—by analogy with the metaphysics of rationalist philosophers of the seventeenth and eighteenth centuries."[8] I fear that

7. See Michael Marissen, *The Social and Religious Designs of J. S. Bach's Brandenburg Concertos* (Princeton: Princeton University Press, 1995); and Michael Marissen, "The Theological Character of J. S. Bach's *Musical Offering*," in *Bach-Studies 2*, edited by Daniel R. Melamed (Cambridge: Cambridge University Press, 1995), 85–106 (reprinted as chapter 7 in this book).

8. John Butt, "Bach's Metaphysics of Music," in *The Cambridge Companion to Bach*, edited by John Butt (Cambridge: Cambridge University Press, 1997), 47; see also, in the same volume, John Butt, "'A Mind Unconscious That It Is Calculating'? Bach and the Rationalist Philosophy of Wolff, Leibniz and Spinoza," 60–71. (Butt himself is, however, by no means unsympathetic to theological concerns.

philosophical approaches to Bach, while intellectually appealing, may involve too many problems of contextual plausibility. Does Bach's thought actually coincide with that of Spinoza and Leibniz? I wonder if the issue is analogous to what Albert Schweitzer had to say about scholars who try to explain the apostle Paul's very Jewish thought primarily on the basis of Hellenism: they are, he says, "like a man who should bring water from a long distance in leaky watering-cans in order to water a garden lying beside a stream."[9]

In any event, there can hardly be any doubt that Bach was familiar with the basic tenets of Lutheran theology. Before he could assume his post as cantor in Leipzig, he had to be tested on his knowledge of Lutheranism as it is systematized in the *Book of Concord* (1580).[10] It is also important to know that Bach owned a large collection of Bible commentaries and sermons,[11] including several sets of Luther's collected German works and the Calov

The question here is one of emphasis.) See also Jeremy Begbie, "Disquieting Conversations: Bach, Modernity, and God," in *Music, Modernity, and God: Essays in Listening* (New York: Oxford University Press, 2013), 41–72.

9. Albert Schweitzer, *The Mysticism of Paul the Apostle* (New York: Seabury, 1968; German orig. 1930), 140; quoted in N. T. Wright, *Christian Origins and the Question of God*, vol. 2, *Jesus and the Victory of God* (Minneapolis: Fortress Press, 1996), 213. That first-century Judaism was more permeated by Hellenism than earlier scholars cared to allow, however, is shown by Martin Hengel, *Judaism and Hellenism: Studies in Their Encounter in Palestine during the Early Hellenistic Period*, translated by John Bowden (Philadelphia: Fortress Press, 1974).

10. Werner Neumann and Hans-Joachim Schulze, eds., *Bach-Dokumente II* (Kassel: Bärenreiter, 1969), no. 134; translation in Christoph Wolff, ed., *The New Bach Reader* (New York: W. W. Norton, 1998), 105. Reference to Bach's knowledge of the "Formula of Concord" (1577, printed in the *Book of Concord*) is found in *Bach-Dokumente II*, no. 136 (not reproduced in *New Bach Reader*), and his knowledge of the "Saxon Visitation Articles" (1592–1593; printed in subsequent editions of the *Book of Concord*) is found in Hans-Joachim Schulze, ed., *Bach-Dokumente III* (Kassel: Bärenreiter, 1972), no. 92a (not in *New Bach Reader*). For a full discussion of the (nontrivial) nature of these theological examinations, see Martin Petzoldt, "Bachs Prüfung vor dem Kurfürstlichen Konsistorium zu Leipzig," *Bach-Jahrbuch* 84 (1998): 19–30.

11. Robin A. Leaver, *Bachs Theologische Bibliothek/Bach's Theological Library* (Neuhausen-Stuttgart: Hänssler-Verlag, 1985). For further comments and

Bible Commentary.[12] Bach's copy of the Calov Bible is now kept at the Concordia Seminary Library in St. Louis, Missouri.[13] Scientific research has determined that the chemical content of the inks in the extensive underlinings in this Bible is the same as that of the many marginal comments whose handwriting characteristics were identified with Bach's by Hans-Joachim Schulze of the Bach-Archiv, Leipzig.[14]

To our examples, then.

The Pastoral and *Meine Seufzer, meine Tränen* (BWV 13)

Grim indeed are the sentiments expressed in the opening aria from Bach's church cantata *Meine Seufzer, meine Tränen* (BWV 13):

Meine Seufzer, meine Tränen	My sighs, my tears
Können nicht zu zählen sein.	are not able to be counted.
Wenn sich täglich Wehmut findet	When melancholy is encountered daily
Und der Jammer[15] nicht verschwindet,	and my misery does not fade away,

some minor revisions, see Johannes Wallman, "Johann Sebastian Bach und die 'Geistlichen Bücher' seiner Bibliothek," *Pietismus und Neuzeit* 12 (1986): 162–181.

12. Abraham Calov, *Die heilige Bibel nach S. Herrn D. Martini Lutheri Deutscher Dolmetschung und Erklärung* (Wittenberg, 1681–1682).

13. For facsimiles of the pages with Bach's notations, see Howard H. Cox, ed., *The Calov Bible of J. S. Bach* (Ann Arbor: UMI Research Press, 1985), 108–393. See also Robin A. Leaver, *J. S. Bach and Scripture: Glosses from the Calov Bible Commentary* (St. Louis: Concordia Publishing House, 1985).

14. Bruce Kusko, "Proton Milloprobe Analysis of the Hand-Penned Annotations in Bach's Calov Bible," in Cox, *Calov Bible*, 31–106.

15. In Bach's own score and separate vocal part, the words *Schmerz noch* ("agony still") replace the librettist's *Jammer* only at bar 42; see Marianne Helms, *Kritischer Bericht* for Johann Sebastian Bach, *Neue Ausgabe sämtlicher Werke*,

Ach! so muß uns diese Pein	ah! then this pain must
Schon[16] den Weg zum Tode	surely set before us the way of
bahnen.	death.[17]

Bach's setting, with its minor mode and pervasive chromaticisms and with its resolute sixteenth-note activity in the oboe part, captures the anxious mood of Georg Christian Lehms's libretto extremely well.

Yet Bach's aria does not wallow in misery. The otherworldly instrumental sonority (two recorders and oboe da caccia[18]) and the instrumental counterpoint (parallel thirds or sixths in duple meter with a triple subdivision of the beat) evoke the Arcadian comfort of the pastoral. The normal way to project the world of the pastoral is, of course, not via the minor mode with chromatic inflections but via the major mode with diatonic harmonies. See, for example, the evocation of Jesus as the Good Shepherd in the aria "Beglückte Herde, Jesu Schafe" from his church cantata *Du Hirte Israel, höre* (BWV 104).[19] In Cantata 13, while Bach's tonality and harmonies express powerfully the surface pessimism of Lehms's poetry, the scoring and counterpoint offer a shepherdly comfort not even hinted at in the aria text, providing an example of what Luther

---

series I, vol. 5, *Kantaten zum Epiphaniasfest bis zum 2. Sonntag nach Epiphanias* (Kassel: Bärenreiter, 1976), 215.

16. In Bach's own score and separate vocal part, the word *nur* ("only") replaces the librettist's *schon* only at bar 46; see Helms, *Kritischer Bericht*, 215.

17. See also Jeremiah 21:8.

18. The first and arguably still the interpretively best recording of Cantata 13 on period instruments, the one directed by Gustav Leonhardt in vol. 4 of Bach's complete church cantatas for Telefunken/Teldec, though listed that way, does not actually feature the oboe da caccia. The true identity of this extraordinary instrument was not discovered until Nikolaus Harnoncourt recorded *Wer weiß, wie nahe mir mein Ende!* (BWV 27) for vol. 7 of the series.

19. For a comprehensive study of Bach and the pastoral, see Renate Steiger, "'Die Welt ist euch ein Himmelreich': Zu J. S. Bachs Deutung des Pastoralen," *Musik und Kirche* 41 (1971): 1–8, 69–79.

would call God's Yes behind his No.[20] It is only later in the cantata, at the soprano recitative, that comfort is made verbally explicit:

Mein Kummer nimmet zu	My affliction gets worse
Und raubt mir alle Ruh,	and robs me of all peace.
Mein Jammerkrug ist ganz	My jar of misery is
Mit Tränen angefüllet.	filled to the brim with tears.
...	...
Doch, Seele, nein,	Yet, soul, no,
Sei nur getrost in deiner Pein:	be only hopeful in your pain:
Gott kann den Wermutsaft	Your wormwood sap God can
Gar leicht in Freudenwein	rather easily change into wine
verkehren	of joy,
Und dir alsdenn viel tausend	and then grant you many
Lust gewähren.	thousand delights.

Lehms's libretto appears to be punning on *weinen* and *Wein*, the initial "tears" wine being transformed into "joy wine" at the end of the recitative. Inspiration for this may have come in part from the gospel reading for the Sunday to which Lehms assigned his poetry[21] (the second after Epiphany), John 2:1–11, the story of Jesus transforming water into wine at a wedding in Cana.[22]

Bach's subtle interpretive strategy of musically though not verbally having projected comfort already in the opening aria agrees to some extent with the commentary on Romans 12:15 in the Olearius Bible Commentary from his personal library (Romans 12:6–16 being the epistle reading for the Second Sunday after

20. See the similar comments on the aria "Ach, mein Sinn" from Bach's *St. John Passion* in Michael Marissen, *Lutheranism, Anti-Judaism, and Bach's St. John Passion* (New York: Oxford University Press, 1998), 17.

21. Georg Christian Lehms, *Gottgefälliges Kirchen-Opffer* (Darmstadt, 1711), 17–18.

22. See also Steiger, "'Die Welt ist euch ein Himmelreich,'" 76. Such sentiments are clearly expressed in Bach's church cantata *Ich hatte viel bekümmernis* (BWV 21/10): "Verwandle dich, *Weinen*, in lauteren *Wein!* / Es wird nur mein Achzen in Jauchzen mir sein" (my emphasis: "Transform yourself, weeping/*whining*, into pure *wine*! / My *moaning* will now become *singing* to me").

Epiphany): "*Weeps* . . . NB. Weeping is a routine of reasonable souls, whereby sadness is displayed. Thence it is also the case that the tears of those who weep are various. For it may even happen that one by chance can shed tears of joy (like Jacob in Genesis 29:11, and Joseph in Genesis 43:30 and 46:29), in that one at the same time considers evil and good; and in that one is glad about the present good and at the same time ponders the former, overcome misfortune."[23]

Justification by Faith and *Es ist das Heil uns kommen her* (BWV 9)

On the face of it, the following text from Bach's church cantata *Es ist das Heil uns kommen her* (BWV 9)—wanting in poetic inspiration, teeming in theological doctrine—hardly seems to cry out for music:

Herr, du siehst statt	Lord, you look, rather than at
guter Werke	good works,
Auf des Herzens	at the heart's strength
Glaubensstärke,	of faith;
Nur den Glauben nimmst du an.	you accept only faith.
Nur der Glaube macht gerecht,	Only faith renders [us] just,
Alles andre scheint zu	all else shines forth[24] too
schlecht,	poorly
Als daß es uns helfen kann.	to be able to help us.

    Bach managed, however, to turn out a musical setting of phenomenal beauty, outdoing himself in generating line after line

---

23. Johann Olearius, *Biblische Erklärung, Darinnen, nechst dem allgemeinen Haupt-Schlüssel der gantzen heiligen Schrifft* (Leipzig, 1678–1681), 5:1118.

24. See also Wisdom of Solomon 3:7 and Matthew 13:43.

of beguiling melody. All the more astounding is the fact that his instrumental pair largely proceeds in canon at the fifth while his vocal pair is also canonic, proceeding likewise at the fifth.

As if the challenges of writing in double canon here and there in the A section of this da capo aria were not formidable enough, Bach in the B section occasionally changed the interval between the canonic entries from the fifth to the fourth (see bars 108, 116, and 124); that is, here the music had to be written in such a way that the first two bars of the initial voice in a new canonic line at the fourth sounds melodically satisfying and harmonizes with the last two bars of the answering voice from the previous canonic line at the fifth and in such a way that the move from the last note in the answering voice at the fifth proceeds smoothly to the first note of the new answer at the fourth.

On first hearing this duet, I was haunted by the opening theme's elusive familiarity. Soon after, listening to the chorale that has come to be performed with Bach's motet *Der Geist hilft unser Schwachheit auf* (BWV 226), I stumbled upon the melodic resemblance between the cantata duet and the chorale "Komm, Heiliger Geist," a prayer to the Holy Spirit for regeneration and hymn of praise[25] (see example 1):

Komm, Heiliger Geist,	Come, Holy Spirit, Lord
Herre Gott,	God.
Erfüll mit deiner Gnaden Gut	Fill with your treasure of grace
Deiner Gläubigen Herz, Mut	the heart, will, and mind of yours
und Sinn.	in the faith.

25. The melodic allusion, it turns out, is also noted by Friedrich Smend, *Johann Sebastian Bach: Kirchen-Kantaten* (Berlin: Christlicher Zeitschriftenverlag, 1947–1949), 2:36–37. Smend sees further allusions to several other chorales elsewhere in Cantata 9, connections I consider coincidental or musically rather unconvincing. It should perhaps be mentioned that the chorale "O Gottes Geist, mein Trost und Rat," sung to the same melody as "Komm, Heiliger Geist," likewise concerns the Holy Spirit.

Dein brünstig Lieb entzünd in ihn'n.	Your ardent love inflame in them.
O Herr, durch deines Lichtes Glanz	O Lord, [you who] through your light's brilliance
Zu dem Glauben versammlet hast	to faith has gathered
Das Volk aus aller Welt Zungen;	people from all the world's tongues—
Das sei dir, Herr, zu Lob gesungen.	for that, Lord, may laud be sung to you.
Alleluja, alleluja.	Alleluia, alleluia.

EXAMPLE 1

Opening phrase of chorale "Komm, Heiliger Geist" with opening phrase of aria "Herr, du siehst statt guter Werke" (BWV 9).

Komm,   hei - li - ger___   Geist

Before drawing interpretive conclusions about Bach's musical setting of the aria, let us consider some doctrinal background. Bach, of course, knew about the ideas on justification put forth by Luther's followers in the *Book of Concord*,[26] and more direct documentation of Bach's familiarity with the subject can be found, for example, in his having highlighted within his Calov Bible Commentary a part of the interpolated commentary on Romans 1:16–17 (verses that are commonly regarded as the central theme of the epistle): "The main cause of blessedness is God whose word and power is the gospel,

26. See note 10.

as the means of blessedness. The effective cause however is Christ; the means on our side is faith which embraces the righteousness of Christ revealed in the gospel which alone belongs to faith. He who is thus vindicated is a sinful man who believes in Christ. The form is the righteousness of Christ which is imputed to us through faith. The final cause is life and eternal blessedness."[27]

Lutheranism never tired of asserting that only Jesus's imputed righteousness can bring about salvation. Robin Leaver sums it up aptly: "Luther will tenaciously hold on to the doctrine [of justification], because if it is overthrown, it would mean that Jesus Christ had been wasting His time on the cross."[28]

As it happens, almost all the essential aspects of the doctrine are laid out in the (sermonic) libretto of Bach's Cantata 9: Jesus has come as mediator, that is, before God the Father (opening chorus); humans were incapable of keeping God's law (first recitative and tenor aria); and so Jesus came to fulfill the law, and his death makes it possible for people to come before God the Father's wrath protected by their trust in Jesus (second recitative); faith, not good works, brings about salvation (duet); after they have recognized their sin from the law, people can find comfort in the gospel, and they need not fear death (third recitative); people should not be troubled if it seems as though God is not with them, for the essence of faith is in things unseen (closing chorale).[29]

The only basic doctrinal aspects missing from the libretto are that Christian faith is a gift from the Holy Spirit and that the fruits of faith, good works—though unnecessary in the sense that they

27. Calov, *Die heilige Bibel*, 6:19; translation taken from Cox, *Calov Bible*, 449–450. Calov earlier on this page makes harsh statements, not highlighted by Bach, about the faithlessness of Jews and their eternal ruin.

28. Robin A. Leaver, *Luther on Justification* (St. Louis: Concordia Publishing House, 1975), 23–24.

29. The libretto quotes stanzas 1 and 12 literally and paraphrases stanzas 2–9 and 11 of Paul Speratus's "Es ist das Heil uns kommen her" (1523), a fourteen-stanza chorale devoted to the subject of justification.

cannot bring about salvation—are necessary in the sense that they are commanded by God[30] and in that they act as testimonies of the Holy Spirit's presence and indwelling.

Bach's musical setting appears to provide the doctrinal aspects missing from the libretto of Cantata 9.[31] This happens in ways that are perhaps not immediately obvious but are easy enough to hear if pointed out. The chorale allusion in the canonic duet conjures up both the notion that it is the Holy Spirit who gathers people to faith (chorale "Komm Heiliger Geist," first stanza, lines 5–8) and the notion that sinners, already justified, need the Holy Spirit to do God's ongoing work of sanctification ("Komm Heiliger Geist," lines 1–4). Canonic writing has associations with law in Bach,[32] and there is a certain Lutheran elegance in Bach's having set uncommonly beautiful, carefree-sounding melodies to such severe forms of counterpoint in Cantata 9. It is as if to say that law and gospel, good works and grace through faith, are inextricably bound up with each other, though they remain distinct. The Lutheranism of Bach's music apparently contends that justified sinners are not to put the law behind them. Regeneration is always incomplete in the present world, and the children of God are still to be guided by the law of God. If the musical setting of the opening aria from Cantata 13 can be understood to express God's Yes behind a No, the setting of the duet from Cantata 9 may express God's No behind a Yes.

An Inverted World

One of the most peculiar movements in Bach's output is the aria "Wie jammern mich doch die verkehrten Herzen" from his church cantata *Vergnügte Ruh, beliebte Seelenlust* (BWV 170). Having

---

30. On this point, see the bass recitative from Bach's church cantata *Wer da gläubet und getauft wird* (BWV 37).

31. These are to be found in stanzas 10 and 13 of Speratus's chorale (see note 29).

32. See Marissen, "The Theological Character," 98–105 (chapter 7 in this book).

gloriously depicted the peace and contentment of heaven in the opening movement, this second aria comments as follows on the intervening recitative's condemnation of the evil and perversity of the present world:

Wie jammern mich doch die verkehrten Herzen,	How I surely pity the froward hearts
Die dir, mein Gott, so sehr zuwider sein;	that toward you, my God, are so very contrary.
Ich zittre recht und fühle tausend Schmerzen,	I truly tremble and feel a thousand agonies,
Wenn sie nur an Rach und Haß erfreun.	when all they do is delight in vengeance and hate.
Gerechter Gott, was magst du doch gedenken,	Righteous God, what would you but have to contemplate,
Wenn sie allein mit rechten Satansränken	when they with truly satanic machinations
Dein scharfes Strafgebot so frech verlacht.	so boldly only laugh at your strict decree of punishment.
Ach! ohne Zweifel hast du so gedacht:	Ah! without a doubt you have thus thought:
Wie jammern mich doch die verkehrten Herzen!	"How I surely pity the froward hearts"!

With its slow tempo, F-sharp minor tonality, pervasive dissonances, and so on, Bach's musical setting fittingly plumbs the depths of the libretto's torment. Some commentators take notice also of Bach's unusual instrumental scoring: three-part counterpoint consisting of a lower line for violins and viola in unison and two upper lines for organ obbligato. Alfred Dürr, for example, suggestively argues that the absence of a proper basso continuo is most likely intentional on Bach's part; the basso continuo is a sort of fundament, and its absence can symbolize either that a Godly foothold is not needed (as, for example, in the aria "Aus Liebe will mein Heiland sterben" from Bach's *St. Matthew Passion*) or that such a foothold has been lost (for example, as here in Cantata 170 and in the aria "Wie zittern und wanken der Sünder Gedanken" from Bach's church cantata *Herr, gehe nicht ins Gericht mit deinem Knecht* [BWV 105]).[33]

Bach's instrumental scoring deserves still closer consideration. The rhythmic activity in the organ lines is typically twice and often four times as great as in the unison strings line. Such textural stratification is rather unusual in Bach, and so this heightened contrast between the upper and lower lines surely commands our attention. Much more than an extreme instrumental contrast, what Bach's music, in fact, sets up here is a *reversal*: criss-crossing, highly expressive lines that have very much the look of solo violin parts were assigned, by the marking *à 2 Clav.* ("for two manuals"), to the large church organ; and a simple, stolid, continuo-like line that has very much the look of a pedals-only organ part was assigned to the upper strings of Bach's ensemble, *in unisono*. For Bach, it would have been a straightforward affair to arrange this aria "properly" by transposing the organ lines as violin parts and by shifting the strings line into the lower octave for organ and furnishing it with continuo figures.[34]

---

33. Dürr, *The Cantatas of J. S. Bach*, 435.

34. For a convenient, brief explanation of Bach's various pitch standards for keyboard, orchestral, and vocal parts, see Melamed and Marissen, *Introduction to Bach Studies*, 142–145. For more on the notion of meaningful reversals of scoring in Bach, see Marissen, *The Social and Religious Designs*. Hans-Joachim Schulze, "Bach in the Early Twenty-first Century," in *The Worlds of Johann Sebastian Bach*, edited by Raymond Erickson (Milwaukee: Amadeus Press, 2009), 297–98, oddly deems this study of Bach's concertos an example of the "types of interpretation [that involve] The Search for Hidden Meanings." (There is, however, in *The Social and Religious Designs* no hint of any search for "*hidden* meanings.") Schulze notes the case in point of the sixth concerto, whose scoring, he says, "[Marissen interprets] as candid criticism of the conditions at the Anhalt-Cöthen court." (There is, however, in *The Social and Religious Designs* no suggestion that the sixth concerto is to be interpreted as criticism of the conditions at the Anhalt-Cöthen court.) Schulze goes on to state that for this concerto, Bach was only following a scoring convention of the previous century. (In fact, however, virtuoso violas accompanied by rudimentary

This aria's curious reversal in scoring may be associated with the time-honored theme of the World Upside Down. The *mundus inversus*—in German, *verkehrte Welt*—has appeared in all cultures in a wide variety of forms.[35] In visual representations, for example, a castle or city hovers above the clouds, a sheep protects the flock of humans grazing in a meadow, a servant rides on horseback while the nobleman has to go behind him on foot, a mouse chases the cat, and so on.

The theme of inversion also plays a significant part in Jewish and Christian biblical writings, often proposing messianic or utopian situations in which the present disordered world will be upended.[36] For example, the statement "all who exalt themselves will be humbled, but all who humble themselves will be exalted" appears frequently in the New Testament[37] (and Bach's powerful, verbatim setting of it appears in the opening chorus from Cantata 47, *Wer sich selbst erhöhet, der soll erniedriget werden*; see also Bach's

gambas was never conventional.) In his wrap-up, Schulze suggests that "[more recent research] showing that Bach was merely perpetuating a scoring convention of the seventeenth century . . . in turn, has led to a disillusionment with such types of interpretation [as were put forward in Marissen's book]." The research cited as having shown that Bach was simply in keeping with earlier convention is Ares Rolf, "Die Besetzung des sechsten Brandenburgischen Konzerts," *Bach-Jahrbuch* 84 (1998): 171–181; see also Ares Rolf, *J. S. Bach, Das sechste Brandenburgische Konzert: Besetzung, Analyse, Entstehung* (Dortmund: Klangfarben Musikverlag, 2002), 25–41, 145–168. The disillusionment Schulze speaks of appears to have been unwarranted, as it happens that Bach's treatment of the instruments in the Sixth Brandenburg Concerto radically differs from all of the seventeenth-century musical examples provided in Rolf's two studies.

35. See Michael Kuper, "Zur Topographie der verkehrten Welt," in *Zur Semiotik der Inversion* (Berlin: Verlag für Wissenschaft und Bildung, 1993), 10–18; David Kunzle, "World Upside Down: The Iconography of a European Broadsheet Type," in *The Reversible World: Symbolic Inversion in Art and Society*, edited by Barbara A. Hancock (Ithaca: Cornell University Press, 1978), 39–94.

36. See Raymond C. Van Leeuwen, "Proverbs 30:21–23 and the Biblical World Upside Down," *Journal of Biblical Literature* 105 (1986): 599–610; and Robert W. Scribner, *For the Sake of Simple Folk: Popular Propaganda for the German Reformation* (Oxford: Clarendon Press, 1994), 164.

37. For a discussion of rabbinic parallels, see Geza Vermes, *The Religion of Jesus the Jew* (Minneapolis: Fortress Press, 1993), 80.

settings of the *Magnificat*). Status reversal is said by various New Testament authors to characterize the Kingdom of God.[38]

Consequently, in religious usage, symbolic inversion can be extreme. While particular examples may seem humorous on the surface (depending on one's point of view), the underlying intent can be very serious. Especially striking examples of this are found in the woodcuts that Luther and his early followers produced to spread Reformation ideas.[39] All the major elements appear in Luther's own wildly polemical series, the *Depiction of the Papacy* (1545).[40] Robert Scribner helpfully analyzes the woodcut *Adoratur Papa Deus Terrenus* ("The Pope Is Adored as an Earthly God") from this collection as follows (see Figure 1):[41]

> [In this picture, the] crossed papal keys have been replaced by a pair of jemmies, which the Germans call "thieves' keys." The papal tiara which should be above the shield has been inverted, and a German mercenary soldier, a *Landsknecht*, defecates into it. Two others adjust their dress after having done the same. The Latin title states satirically: "The pope is adored as an earthly god." The German inscription comments that the pope has treated the kingdom of Christ as the pope's crown is treated here. But do not despair, it continues, for God has promised comfort through his spirit. A reference to Apocalypse 18 [that is, the final book in the New Testament] shows what that comfort is to be: the proclamation that Babylon has been overthrown, that is, that the

---

38. See, for example, Matthew 18:4, 20:26–27, 23:11–12; Mark 9:35, 10:42–44; Luke 9:48, 14:11, 18:14, 22:26; Philippians 2:5–11; James 4:4–10; 1 Peter 5:5.

39. See the fascinating discussion by Scribner, *For the Sake of Simple Folk*, 163–189.

40. Martin Luther, "Abbildung des Pabsttums (1545)," in *D. Martin Luthers Werke: Kritische Gesamtausgabe*, vol. 54, edited by O. Clemen and J. Luther, 346–373 (Weimar: Böhlau, 1928), this illustration (no. 11) at p. [542].

41. Scribner, *For the Sake of Simple Folk*, 81–82.

ADORATVR PAPA DEVS TERRENVS.

𝕭apſt hat dem reich Chriſti gethon
𝕸ie man hie handelt ſeine Cron.
𝕸achts jr zweifeltig: ſpricht der geiſt Apoc.18.
𝕾chenckt getroſt ein: Gott iſts ders heiſt.
𝕸art: Luth: D.

11. Adoratur Papa Deus Terrenus.
("Tiara".) Brieg, Gymnaſialbibliothek.

FIGURE 1

"Adoratur Papa Deus Terrenus," from Martin Luther, *Depiction of the Papacy* (1545).

downfall of the papacy [indeed, the end of the world][42] is at hand. . . . The written text adds two varying messages to the visual message. The German text provides a quasi-doctrinal

42. That Luther's various polemics in part reflect a belief that he was living in the end times is argued in great detail by Heiko A. Oberman, *The Roots of Anti-Semitism in the Age of Renaissance and Reformation*, translated by James I. Porter (Philadelphia: Fortress Press, 1984).

commentary; the Latin title, however, captures the wood-cut's intention more closely: it is an ironic inversion.

In the context of religious symbolic inversion, then, Bach's strange scoring in Cantata 170 could be understood to extend substantially the meaning of Lehms's aria text. While Lehms's poetry depicts only this-worldly despair, Bach's musical setting, by virtue of its extreme World Upside Down scoring, inspirits also next-worldly comfort.

As a second example of the *mundus inversus*, let us briefly consider the duet from Bach's church cantata *Wer nur den lieben Gott läßt walten* (BWV 93). Bach lovers tend to be familiar not with the cantata movement but with its arrangement for solo organ as the Schübler chorale *Wer nur den lieben Gott läßt walten* (BWV 647). When, for example, I played recordings of the two versions in a lecture for a Philadelphia meeting of the American Guild of Organists, many in the audience registered great surprise at Bach's scoring in the cantata. They altogether reasonably assumed that the two soprano lines of the right-hand part in the organ version originated in a standard treble scoring for strings or woodwinds and that the chorale line of the pedal part (designated in the four-foot range) originated in a single vocal line, more or less corresponding to the situation for the extremely well-known fourth movement from Bach's church cantata *Wachet auf, ruft uns die Stimme* (BWV 140) and its arrangement in the Schübler chorales (BWV 645). The situation in Cantata 93 turns out to be exactly the reverse: to the unaltered, well-known words of the fourth chorale stanza, the singers render various quasi-"instrumental" interludes, and word-lessly in unison the violins and viola "sing" in longer note values the phrase-by-phrase entries of the chorale melody.[43]

43. Instrumental renderings of chorale melodies are not so unusual in the Bach cantata repertory. It is unusual, however, to find chorale poetry sung verbatim to new or varied melodic material while instruments alone provide the corresponding chorale melody in longer note values. For another example of this sort of reversal, see the duet from Bach's church cantata *Meine Seele erhebt den Herren* (BWV 10). Compare also the fourth movement from *Lobe den Herren, den mächtigen König der Ehren* (BWV 137) and the opening movements from *Wär Gott nicht mit uns diese Zeit* (BWV 14) and *Ein feste Burg ist unser Gott* (BWV 80).

The text of the employed chorale stanza reads as follows:

Er kennt die rechten Freudenstunden,	He knows the right times for joy,
Er weiß wohl, wenn es nützlich sei;	he knows well, when it may be beneficial;
Wenn er uns nur hat treu erfunden	if he only has found us faithful
Und merket keine Heuchelei,	and notes no hypocrisy,
So kömmt Gott, eh wir uns versehn,	then God comes, before we are aware of it,
Und lässet uns viel Guts geschehn.	and lets much good happen to us.

With the miniature *mundus inversus* of this cantata duet, Bach's music appears to be deliberately working against human expectations, as if, again, to give expression to the idea that God's heavenly ways do not correspond to humans' earthly ways.

Such ideas are readily found in the sermon literature from Bach's library. Bach owned two copies of Luther's *Hauspostille*,[44] a collection of sermons on the biblical readings specified for the various Sundays and festivals of the church year in the Lutheran liturgy. The sermon for the Fifth Sunday after Trinity (the Sunday for which Cantata 93 was written), based on the gospel reading of Luke 5:1–11,[45] contains the following illuminating passage (my emphasis):

We are commanded ... to wait patiently for success, and God's blessing shall be experienced in due time.... [Peter]

44. Wolff, *New Bach Reader*, 253–254. The *Hauspostille* was issued in the sixteenth century in two somewhat different versions, one edited by Veit Dietrich and the other by Georg Rörer. Both were frequently reprinted, and, as Robin Leaver points out, the fact that Bach owned two copies of the *Hauspostille* suggests that he had both versions; see Robin Leaver, "Bach's Understanding and Use of the Epistles and Gospels of the Church Year," *Bach* 6, no. 4 (1975): 5.

45. The gospel reports that after his disciples had caught no fish all night, Jesus tells them the next day to go out to sea and cast their nets; their ships nearly sink from the massive intake.

must have had a pious heart, that he so subdued his natural inclinations and held firmly to the Word of Christ. Here
as under many other circumstances the commands and
dealings of God seem to our reason to be all wrong or even
foolish. The best time for catching fishes is ordinarily not
mid-day, but night. Neither is it the custom of fishermen to
launch out into the deep, that is, in the midst of the sea, but
they remain near the shore, for they well know that here
many fish are to be found. *This is reversed by the Savior.*[46]

Conclusion

It seems from these selected church cantata examples, then, that
we might not be fully appreciating Bach's output if we take him
simply or essentially to be a supplier of pitches, rhythms, and tone
colors, however marvelous or magnificent these rich aspects of his
works may indeed be. Likewise, we might not fully appreciate the
range of plausible meanings projected by Bach's works if we simply
analyze the verbal content of his librettos. Accepting the idea that
Bach's musical settings can theologically expand upon and interpret his librettos need not involve downplaying the aesthetic splendor of his works. I would like to suggest, moreover, that insisting
on exclusively aesthetic contemplation of Bach's music potentially
diminishes its meanings and actually reduces its stature.

46. Martin Luther, "Fifth Sunday after Trinity," in *Dr. Martin Luther's House-Postil*,
vol. 3, edited by Matthias Loy, translated by E. Schmid (Columbus: J. A. Schulze,
1884), 123 (this is the Dietrich version of the *Hauspostille*); Martin Luther, "Am
Fünfften Sontag nach der Trifeltigkeyt—Evangelion Luce 5," in *D. Martin Luthers
Werke: Kritische Gesamtausgabe*, vol. 52, *Hauspostille*, edited by Georg Buchwald
(Weimar: Böhlau, 1915), 399.

Chapter 2

Historically Informed Readings
of the Librettos from Bach's Cantatas

Neither traditional Bach scholarship nor historically informed performance has generally given enough attention to an essential problem: what do the German texts that Bach set in his church cantatas actually mean? When preparing English translations, of course, this question cannot properly be ignored, and historical work in religion, Bible, and language can provide well-founded answers. I propose here new findings in five categories: (1) where the text seems straightforward but has a different meaning when viewed biblically, (2) where the text assumes specific biblical knowledge on the part of the listener to complete its thought, (3) where the text assumes specific knowledge of Lutheran theology, (4) where the text contains archaic language, and (5) where the text may on the face of it seem well nigh impossible to understand.

Meanings Made Clear by Biblical References

For a first example, consider the following italicized passage in the bass recitative from Bach's Cantata 122, *Das neugeborne Kindelein:*

Dies ist ein Tag, den selbst der Herr gemacht,
Der seinen Sohn in diese Welt gebracht.
O selge Zeit, die nun erfüllt!

O gläubigs Warten, das nunmehr gestillt!
O Glaube, der sein Ende sieht!
O Liebe, die Gott zu sich zieht!
O Freudigkeit, so durch die Trübsal dringt
Und Gott der Lippen Opfer bringt!

TERRY[1] (1926)
O love, enter in God's light!

DRINKER[2] (1942)
Oh staunchness, to God and
    His will!

HARNONCOURT, CD[3] (1982)
Oh staunchness, to God and
    His will!

AMBROSE[4] (1984)
O love here, which doth draw
    God nigh!

HERREWEGHE, CD[5] (1996)
O love, that God has accepted!

UNGER[6] (1996)
O love, which God to itself
    draws!

---

1. Charles Sanford Terry, *Joh. Seb. Bach: Cantata Texts, Sacred and Secular; with a Reconstruction of the Leipzig Liturgy of His Period* (London: Constable, 1926).

2. Henry S. Drinker, *Texts of the Choral Works of Johann Sebastian Bach in English Translation* (New York: Association of American Colleges, Arts Program, 1942–1943). On the whole, neither Terry's nor Drinker's translation promotes historically informed understanding of the librettos that Bach set to music. Drinker's intent was to make acceptable singing translations, not to convey essentially literal meanings to listeners following the German; nonetheless, many early-music recordings have adopted his readings for their CD booklets.

3. Teldec 242609. Record companies often claim historical "authenticity" for their productions. For convenience, I have identified recordings by their conductors, but this is not meant to suggest that conductors always have control over all aspects of their recordings, including the libretto translations.

4. Z. Philip Ambrose, trans., *The Texts to Johann Sebastian Bach's Church Cantatas* (Neuhausen-Stuttgart: Hänssler-Verlag, 1984).

5. Harmonia mundi France 901594.

6. Melvin P. Unger, *Handbook to Bach's Sacred Cantata Texts* (Lanham: Scarecrow Press, 1996). This is by far the best translation of the librettos from Bach's cantatas.

STOKES[7] (1999)
O Love, that draws God
    to itself!

KOOPMAN, CD[8] (2003)
O love here, which doth
    draw God nigh!

MILNES, CD[9] (2008)
O love, which draws God
    to itself!

KUIJKEN, CD[10] (2010)
O love here, which doth
    draw God nigh!

For Cantata 122, our translators agree that the bass recitative speaks of love that draws God to itself. On solely grammatical grounds, however, the thought could just as easily be that the "drawing" is being performed by "God," not by "love." From a Lutheran theological perspective—where God initiates, people respond—this is more likely to be the intended reading, seeing that the biblical passage it presumably alludes to, Jeremiah 31:3, says in the Luther Bibles of Bach's day:[11]

> Der HErr ist mir erschienen von fernen: Ich [*Gott*] habe dich je und je *geliebet*, darum hab ich dich *zu mir gezogen* aus lauter Güte.

> The LORD has appeared to me from afar: "I [that is, *God*] have *loved* you forever and ever; therefore have I *drawn* you *to me* out of pure kindness."

Thus, the Cantata 122 passage should probably best be rendered, "O love which God draws to himself."

7. Richard Stokes, trans., *Johann Sebastian Bach: The Complete Church and Secular Cantatas* (Ebrington: Long Barn Books, 1999).

8. Challenge Classics 72213.

9. Atma Classique 2403.

10. Accent 25314.

11. Allusion noted in Ulrich Meyer, *Biblical Quotation and Allusion in the Cantata Libretti of Johann Sebastian Bach* (Lanham: Scarecrow Press, 1997), 15. See also John 6:44. This does not, however, make for good poetry: in the surrounding lines, it is the noun at the beginning of the line that initiates the action.

As a second, more involved example, consider the alto aria from Cantata 12, *Weinen, Klagen, Sorgen, Zagen*.

Kreuz und Kronen[12] *sind verbunden,*
Kampf und Kleinod sind vereint.
Christen haben alle Stunden
Ihre Qual und ihren Feind,
Doch ihr Trost sind Christi Wunden.

TERRY (1926)
Cross and crown are one
    together,
only striving victory gives.

DRINKER (1942)
Cross and Crown are bound
    together,
palm and war together go.
[*or* palm and battle gether go.]

LEONHARDT, CD[13] (1971)
Cross and crown are joined
    together,
struggle and gem are united.

AMBROSE (1984)
Cross and crown are joined
    together,
gem and conflict are made one.

KOOPMAN, CD[14] (1995)
Cross and crown are joined
    together,
struggle and gem are united.

THOMAS, CD[15] (1995)
Cross and crown are joined
    together,
conflict and gem are combined.

12. This text has traditionally been given in editions and thus in many performances not as *Kronen* (plural) but as *Krone* (singular). Transcribing the text from Bach's original score (http://www.bach-digital.de/receive/BachDigitalSource_source_00000876) and his separate performing part (http://www.bach-digital.de/receive/BachDigitalSource_source_00002443), I read the following: *Creutz und Krohnen* [sometimes *X. und Krohnen*] *sind verbunden, Kampf u. Kleinod* [sometimes *Kampf und Kleinod*] *sind vereint.* As it happens, though, the aria's biblical-theological import will be basically unaffected by whether this particular noun is singular or plural.

13. Teldec 2425000.

14. Erato 0630–12598.

15. Koch 3–7332–2H1.

SUZUKI, CD[16] (1996)
Cross and crown are linked
together,
struggle and jewel are united.

UNGER (1996)
Cross and crown are tied
together,
battle and treasure are united.

STOKES (1999)
Cross and crown are bound
together,
conflict and jewel are united.

JUNGHÄNEL, CD[17] (2000)
Cross and crown [German
here, *Kronen*] are joined
together,
struggle and gem are united.

CLEOBURY, CD[18] (2000)
Cross and crown are joined
together,
struggle and gem are united.

RIFKIN, CD[19] (2001)
Cross and crown [German
here, *Kronen*] are bound
together,
struggle and the jewel are one.

GARDINER, CD[20] (2005)
Cross and crown are bound
together,
conflict and jewel are united.

HERREWHEGE, CD[21] (2005)
Cross and crown [German here
in booklet, *Kronen*; but in performance, *Krone*] are joined
together,
struggle and gem are united.

16. BIS 791.

17. Harmonia mundi France 901694.

18. EMI 56994.

19. Dorian 93231.

20. SDG 107.

21. Harmonia mundi France 901843.

PURCELL QUARTET, CD[22] (2007)
Cross and crown [German
  here in booklet, *Kronen*; but
  in performance, *Krone*] are
  closely bound,
strife and jewel are the same.

HENGELBROCK, CD[23] (2009)
Cross and crown [German here,
  Kronen] are joined together,
gem and conflict are made one.

KUIJKEN, CD[24] (2010)
Cross and crown are joined
  together,
struggle and gem are united.

Each translation makes good Lutheran sense of the first line, but what does it mean to say that "conflict and jewel are united"? That one can win valuable booty in war? To get a better sense of the meaning of the second line, we can turn to Luther's rendering of 1 Corinthians 9:24–25.[25]

> Wisset ihr nicht, daß die, so in den Schranken laufen, die laufen alle, aber Einer erlanget das *Kleinod*? Laufet nun also, daß ihr es ergreifet. Ein jeglicher aber, der da *kämpfet*, enthält sich alles Dinges: jene also, daß sie eine vergängliche *Krone* empfangen; Wir aber eine unvergängliche.

> Do you not know that they who run in the course, run all; but one gets the *[prize] medal*? Now then, run, that you may obtain it. But each man who *competes*, abstains from all things: those men [will exercise this self-control], then, that they may receive a perishable *crown* [that is, a victory wreath]; but we [abstain so that we may receive] an imperishable one.

22. Chandos 0742.

23. Deutsche harmonia mundi 88697526842.

24. Accent 25311.

25. The allusion is noted in Meyer, *Biblical Quotation*, 56; also in Unger, *Handbook*, 43.

In light of this passage, then, the *Kleinod* of Cantata 12 would be not a jewel or gem but the bronze, silver, or gold medal a winner receives in a sports contest. (In other contexts, however, such as in the bass aria from Cantata 197a, *Ehre sei Gott in der Höhe*, the word *Kleinod* can indeed mean "jewel" or "gem.") Likewise, the *Kampf* in line 2 is not primarily a battle, struggle, or conflict but a contest or competition, that is, a *Wettkampf*. And the *Kronen* have to do not primarily with regal, diamond-studded crowns of metal but with crowns of victory, that is to say, with wreaths whose leaves would be expected eventually to decay.[26] (Yet note that the aria does go on to speak of the Christian's everlasting "enemy," just as 1 Corinthians 9:26 goes on to speak of "fighting" [Luther: *fechten*, literally "fencing"].) Thus, a historically informed rendering of these lines would read, "Cross and victory wreaths are bound together, contest and prize medal are united."

This reading would jibe well with Bach's musical setting, too. For a start, in this aria, the first vocal solo is accompanied by the whole of the oboe line that had preceded it—thus, ritornello and episode, too, are *vereint*.[27] Furthermore, a long-standing editorial quandary becomes unperplexing when the libretto is understood biblically. The great music historian Arnold Schering could not believe that Bach intended the alto to continue singing at the pickup to bar 17 and for the oboe to follow with its canon at the pickup to beat *two*

26. See also Revelation 2:10, where suffering and the "crown of life" are linked. Compare also, for example, the early-eighteenth-century picture of God holding out a crown and cross for the follower of Christ reproduced in Lucia Haselböck, *Bach Textlexikon: Ein Wörterbuch der religiösen Sprachbilder im Vokalwerk von Johann Sebastian Bach* (Kassel: Bärenreiter, 2004), 127.

27. See the either/or analysis of ritornellos and episodes in Laurence Dreyfus, *Bach and the Patterns of Invention* (Cambridge: Harvard University Press, 1996), 59–102. Perhaps Dreyfus is too rigid in saying that segments of Bach's concerto-style music belong to one or the other category. Are not, for example, bars 46–47 of the first movement from Bach's Second Brandenburg Concerto working simultaneously as the final segment of an episode (see the sequence from D–g–C–F at bars 40–47) *and* as the first segment of the ensuing ritornello (see the ritornello segments 1 and 2 at bars 46–50)?

in bar 17.[28] Schering emended the passage so that the *oboe* takes the reading of the alto entry at the pickup to bar 17, and the alto follows in canon not at the pickup to beat two in bar 17 but at the pickup to beat *three* in bar 17. (Incidentally, Cleobury's, Hengelbrock's, Junghänel's, and Kuijken's recordings adopt Schering's contrapuntal emendation but switch his scoring around so that the oboe follows the alto.[29]) But in Bach's notation, the alto and the oboe engage in a brief canonic chase where they appropriately end together, *vereint*, on the final note of the third beat in bar 17.

Meanings Made Clear by Implied Biblical Phrases

This category involves passages that are verbally incomplete (knowingly) and thus can easily be misunderstood.

Consider the first bass recitative from Cantata 152, *Tritt auf die Glaubensbahn*:

Der Heiland ist gesetzt
In Israel zum Fall und Auferstehen.
Der edle Stein ist sonder Schuld,
Wenn sich die böse Welt
So hart an ihm verletzt,
Ja, über ihn zur Höllen fällt,
Weil sie boshaftig an ihn rennet
Und Gottes Huld
Und Gnade nicht erkennet!
Doch selig ist
Ein auserwählter Christ,

28. J. S. Bach, *Kantate 12: Weinen, Klagen*, edited by Arnold Schering (Zurich: Eulenberg, 1926).

29. This is the way the passage was printed, without editorial comment, in J. S. Bach, *Weinen, Klagen, Sorgen, Zagen BWV 12*, edited by Ulrich Leisinger (Stuttgart: Carus, 1996).

Der seinen Glaubensgrund auf diesen Eckstein legt,
Weil er dadurch Heil und Erlösung findet.

TERRY (1926)
The Saviour now is set
in Israel for fall and
rise of many.

DRINKER (1942)
A symbol is this child
in Israel, of death and
Resurrection!

AMBROSE (1984)
The Savior is in charge
in Israel o'er fall and
resurrection.

HARNONCOURT, CD[30] (1985)
A symbol is this child
in Israel, of death and
Resurrection!

RICERCAR, CD[31] (1989)
The saviour was condemned
to death in Israel,
and there also to be
resurrected!

THOMAS, CD[32] (1993)
The Savior rules
in Israel over fall and
resurrection.

KOOPMAN, CD[33] (1995)
A symbol is this child
in Israel, of death and
Resurrection!

UNGER (1996)
The Savior has been
established
in Israel for falling and rising.

SUZUKI, CD[34] (1997)
The saviour is sent
to Israel, to fall and be
resurrected!

STOKES (1999)
The Saviour has been placed
in Israel
for the fall and resurrection.

30. Teldec 242632.

31. Ricercar 061041.

32. Koch 3–7164–2H1.

33. Erato 0630–12598.

34. BIS 841.

TAYLOR, CD[35] (2002)
A symbol is this child
in Israel, of death and
    Resurrection!

GARDINER, CD[36] (2007)
The Saviour has been placed
    in Israel
for the fall and resurrection.

Here our translators give a striking variety of readings for the opening lines. Nonetheless, this movement is most likely neither about Jesus's falling and rising, nor about his being placed or set in Israel (as opposed to, say, in Egypt), nor about his being a symbol, nor about his being condemned in Israel. Bach's congregations would have just heard a pericope from Luke 2 chanted in the liturgy,[37] which at verse 34b reads:

> Siehe, dieser wird gesetzt zu einem Fall und Auferstehen vieler in Israel.

> Look, this one is set for a fall and rising again of many in Israel.

That is to say, according to the Gospel of Luke, Jesus was placed by God for the fall and rising again of *many people in Israel.* The recitative lines from Cantata 152 would thus be best rendered, "The Savior is set for the fall and rising again [of many] in Israel!" in recognition of the scriptural passage it is meant to echo.

For a second example, consider the bass aria from Cantata 98, *Was Gott tut, das ist wohlgetan*:

Meinen Jesum laß ich nicht,
Bis mich erst sein Angesicht
Wird erhören oder segnen.

35. Atma 2–2279.

36. SDG 137.

37. Noted in Terry, *Cantata Texts*, 101; Meyer, *Biblical Quotation*, 13; and Unger, *Handbook*, 521.

Er allein
Soll mein Schutz in allem sein,
Was mir Übels kann begegnen.

TERRY (1926)
Never Jesus will I leave
till He shall upon me breathe
words of comfort and His
   blessing.

DRINKER (1942)
Jesus will I never leave
'til His blessing I receive,
he will aid me and abet me.

LEONHARDT, CD[38] (1979)
Jesus will I never leave
'til His blessing I receive,
he will aid me and abet me.

AMBROSE (1984)
I my Jesus shall not leave
till me first his countenance
shall give favor or its blessing.

UNGER (1996)
I will not my Jesus go,
until his countenance
will grant favorable hearing
   (to me) or bless (me).

STOKES (1999)
I shall not forsake my Jesus,
until He
hear me and bless me.

GARDINER, CD[39] (2000)
I shall not let my Jesus go
until His face
shall hear my prayer or bless me.

KOOPMAN, CD[40] (2005)
I my Jesus shall not leave
till me first his countenance
shall give favor or its blessing.

KUIJKEN, CD[41] (2006)
I will not let go of my Jesus,
until His countenance first
heeds me or blesses me.

GARDINER, CD[42] (2010)
I shall not forsake my Jesus,
until He
hear me and bless me.

38. Teldec 2292–42583.

39. Archiv 463586.

40. Challenge Classics 72218.

41. Accent 25301.

42. SDG 168.

SUZUKI, CD[43] (2011)
I shall not leave my Jesus,
until his face at last
will pay heed to me or bless me.

Only the renderings in the Kuijken and the first of the two Gardiner CDs catch fully the apparent allusion to Genesis 32:26, with both the verb *to go* and its auxiliary *let*.

Und er sprach: *Laß* mich *gehen*, denn die Morgenröte bricht an. Aber er antwortete: Ich *lasse* dich nicht *[gehen]*, du segnest mich denn.

And he [the man/angel/God] said: "*Let* me *go*, for the rubescence of the morning [sky] is breaking in." But he [Jacob] answered: "I will not *let* you *[go]*, unless you bless me."

In Cantata 98, then, the text does not speak of "leaving" Jesus, much less of "forsaking" him. It suggests, rather, that followers of Jesus metaphorically relive the experience of Jacob: they are in a profound spiritual struggle, and they will not let go in this wrestling match until they are blessed. (According to Luther's radically Christocentric reading of the Hebrew scriptures, it was actually Christ himself whom Jacob wrestled with at Peniel.)[44] An informed translation would thus read: "I shall not let my Jesus [go], until his face gives heed to me or blesses me."

---

43. BIS 1881.

44. Martin Luther, *Luther's Works*, vol. 6, *Lectures on Genesis: Chapters 31–37*, edited by Jaroslav Pelikan, translated by Paul D. Pahl (St. Louis: Concordia Publishing House, 1970), 144, where Luther states: "Without any controversy we shall say that this man [with whom Jacob wrestled] was not an angel but our Lord Jesus Christ, eternal God and future Man, to be crucified by the Jews."

Meanings Made Clear from Biblical/ Theological References

The soprano aria from Cantata 80, *Ein feste Burg ist unser Gott*, seems straightforwardly to affirm that God's image should "shine once again in me," and most translators appear to agree.

Komm in mein Herzenshaus,
Herr Jesu, mein Verlangen!
Treib Welt und Satan aus
Und laß dein Bild in mir erneuert prangen!
Weg, schnöder Sündengraus!

TERRY (1926)
And make my soul Thine own
   new garnished dwelling!

DRINKER (1942)
And let Thine image ever shine
   before me.

HARNONCOURT, CD[45] (1978)
And let Thine image ever shine
   before me.

AMBROSE (1984)
And let thine image find in me
   new glory!

RIFKIN, CD[46] (1987)
And let thy image shine
   renewed within me.

HERREWHEGE, CD[47] (1990)
And let your image shine again
   within me!

UNGER (1996)
And let thine image be
   resplendent anew in me!

THOMAS, CD[48] (1996)
And let your image shine in me
   renewed!

45. Teldec 242577.

46. Editions de l'Oiseau-Lyre 417250

47. Harmonia mundi France 901326.

48. Koch 3–7234–2H1.

STOKES (1999)
And let your image gleam in
  me anew!

GARDINER, CD[49] (2005)
And let you[r] image gleam in
  me anew!

SUZUKI, CD[50] (2005)
And let your image be
  resplendent in me anew!

KOOPMAN, CD[51] (2006)
And let thine image find in me
  new glory!

BELDER, CD[52] (2012)
And let your image shine forth
renewed in me!

But with its use of *erneuert*, however, the text more likely projects a somewhat different sense, namely: "And let your image shine forth in a renewed me" (the Thomas CD can be read as having captured this sense). Such a reading reflects Luther's subtle but theologically significant understanding of Colossians 3:9–11:[53]

> Lüget nicht untereinander; ziehet den alten Menschen mit seinen Werken aus und ziehet den neuen an, der da *erneuert*[54] wird zu der Erkenntnis, nach dem Eben*bilde* des, der ihn geschaffen hat: da nicht ist Grieche, Jude, Beschneidung, Vorhaut, Ungrieche, Scythe, Knecht, Freier; sondern alles und in allen Christus.

> Do not lie to one another; put off the old man [that is, the fallen Adam] and his works and put on the new [that is, the

---

49. SDG 110.

50. BIS 1421.

51. Challenge Classics 72222.

52. Etcetera KTC–1442.

53. This allusion is noted in Meyer, *Biblical Quotation*, 159.

54. In other Luther Bibles of Bach's day, *verneuert*.

sinless Christ, who is the new man], which is being *renewed* in knowledge according to the *image* of him who has created him: where there is no Greek, Jew, circumcision, foreskin, non-Greek, Scythian, servant, free man; rather all, and in all, is Christ.

In this reading of Paul's letter, a person who has put on the new man (Christ, the "new Adam") is renewed according to the image of God (that is, a person's whole being as the "image of God" is restored by union with Christ, who is the very "image of the invisible God," according to Colossians 1:15; it is not God's image itself that is renovated, rather, fallen human beings are made new into God's image).[55] The text from Bach's cantata, then, would be speaking of a renewed person, not of a radiance anew or of God's image being made new. A meticulous translation would thus be: "And let your image shine in me [who is being] renewed [in knowledge after the image of the creator]."

A second example: in the closing chorale from Cantata 190, *Singet dem Herrn ein neues Lied,* there is some confusion among translators about the sense of the third line from the end:

Laß uns das Jahr vollbringen
Zu Lob dem Namen dein,
Daß wir demselben singen
In der Christen Gemein;
Wollst uns das Leben fristen
Durch dein allmächtig Hand,
Erhalt deine lieben Christen
Und unser Vaterland.
Dein Segen zu uns wende,

---

55. Also, Paul's "renew" (Greek, *anakainoo*) means "made new in [something's] *nature*," as opposed to "new in time" (*neos*). Hence Luther's rendering as "[v]*er*neuert."

Gib Fried an allem Ende;
Gib unverfälscht im Lande
Dein seligmachend Wort.
Die Heuchler[56] *mach zuschanden*
Hier und an allem Ort!

TERRY (1926)
Stablish among
    believers
thine own Almighty realm,
and all earth's vain
    deceivers
right utterly o'erwhelm!

DRINKER (1942)
Let truth and simple
    candor
to honor be restored,
hypocrisy and slander
be ev'rywhere abhorred.

AMBROSE (1984)
Give unalloyed this country
thy grace-inspiring word.
To hypocrites bring ruin
both here and ev'rywhere!

UNGER (1996)
Grant unadulterated in
    this land
thy beatific Word.
Confound all hypocrites
here and in every place!

KOOPMAN, CD[57] (1998)
Spread thy beatific word
unadulterated throughout
    the land.
Confound the
    hypocrites
here and everywhere!

STOKES (1999)
Give throughout the land
thy pure and
    joy-inspiring Word.
Destroy all the
    hypocrites
here and everywhere!

56. In most contemporary hymn books, not *die Heuchler* (the hypocrites) but *die Teufel* (the demons, plural; *der Teufel*, "the demon," singular, is "the devil," Satan); see Werner Neumann, ed., *Sämtliche von Johann Sebastian Bach vertonte Texte* (Leipzig: VEB Deutscher Verlag für Musik, 1974), 40.

57. Erato 3984–21629.

SUZUKI, CD[58] (2003)	GARDINER, CD (2007)
Give unfalsified to the world	Give throughout the land
your blessed word.	thy pure and
Destroy the devil[59]	joy-inspiring Word.
here and throughout	Destroy all the hypocrites
the world.	here and everywhere!

Is God's *seligmachend* Word "grace-inspiring," "pure," "joy-inspiring," "blessed," or "beatific"? Only the rendition "beatific" (whose precise meaning is *"making* blessed") approaches the right idea, but even it is probably not quite correct. Bach's librettist most likely alludes to a notion of God's Word as *salvific* (that is, *selig* in the sense of *"eternally* blessed," though this would be, of course, a heavenly blessedness experienced proleptically in the services in Bach's Leipzig churches), something that is proclaimed at James 1:21:[60]

> Darum so leget ab alle Unsauberkeit und alle Bosheit und nehmet das Wort an mit Sanftmut, das in euch gepflanzet ist, welches kann eure Seelen selig machen.

> Therefore lay aside all filthiness and all evil, and accept with meekness the Word that is planted in you, which is able to make your souls blessed [that is, which is able to save your souls].

The Cantata 190 passage is thus best translated as: "Grant uncorrupted[61] in the land your saving Word. Put the hypocrites to shame here and in every place!"

---

58. BIS 1311.

59. See note 56, above.

60. The allusion is noted in Meyer, *Biblical Quotation,* 17.

61. For *unverfälscht,* see the "uncorrupted doctrine" (Luther, *unverfälschte Lehre*) of Titus 2:7.

As a final, more involved example of questions of theological understanding, consider the tenor recitative from Cantata 31, *Der Himmel lacht! die Erde jubilieret,* which presents the additional problem of having several different readings for the German text in modern editions. Bach's own score does not survive; the earliest source is the set of vocal parts that Samuel Gottlieb Heder, a student at the Thomasschule, copied in 1731.[62] Heder was evidently confused by Bach's score (from which he apparently copied), and modern editors have sometimes ventured further improvements on Heder's solutions to the problems in his model. Here is the German text as it most likely should read, along with various translations (and their German sources, if different from the italicized lines 4–6):

So stehe dann, du gottergebne Seele,
Mit Christo geistlich auf!
Tritt an den neuen Lebenslauf!
Auf! von den toten Werken!
Laß, daß dein Heiland in dir lebt,
An deinem Leben merken!
Der Weinstock, der jetzt blüht,
Trägt keine tote Reben!
Der Lebensbaum läßt seine Zweige leben!
Ein Christe flieht
Ganz eilend von dem Grabe!
Er läßt den Stein,
Er läßt das Tuch der Sünden
Dahinten
Und will mit Christo lebend sein.

---

62. For the details, see Alfred Dürr, *Kritischer Bericht* for Johann Sebastian Bach, *Neue Ausgabe sämtlicher Werke,* series I, vol. 9, *Kantaten zum 1. Ostertag* (Kassel: Bärenreiter, 1986), 37–39.

TERRY (1926)
Flee all the works of
   darkness!
Soul, let thy Saviour now
   above
remark thy love and
   goodness!

DRINKER (1942)
Up! follow now thy Savior.
Stay, let Him ever live in thee,
and mark well thy behavior!
Auf! von den toten [*or* Todes]
   Werken!
Lass, lass [*sic*] dein Heiland in dir
   [*sic*] Welt,
an deinem Leben merken!

HARNONCOURT, CD[63] (1974)
Up! follow now thy Saviour.
Stay, let Him ever live in thee,
and mark well thy behaviour!
[*booklet and performance:*]
Auf! von des Todes Werken!
Laß, daß dein Heiland in
   der Welt,
An deinem Leben merken!

AMBROSE (1984)
Rise, leave the works of dying!
Make thine own Savior in
   the world
be in thy life reflected!
Auf! von den toten Werken!
Laß, daß dein Heiland in
   der Welt,
An deinem Leben merken!

KOOPMAN, CD[64] (1995)
Up! follow now thy Saviour.
Stay, let Him ever live in thee,
and mark well thy behaviour!
[*booklet:*]
Auf! von des Todes Werken!
Laß, daß dein Heiland in der
   Welt, an deinem Leben
   merken!
[*performance:*]
. . . von des Todes Werken . . .
. . . in dir weiht [?], . . .

UNGER (1996)
Up from thy dead works!
Allow thy Savior to live in thee,
to be observed in thy life!
Auf! von den toten Werken!
Laß, daß dein Heiland in dir lebt,
An deinem Leben merken!

63. Teldec 242505.

64. Erato 4509–98536.

SUZUKI, CD⁶⁵ (1998)
Up, from the works of death.
May the saviour in the world
regard your life.
[*booklet:*]
Auf! von des Todes Werken!
Laß, daß dein Heiland in
    der Welt,
an deinem Leben merken!
[*performance:*]
. . . von den toten Werken!
. . . in dir lebt, . . .

STOKES (1999)
Rise! Abandon the pursuit
    of death!
Let the existence of the Saviour
    in this world
be reflected in your life!
Auf! von des Todes Werken!
Laß, daß dein Heiland in
    der Welt,
An deinem Leben merken!

GARDINER, CD⁶⁶ (2007)
Rise up from your dead works,
let your Saviour live in you,
to be reflected in your life!
[*booklet and performance:*]
Auf! Von den toten Werken!
Lass, dass dein Heiland in dir lebt,
An deinem Leben merken!

The libretto booklets distributed in Bach's churches for renderings of the cantata in 1724 and 1731 both provide the surely correct
reading, "von den toten Werken," a phrase presumably alluding to
Luther's translation of Hebrews 9:14:⁶⁷

> Denn so der Ochsen und der Böcke Blut, und die Asche, von
> der Kuhe gesprenget, heiliget die Unreinen zu der leiblichen

65. BIS 851.

66. SDG 2007.

67. The allusion is noted in Dürr, *Kritischer Bericht*, 52; Unger, *Handbook*, 112; and
Meyer, *Biblical Quotation*, 47.

Reinigkeit, wie vielmehr wird das Blut Christi, der sich selbst ohne allen Wandel durch den Heiligen Geist GOtt geopfert hat, unser Gewissen reinigen *von den toten Werken*, zu dienen dem lebendigen GOtt!

For if the blood of oxen and goats and the sprinkled ashes of the heifer sanctify the impure person unto bodily purity, how much more will the blood of Christ, who through the Holy Spirit offered himself immutable to God, purge our conscience *from dead works*, to serve the living God?

Cantata 31, then, speaks not of the "works of darkness," the "works of dying," the "works of death," a "pursuit of death," or "*your* dead works" but, rather, of "works that are [per se] dead." Luther's notion here is that works are "dead" because they can do nothing to justify a person in the face of God's wrath. According to Luther, persons can be justified before God only by having Christ's righteousness imputed to them, as appropriated through the unmerited gift of faith. Good works are the *fruit* of right faith; they are of no help in justification.[68]

The more likely reading of line 5, "Laß, daß dein Heiland *in dir lebt*"[69] (not *in der Welt*), advocates humans' focusing only on Christ's imputed righteousness (that is, because the Savior "lives in you"). The passage from Cantata 31—best translated as: "Up, from dead works! Let [the fact] that your Savior lives in you be observed in your life!"—in true Lutheran fashion does not advocate reward for good works or for any ritual acts of purification.

---

68. For a full discussion, see Robin A. Leaver, *Luther on Justification* (St. Louis: Concordia Publishing House, 1975); and Alister E. McGrath, *Iustitia Dei: A History of the Christian Doctrine of Justification* (Cambridge: Cambridge University Press, 1998).

69. See also Galatians 2:20, . . . *Christus lebet in mir* ("Christ lives in me"); noted in Meyer, *Biblical Quotation*, 47.

Passages Obscured by Archaic Language

For the bass recitative from Cantata 39, *Brich dem Hungrigen dein Brot*, many translators render *milde* as "gentle."

Der reiche Gott wirft seinen Überfluß
Auf uns, die wir ohn ihn auch nicht den Odem haben.
Sein ist es, was wir sind; er gibt nur den Genuß,
Doch nicht, daß uns allein
Nur seine Schätze laben.
Sie sind der Probestein,
Wodurch er macht bekannt,
Daß er der Armut auch die Notdurft ausgespendet,
Als er mit milder Hand,
Was jener nötig ist, uns reichlich zugewendet.
Wir sollen ihm für sein gelehntes Gut
Die Zinse nicht in seine Scheuren bringen;
Barmherzigkeit, die auf dem Nächsten ruht,
Kann mehr als alle Gab ihm an das Herze dringen.

TERRY (1926)
They are a trust, indeed,
in that He asks our care
to give from out our plenty
    where our help is needed,
as He, with favour rare,
to meet our daily need
with lavish hand's
    provided.

DRINKER (1942)
They are the touchstones, too,
by which He tells to you
that what He gives is not alone
    to fill your need,
but that for poorer folk you
    have the wherewithal
their hungry mouths
    to feed.

LEONHARDT, CD[70] (1975)
They are the touchstones, too,
by which He tells to you

AMBROSE (1984)
They as a touchstone serve,
by which he hath revealed

70. Teldec 8.35269.

that what He gives is not
   alone to fill your need,
but that for poorer folk you
   have the wherewithal
their hungry mouths to feed.

that he to poor men also need
   hath freely given,
and hath with open hand,
whate'er the poor require, to us
   so richly proffered.

HERREWEGHE, CD[71] (1993)
They are the touchstone
by which he makes known
that he alleviates poverty
   as well as necessity,
since he richly bestows
   whatever is necessary
with gentle hand.

UNGER (1996)
They are the touchstone,
by which he makes known
that he has also provided the
   poor with their necessities,
when he with liberal hand,
richly bestows on us what is
   needful to them.

STOKES (1999)
They are the touchstone,
by which He reveals
that He provides the bare
   necessities even for the poor,
when He with gentle hand
showers upon us all that they
   need.

KOOPMAN, CD[72] (2004)
They as a touchstone serve
by which he hath revealed
that he to poor men also need
   hath freely given,
and hath with open hand,
whate'er the poor require, to us
   so richly proffered.

SUZUKI, CD[73] (2009)
They are the benchmark
through which he makes it known
that he has also given what is
   needed to those in poverty.
When, with gentle hand,
he lavishly provides us with whatever we need.

---

71. Virgin Classics 7–59320.

72. Challenge Classics 72216.

73. BIS 1801.

In the eighteenth century, however, this word had several meanings, including *freigebig* ("generous"). This is the understanding that readers in Bach's day would have brought to such passages as Psalm 37:21 (which speaks of the righteous person, who is generous),[74] Ecclesiastes 7:7 (which speaks of corrupting a generous heart),[75] and Ezekiel 16:36–37 (which speaks of the wanton [that is, an ironic "generous"] outpouring of one's wealth).[76] In Cantata 39, *milde* as "generous" makes a great deal more sense than as "gentle."

For a second example, even in Bach's day, *mildiglich* was an archaism, an older form for *milde*. Thus, the last line of the closing chorale from Cantata 28, *Gottlob! nun geht das Jahr zu Ende*, should most likely be translated "And feed us *generously*," rather than "gently" or "tenderly."

All solch dein Güt wir preisen,
Vater ins Himmels Thron,
Die du uns tust beweisen
Durch Christum, deinen Sohn,
Und bitten ferner dich:
Gib uns ein friedsam Jahre,
Für allem Leid bewahre
Und nähr uns mildiglich.

74. Luther, "Der Gottlose borget und bezahlet nicht; der Gerechte aber ist barmherzig und *milde*."

75. Luther (verse 8 in the Bibles of Bach's day), "Ein Widerspenstiger machet einen Weisen unwillig und verderbet ein *mild* Herz."

76. Luther, "So spricht der HERR HERR: Weil du denn so *milde* Geld zugibst, und deine Scham durch deine Hurerey gegen deine Bulen entblößest und gegen alle Götzen deiner Greuel; und vergeußest das Blut deiner Kinder, welche du ihnen opferst; darum siehe, will ich sammeln alle deine Bulen, mit welchen du Wohllust getrieben hast, samt allen, die du für Freunde hieltest, zu deinen Feinden; und will sie beyde wider dich samlen allenthalben und will ihnen deine Scham blößen, daß sie deine Scham gar sehen sollen." In other Bibles, not "wealth" (Luther, *Geld*) but "lust."

TERRY (1926)
We beg a further prayer:
"Peace with the New Year
   send us,
from every ill defend us,
and hold us in Thy care!"

DRINKER (1942)
Do Thou our prayer hear:
"In paths of peace direct us,
from ev'ry ill protect us,
thruout this coming year."

HARNONCOURT, CD[77] (1974)
Do Thou our prayer hear:
In paths of peace direct us,
from ev'ry ill protect us,
thruout this coming year.

AMBROSE (1984)
And further ask of thee:
Give us a peaceful year now,
from ev'ry woe defend us
and us with kindness feed.

UNGER (1996)
And ask furthermore of thee:
give us a peaceful year;
from all harm protect
and feed us tenderly.

STOKES (1999)
And beseech Thee now as well
to grant us a peaceful year,
to protect us from all sorrow
and gently to sustain us.

KOOPMAN, CD[78] (2004)
And further ask of thee:
Give us a peaceful year now,
from ev'ry woe defend us
and us with kindness feed.

GARDINER, CD[79] (2007)
And we beseech Thee now as well
to grant us a peaceful year,
to protect us from all sorrow
and gently to sustain us.

SUZUKI, CD[80] (2008)
And furthermore we ask you:
Give us a peaceful year,
protect us from all suffering
and nourish us charitably.

77. Teldec 242504.

78. Challenge Classics 72215.

79. SDG 137.

80. BIS 1641.

Passages That Are Simply Difficult

Some passages in the librettos from Bach's church cantatas are, on the face of it, simply difficult.[81] One notorious line that has plagued many readers appears in the closing movement from Cantata 60, *O Ewigkeit, du Donnerwort*, a four-part chorale inevitably encountered in undergraduate harmony and counterpoint classes. What does it mean to exclaim, as this text does, "Herr, wenn es dir gefällt, *so spanne mich doch aus*"?

Es ist genung;
Herr, wenn es dir gefällt,
So spanne mich doch aus!
Mein Jesu kömmt;
Nun gute Nacht, o Welt!
Ich fahr ins Himmelshaus,
Ich fahre sicher hin mit Frieden,
Mein großer Jammer bleibt danieden.
Es ist genung.

TERRY (1926)
It is enough!
Lord, brace me to the test
when toward me Death shall nod!

DRINKER (1942)
It is enough:
Lord, when it pleases Thee
do Thou unshackle me.

HARNONCOURT, CD[82] (1976)
It is enough;
Lord, when it pleases Thee
do Thou unshackle me.

AMBROSE (1984)
It is enough;
Lord, if it be thy will,
then let me rest in peace!

---

81. For example, even Werner Neumann, a German specialist on the librettos that Bach set, says of the poetry in the thirteenth movement from Cantata 76, *Die Himmel erzählen die Ehre Gottes*: "it is hard to understand." Werner Neumann, *Sämtliche*, 100.

82. Teldec 8.43745.

UNGER (1996)
It is enough;
Lord, if it pleases thee,
then indeed put me to rest!

KOOPMAN, CD[83] (1999)
It is enough,
Lord, when it pleases Thee
do Thou unshackle me.

STOKES (1999)
It is enough:
Lord, if it be Thy will,
free me from my burden!

SUZUKI, CD[84] (2001)
It is enough:
Lord, if it pleases you
let me relax.

GARDINER, CD[85] (2010)
It is enough:
Lord, if it be Thy will,
free me from my burden!

KUIJKEN, CD[86] (2012)
It is enough,
Lord, when it pleases Thee
do Thou unshackle me.

I suspect that Drinker and Stokes are closest to the sense of this passage and its use of the word *ausspannen*. Luther's translation of Job 30:11 may provide a helpful clue:

> Sie haben mein Seil ausgespannet, und mich zunichte gemacht, und das Meine abgezäumet.

> They have unharnessed my rope, and ruined me, and unbridled what is mine.

Ausspannen otherwise appears in the Old Testament of the Luther Bibles of Bach's day only at Ezekiel 26:4, 26:5, 26:14, and Hosea 5:1, each time having to do with the spreading out of fishnets; the verb does not show up in Luther's New Testament.

Considering Luther's use in Job 30:11 of *abgezäumet* ("unbridled") and considering the standard German expression *Die*

83. Erato 3984–25488.

84. BIS 1111.

85. SDG 171.

86. Accent 25315.

Pferde ausspannen ("unharness the horses"), I would offer as a best construal for Cantata 60's vexing *So spanne mich doch aus* the rendering "Then do unharness me [of the world's "trappings," and from the yoke of the world's endless sorrows, trials, and burdens]."[87] These sentiments were certainly explored fully in many Lutheran sermons of Bach's day and earlier. For example, in a late-seventeenth-century collection of funeral sermons, Heinrich Müller wrote:

> Simeon nennet den Tod eine Außspannung. [In marg. Luc 2/29.] Hie sind wir eingespannet in das Joch der Mühe / deß Jammers und Leidens. Der Tod spannet uns auß aus dem Leidens- und Angst-Joch.[88]

> Simeon calls death an unharnessing [margin: "Luke 2:29"].[89] Here [in the present world] we are harnessed in the yoke of trouble, misery, and suffering. Death unharnesses us out from the yoke of suffering and fear.

Conclusion

Each of these new suggested renderings for the librettos from Bach's cantatas arises out of insights that are likely to occur to us

87. See the penultimate line of the chorale stanza ("Mein großer Jammer bleibt danieden").

88. Heinrich Müller, *Gräber der Heiligen, Mit Christlichen Leich-Predigten* (Frankfurt, 1685), 478–479; quoted in Renate Steiger, *Gnadengegenwart: Johann Sebastian Bach im Kontext lutherischer Orthodoxie und Frommigkeit* (Stuttgart-Bad Cannstatt: Frommann-Holzboog, 2002), 113. In Dietrich Buxtehude's cantata *Ich habe Lust abzuscheiden* (BuxWV 47), *ausspannen* is employed to express these same sentiments.

89. That is, referring to the Greek word *apolyo*, "dismiss" or "set free." Note, too, that the line "Ich fahre sicher hin mit Frieden" at the end of the chorale from Cantata 60 alludes to Luther's translation of Luke 2:29 ("HErr, nun lässest du deinen Diener im Frieden fahren").

only with a knowledge of the broader religious contexts of Bach's music and poetry. Unlike us, Bach lived and worked in a biblically literate culture. We cannot hope adequately to understand his output unless we aim to become historically informed about his religious *Sitz im Leben,* whatever our own predilections might be.

PART II

Taking Up Anti-Judaism in Cantatas

Chapter 3

Bach's Cantata on
the Destruction of Jerusalem

And never be joyful, save when you look in love upon your brother.

*A probably authentic saying of Jesus that was recorded
in the now lost Gospel of the Hebrews*

On the east wall of the south balcony in the St. Thomas Church
of Leipzig, one of the principal churches where J. S. Bach worked
as musical director from 1723 to 1750, there hangs in memory of
one Bartholomæus Helmut a large, anonymous sixteenth-century
painting now known by the title *Gesetz und Gnade* ("law and grace")
or *Gesetz und Evangelium* ("law and gospel").[1] The picture presents
a powerful series of theologically conventional contrasts of type
with antitype. At the far left, Moses is shown on his knees at the
edge of a precipice, receiving stone tablets—the law—from a pair
of hands sticking out of a cloud. At the far right, in a roughly parallel position, Mary, with wavy blond hair, is shown receiving a

My thanks to Shaye Cohen, Paula Fredriksen, Christopher Leighton, Daniel
Melamed, Martin Petzoldt, and Renate Steiger for their encouragement or con-
structive discouragement.

1. A badly mangled reproduction, with many important elements cut off from
all four edges, can be found in Herbert Stiehl, "Das Innere der Thomaskirche zur
Amtszeit Johann Sebastian Bachs," *Beiträge zur Bachforschung* 3 (1984): 91; a serv-
iceable one is in Ernst-Heinz Lemper, *Die Thomaskirche zu Leipzig: Die Kirche Johann
Sebastian Bachs als Denkmal deutscher Baukunst* (Leipzig: Koehler & Amelang,
1954), 213; and a good one is in Landesamt für Denkmalpflege Sachsen, ed., *Die
Bau- und Kunstdenkmäler von Sachsen: Stadt Leipzig, Die Sakralbauten* (Munich and
Berlin: Deutscher Kunstverlag, 1995), 1:280.

cross-bearing baby Jesus—the gospel—from a fully visible God. At the left, farther below, the Fall of humanity is depicted: Adam and Eve break God's law by eating the forbidden fruit (from the Tree of the Knowledge of Good and Evil) and are shown thus bringing death into the world. At the right, divine redemption is depicted: Jesus, with heavenly rays beaming from his head, suffers on the cross (a sort of tree) and is shown conquering death. Likewise, at the left is found the bronze serpent amid exodus encampments of the Hebrew people in the wilderness.[2] At the right is a large church of Christian worship amid the established city of God, the New Jerusalem.

All of this is backdrop for a grouping of three disproportionately large figures at the center of the picture: on the left, a neatly long-bearded, fancy-headdress-bearing, unidentified prophet, richly clad in red; on the right, a scraggily short-bearded, nimbus-bearing John the Baptist, poorly clad in red; and offset between them, a seminaked man. The three are standing on stone blocks chiseled with explanatory inscriptions. The prophet's right foot is poised on one slab, inscribed PROPHETEN ("prophets"), his left foot on a second slab (which likewise appears to the left of the picture's center), inscribed *MEN[SCH] [O]N*[3] / *GNAD[*] ("man without grace").[4] John the Baptist stands with his left foot on a third slab, inscribed *ANZEIGER / CRISTI* ("proclaimer of Christ"). And below a depiction of Jesus's crucifixion appears a fourth slab, inscribed *VNSER RECHTFER / TIGVNG* ("our justification"). The seminaked man stands in an awkward position: below the neck, he is turned to the left, but above the neck, he is turned to the right; in other words,

2. See Numbers 21:4–9; see also 2 Kings 18:4.

3. *On* is Old German for *ohne*.

4. The painting is partly damaged, and restorations were attempted in the 1910s and 1960s. The inscriptions are no longer entirely legible, but they can be retrieved by consulting Salomon Stepner, *Inscriptiones Lipsiensis: . . . Verzeichniß allerhand denckwürdiger Vberschrifften, Grab- und Gedächtniß-Mahle in Leipzig* (Leipzig, 1675), 161, inscr. 639. At the second word in the painting, the right third of the letter O is still visible just next to the N.

his body or flesh is inclined toward the law and those things here associated with it (human sin and death), his mind or spirit toward the gospel of grace and those things associated with it (divine justification and life).

The picture appears to show humanity per se presented with a Hercules-like choice between the virtues of redemption and life on the one hand and the vices of sin and death on the other—what is believed to be, *post Christi adventum*, a choice between the negative ways of humanity remaining under the old covenant and the possibility of positive ways that are effected by the grace of the new covenant. As if all of these contrasts and what is spiritually to be made of them were not depicted clearly enough, at the center of the painting, directly behind the seminaked man, there shoots up to the heavens, as a sort of *axis mundi*, an extraordinary tree; its right side teems with foliage, while its left side is completely withered.

This subject matter—including the strange half-withered and half-foliated tree at the center—was common in Reformation art.[5] Not surprisingly, another painting, displayed before the 1780s in the other main Leipzig church where Bach worked, St. Nicholas, apparently featured much the same content. The fragment now known as *Moses mit den Gesetzestafeln* ("Moses with the Tablets of the Law"),[6] currently housed in the *Museum der bildenen Künste Leipzig*, presumably was once part of the large, anonymous painting that Salomon Stepner in the 1670s described as having been

---

5. See Günter Schade, ed., *Kunst der Reformationszeit* (Berlin: Henschelverlag Kunst und Gesellschaft, 1983), 328, 357–360, 402, 414. Luther Bible woodcuts will sometimes illustrate Matthew 7:15 in a related way; see, for example, Ph. Schmidt, *Die Illustrationen der Lutherbibel 1522–1700* (Basel: Reinhardt, 1962), 343. For a detailed discussion of the artistic reception of Lucas Cranach the Elder's law-and-grace paintings, see Richard Foerster, "Die Bildnisse von Johann Hess und Cranachs 'Gesetz und Gnade,'" *Jahrbuch des Schlesischen Museums für Kunstgewerbe und Altertümer* 5 (1909): 117–143, 205–206.

6. See Herwig Guratzsch, ed., *Vergessene altdeutsche Gemälde: 1815 auf dem Dachboden der Leipziger Nikolaikirche gefunden* (Heidelberg: Braus, 1997), 64–65.

accompanied by the following inscriptions: at the left, *Moses mit dem Gesetz. / Der Sünder. / Propheten* ("Moses with the law. / The sinner. / Prophets"); and at the right, *Unsere Rechtfertigung. / ... Anzeiger Christi* ("our justification. / ... proclaimer of Christ").[7] In addition to a concerned-looking Moses holding the law tablets, with the exodus encampment and the bronze serpent as background, one finds at the edge of the fragment a tree whose left side is leafless.

Perhaps only the insistent apologist will fail to see that these pictures from Bach's main churches represent not merely a juxtaposition of sin and redemption in general but also a sharp value judgment about the progress made in moving narratively from the historical failings of an old Israel under the law—why not, for example, depict the sins of Jesus's followers as narrated in the gospels?—to the triumphs made possible for a new Israel grounded in faith through God's grace.[8] That is to say, the law is considered "good" only insofar as it is a necessary step leading forward to the inclusion of the grace of the gospel; the way of the law by itself, however, is "dead." As Martin Luther put it most succinctly in his sermon of 1532 on the difference between the law and the gospel: "[Knowing and being able to state the] difference between the law and gospel is the height of ability in Christendom. . . . For if this piece is lacking, then one cannot discern a Christian from a heathen or Jew; so much hinges on this difference."[9]

7. Stepner, *Inscriptiones Lipsiensis*, 126, inscr. 442.

8. For another example of presenting a half-withered tree at the center as a symbol that divides the negative from the positive, see "The Blessings of Peace and the Horrors of War," an entry by Johann Zaulich in the autograph book of Johannes Frentzel, professor of poetics at the University of Leipzig in the seventeenth century; an excellent reproduction can be found in Wolfgang Schneider, *Leipzig: Streifzüge durch die Kulturgeschichte* (Leipzig: Gustav Kiepenhauer, 1995), 131. In fall 2001, there was displayed in the Leipzig St. Thomas Church's fellowship hall, the *Selneckersakristei*, a huge drawing by the *Jugendgemeinde* (youth group) that featured a central half-withered tree dividing pollution and an army tank on its left side from sunshine and the tranquility of nature on its right.

9. Martin Luther, "Wie das Gesetz und Euangelion recht grundlich zu unterscheiden sind . . . nach der Jenaer Gesamtausgabe (1532)," in Georg Buchwald, ed.,

Thesis

Bach's largely unfamiliar masterpiece, *Schauet doch und sehet, ob irgendein Schmerz sei wie mein Schmerz* (BWV 46), the church cantata composed for the Tenth Sunday after Trinity in the St. Thomas Church during his first year in Leipzig, presents a series of uncommonly strong contrasts between the first three and the last three of its six movements. Without alleging any direct connection, I claim that Bach's musical setting of Cantata 46 projects a theological anti-Judaism similar to that of the St. Thomas and St. Nicholas law-and-grace paintings[10] and that in doing so the cantata was very much in keeping with the specific liturgical demands for the Tenth Sunday after Trinity in the Lutheranism of Bach's day. Indeed, this chapter is by and large a response to a highly emotional and, in my view, alarmingly ill-informed 1998 academic conference discussion

D. Martin Luthers Werke: Kritische Gesamtausgabe, vol. 36 (Weimar: Böhlau, 1909), 25. For all quotations in this chapter, material in brackets has been added editorially for clarification; material in parentheses, however, appears that way in the original sources.

10. One might counter that the pictures are not really anti-Judaic, because withered trees should be understood to represent all who are without Christ. For example, commenting on Luke 23:31, Johann Gerhard links Psalm 1[:3–4] with John 15[:5, 16], Revelation 22[:2], and Psalm 92[:13–15] and teaches that "without Christ all people are dry, decayed trees." Johann Gerhard, *Erklährung der Historien des Leidens vnnd Sterbens vnsers HErrn Christi Jesu (1611)*, edited by Johann Anselm Steiger (Stuttgart-Bad Cannstatt: Frommann-Holzboog, 2002), 325–326; my thanks to Renate Steiger for this reference. But surely it is worth asking why the Leipzig paintings depict only figures from Old Israel as dry or decayed. Old Israel appears, at the very least, to be the quintessential example of being without grace or redemption. Consider in this regard Luther's own, much more restrictive comments on the "withered leaves" and "Godless chaff" of Gerhard's first cited passage, Psalm 1: "note here especially that he does not speak of chaff that lies there in tranquility but that the wind disperses.... [The psalmist's likening to "Godless chaff" is one] which in the first instance [see also Romans 2:9?] is to be understood of the Jews [*Welchs erstlich von den Jüden ... zuuerstehen ist*] ... since they are not secured in faith in Christ ... they have been driven about by various winds of teaching through their harmful and poisonous teachers, the rabbis.... On Judgment Day the Jews will be driven out and dispersed with the eternal horror and despair of God's unbearable wrath, so that they shall have peace

in which several distinguished theologians claimed that neither Bach's Cantata 46 nor its relevant contexts contain anti-Jewish sentiment.[11]

One might reasonably ask why this particular cantata had been chosen by the conference for a study of questions concerning possible theological anti-Judaism in Bach. The immediate answer is that in Bach's day, the Tenth Sunday after Trinity was the one time in the Lutheran church year when the liturgy focused specifically on the matter of historical and spiritual "Israel," and Cantata 46 was

---

nevermore, for all eternity, not even for a moment." Martin Luther, *Der Dritte Teil der Bücher* ... *Lutheri, darin zusamen gebracht sind Christliche vnd tröstliche erklerung vnd auslegung der fürnemesten Psalmen* (Wittenberg, 1550), 1:82r.

11. In the session "Antijudaismus in Bachs Passionen?" at the *Tagung der Internationalen Arbeitsgemeinschaft für theologische Bachforschung*, June 6–8, 1998, during the *Arolser Barockfestspiele*, Bad Arolsen, Germany. The discussion followed principally from the (as yet unpublished) contribution by Martin Petzoldt, "Zur Theologie der Kantate BWV 46 'Schauet doch und sehet, ob irgendein Schmerz sei': Entwurf zum Vortrag in Arolsen, 5./6. Juni 1998," a printout of which was distributed at the conference. A much longer but in my view likewise oversanguine study, similarly denying anti-Judaism in Bach's cantata, has now been provided by Renate Steiger, "Johann Sebastian Bachs Kantaten zum 10. Sonntag nach Trinitatis und die Frage nach dem Antijudaismus," in *Festschrift Georg Christian Macholz zum 70. Geburtstag*, edited by Angelika Berlejung and Arndt Meinhold (Neukirchen-Vluyn: Neukirchener-Verlag, 2004), 283–323. Both Petzoldt and Steiger actually give fairly short shrift to the issue of anti-Judaism (for the specifics of their argument, see this chapter's note 97 and note 108). Martin Petzoldt, *Bach-Kommentar*, vol. 1, *Die Geistlichen Kantaten des 1. bis 27. Trinitatis-Sonntages* (Kassel: Bärenreiter, 2004), 222, states that it is wrong to contend that Cantata 46 is anti-Judaic, because the libretto also censures Christians and because the libretto does not explicitly say what the fate of Jews will be. As we shall see, this first reason is ungermane, whereas the second is untrue: the cantata's first recitative chillingly speaks of Old Jerusalem facing "an *irreparable* loss of the Most High's favor" (see note 114 here). Don O. Franklin, "Konvention und Invention in Kantate 46: Johann Sebastian Bachs Kantate für den 10. Sonntag nach Trinitatis," in the conference report of the above-mentioned 1998 meeting, *Hof- und Kirchenmusik in der Barockzeit: Hymnologische, Theologische und Musikgeschichtliche Aspekte*, edited by Friedhelm Brusniak and Renate Steiger (Sinzig: Studio, 1999), 181–205, makes many insightful musical and theological points but does not engage the issue of anti-Judaism at all. As will become clear in the present discussion, by "theological anti-Judaism" I mean not disagreement with or critique of Judaism but rather

Bach's first composition for this particular Sunday.[12] I should perhaps note here that I proceed not from the biographical question "Did Bach personally espouse anti-Jewish contempt?" but from the exegetical question "What does Bach's church cantata mean?"

Lucan and Josephan Background for Bach's Cantata 46

The gospel pericope for the Tenth Sunday after Trinity was Luke 19:41–48, the story in which Jesus is depicted weeping over the future destruction of Jerusalem and driving merchants out of the Temple. For the morning service on that day, Bach would be expected to provide music appropriate to this gospel reading. Here is a direct translation of Luther's rendering of the gospel's Greek text:

> And as [Jesus] came near, he looked upon the city and wept over it, and declared, "If you knew what they were, then you

the teaching of marked contempt for the religion of Judaism and its practitioners. I do not agree with those colleagues of mine from the 1998 conference who claim that so long as one does not exclude Luther's possibility of Jewish persons' converting to Christ as late as at the Second Coming of Jesus, there can be no real problem or even instance of anti-Judaism. For a full exploration of Luther's anti-Jewish polemics and their contexts, see Heiko A. Oberman, *The Roots of Anti-Semitism in the Age of Renaissance and Reformation*, translated by James I. Porter (Philadelphia: Fortress Press, 1984); and Achim Detmers, *Reformation und Judentum: Israel-Lehren und Einstellungen zum Judentum von Luther bis zum frühen Calvin* (Stuttgart: Kohlhammer, 2001).

12. For a convenient overview of the central liturgical materials, see K. Eberhard Oehler, "Die Historie von der Zerstörung Jerusalems," *Jahrbuch für Liturgik und Hymnologie* 38 (1999): 88–98. For a list of liturgical items in the main service and vespers, see table 3.1 in this chapter. Regarding the Passion season, see the comments in note 107. There are two other extant Bach cantatas meant for the Tenth Sunday after Trinity, Cantatas 101 and 102. Unlike Cantata 46, these later works do not engage anti-Jewish polemic; it was Bach's practice to focus on different

would also consider, at this time of yours, the things that
serve you for peace. But now they are hidden from your eyes.
For the time will come upon you, when your enemies will
strike up an enclosure around you and your children with
you, when they will besiege you, and at all places hem you
in; and they will raze you to the ground, and leave no stone
upon another: this, because you have not recognized the
time of your visitation." And he went into the Temple, and
began to drive out those who were selling and buying there,
and declared to them, "It is written: 'My house is a house of
prayer'; you, however, have made it into a den of murderers
[Luther: Mördergrube]." And he taught daily in the Temple.
But the chief priests and scribes [Luther: Schriftgelehrten],
and the leaders among the people [Luther: die Vornehmsten
im Volck], sought after him, that they might kill him; and
they did not find a way they might do it to him, for all the
people followed him and listened to him. (Luke 19:41–48)

Jerusalem and its Temple were indeed destroyed by the Romans
in the first century, and from early Christian understanding of the
event, it was widely agreed that this represented God's punishment
of Old Jerusalem for its sin of rejecting Jesus.[13] The pastoral sermons on the Tenth Sunday after Trinity in Bach's churches, then,
were expected to focus primarily on sternly warning the Lutheran
parishioners of their own similar sinfulness and possible similar
punishment.

aspects of the gospel reading in his multiple cantatas for the same liturgical occasion. Strong anti-Jewish sentiments are expressed in, for example, several of the
many cantata librettos for the Tenth Sunday after Trinity that were set by Bach's
Hamburg colleague Georg Philipp Telemann.

13. See Paula Fredriksen, "The Holy City in Christian Thought," in *City of
the Great King: Jerusalem from David to the Present*, edited by Nitza Rosovsky
(Cambridge: Harvard University Press, 1996), 74–92.

The Christian scriptures do not contain a story of the destruction itself, and so it was established that Johann Bugenhagen's extended summary, "The Destruction of Jerusalem" (mostly drawing on book 6 of Flavius Josephus's first-century *The Jewish War*),[14] which was also widely printed in contemporary Lutheran devotional books and hymnals, should be read in all its gruesome details as a further warning for those attending the Leipzig churches. As the *Leipziger Kirchen-Staat*, a contemporary guide to the Leipzig liturgies, explains:

> For some of these [Sundays after Trinity] there is something special to be aware of, as . . . [for example, the fact that on] the 10th Sunday after Trinity in the sermon at vespers the story of the destruction of the city of Jerusalem is read . . . at which the preacher, too, exhorts concerning repentance and mending of one's ways.[15]

That the story was indeed read in St. Thomas at vespers in the early eighteenth century is confirmed by entries in a manuscript liturgical notebook maintained for the church by Johann Christoph Rost.[16] Rost wrote concerning the liturgy for that Sunday:

> *Destruction of Jerusalem.*
> When in the vespers sermon the "Our Father"[17] is prayed, at the place of the Epistle the Destruction [of Jerusalem and

---

14. I used Johann Bugenhagen, "Zerstörung der Stadt Jerusalem, wie sie von Josepho, Egesippo, und andern beschrieben worden," in *Vollständiges Kirchen-Buch* (Leipzig, 1731), 369–392.

15. *Leipziger Kirchen-Staat: Das ist Deutlicher Unterricht vom Gottes-Dienst in Leipzig* (Leipzig, 1710), 37.

16. Johann Christoph Rost, *Nachricht, Wie es, in der Kirchen zu St. Thom: allhier, mit dem Gottes Dienst . . . pfleget gehalten zu werden* (manuscript, 1716–[1739], Archiv der ev.-luth. Thomas-Matthäi-Gemeinde Leipzig, no call number). My thanks to Pastor Christian Wolff of the St. Thomas Church for allowing me to borrow this manuscript and study it in the Bach-Archiv, Leipzig.

17. The Lord's Prayer, Matthew 6:9–13.

its Temple] is read. This is always read on the 10th Sunday in Trinity at vespers.

At that point only a prologue is rendered, as then, after the "Our Father," in place of the Epistle, the Destruction is read. As soon as the [specially handwritten] words *Hic populus sedere jubeatur*, etc.,[18] appear within the [printed] text: at that point the priest pauses only a little, as though the text were over, [and] at this point the people [in the pews] sit down. Next there is further reading. When the [story of the] Destruction is over, an application to the listeners is rendered in addition.[19]

General Theological Background for Bach's Cantata 46

Bach owned a large number of books on religion and theology,[20] and his various biblical commentaries, collections of sermons, and other related works are here drawn on heavily as contextual material that is helpful for understanding his liturgical vocal music; indeed, I deliberately restrict citation from the vast literature of

---

18. These words are written into the very exemplar of Bugenhagen's "Zerstörung der Stadt Jerusalem" that was used in the St. Thomas Church services during Bach's tenure there, right before the sentences reading: "Now we want also to speak briefly about the destruction itself. Since the Jews, like Stephen says [Acts 7:52], had as murderers and betrayers killed the righteous and innocent Christ ..." This book, in its current state, is a rebound volume of only part of an edition of the *Vollständiges Kirchen-Buch*, once cataloged in the church's library as "St.Thomas.1074" under the title *Kirchen-Buch für die Chur-Sächsischen Länder* (Leipzig, 17[2]1) and now kept under that call number on permanent loan to the library of the University of Leipzig. My thanks to Pastor Christian Wolff of the St. Thomas Church for allowing me to borrow the book from a temporary exhibit in the church in fall 2001.

19. Rost, *Nachricht*, f. 76r (complete); my thanks to Peter Wollny of the Bach-Archiv, Leipzig, for transcribing this passage.

20. As explained and documented in the opening section of chapter 1.

Lutheranism to those books that were in Bach's library and whose relevant information is easy to find. To some readers, the extent of the citations may seem excessive, but my own experience from conferences and lecturing for various audiences suggests unambiguously that for many other readers, it will not seem so.[21]

Quotations from several of Bach's books can be culled already as general conceptual material to help set the stage for the often harsh tone encountered in the first half of Cantata 46. Luther himself, for example, in a widely disseminated sermon for the Tenth Sunday after Trinity, has the following to say concerning the broad warning value of the horrible event of Jerusalem's destruction:

> When one cannot endure forgiveness of sins and God's grace, there is no longer counsel or salvation.
>
> And this is the reason that the wrath of God is so exceedingly great and horrible. For just as the Jews want neither to see nor hear his Word, God therefore subsequently wants also neither to see nor hear their shouting, praying, worship services, and other affairs; and not until Jerusalem is utterly wiped out does his wrath want to subside. . . . This is, then, the horrible example which the evangelist [Luke] has written for the mending of our ways, so that we shall not despise God's Word, and should not let the time of our visitation pass by unfruitfully.[22]

---

21. Most especially when I delivered a version of this essay in the conference session, "'... Das also dringe vnd klinge ynns hertz ...'—Luther und Bach als Übersetzer der biblischen Botschaft," at the *Tagung der Internationalen Arbeitsgemeinschaft für theologische Bachforschung e.V. in Verbindung mit der Evang.-Luth. Kirchgemeinde Eisenach, der Gesellschaft "Thüringer Bach-Wochen" und dem Bachhaus Eisenach, 14.–17. März 2002 in Eisenach.*

22. Martin Luther, *Hauß-Postilla, Über die Sonntags- und fürnehmsten Fest-Evangelien durchs gantze Jahr* (Leipzig, 1692), 525. Please note that in aiming throughout for exact translation of Bach's sources, I have also retained their gender-exclusive language in my rendering of their pronouns for God.

Heinrich Müller, a seventeenth-century Lutheran theologian, in a printed sermon for the same Sunday, brings matters even more clearly into the present:

> If the Jews had repented still [as late as] on the day when Christ entered [Jerusalem,[23] leading to his crucifixion], then the stern judgment would not have been pronounced upon them. Since, however, even there they *did not want* [to repent], they subsequently no longer found mercy. Hence anyone is able to have, in good time, a perception of his blessedness [*Seligkeit*].[24]

Johann Olearius, another seventeenth-century Lutheran theologian, sums up succinctly in his massive biblical commentary the issues associated with Luke 19 as a whole:

> Summa: . . . God warns: render yourself open to repentance, or else God will punish; it is high time.[25]

The Libretto from Bach's Cantata 46 and Its Specific Theological, Biblical, and Liturgical Contexts

The libretto of Bach's Cantata 46, whose authorship is unknown,[26] to a certain extent divides its subject matter in two. (See the end

---

23. See Matthew 21:10.

24. Heinrich Müller, *Evangelische Schluß-Kette . . . Gründliche Außlegung der gewöhn-lichen Sonntags-Evangelien* (Frankfurt, 1672), 903. *Seligkeit* refers to blessedness—or lack of it—in the afterlife.

25. Johann Olearius, *Biblische Erklärung: Darinnen, nechst dem allgemeinen Haupt-Schlüssel der gantzen heiligen Schrifft* (Leipzig, 1678–1681), 5:545.

26. Bach, however, as ordained staff in the Lutheran church, was personally responsible for the theological content of the librettos that he set for the Lutheran

of this chapter for the full libretto, with direct translation.) The opening chorus with recitative-aria pair, so far as the narrative itself is concerned, may also be thought of as a musical counterpart to the Bugenhagen-Josephus vespers reading of the destruction of Jerusalem; and the second recitative-aria pair with closing choral movement may be thought of as a counterpart to the pastor's further but now even more immediate spiritual application of the story to the daily lives of his listeners.[27] Anyone who went to church in the morning and again at vespers that particular Sunday would most likely have heard several sermons with more or less the same messages; for a liturgical overview of the two services, see table 3.1.

More specifically, the outer movements of Bach's cantata may be seen as a sort of old song/new song or, to use the language more typical of contemporary Lutheranism, law/grace frame for the internal contrasting recitative-aria pairs. The choral lines of the first movement are a massive, motet-style, canonic (that is, "law"-like) prelude-and-fugue setting of Lamentations 1:12 verbatim. The last movement is a typical four-part Lutheran chorale harmonization, with extremely atypical short instrumental interludes,[28] of the final stanza from Johann Matthäus Meyfart's hymn "O großer Gott von Macht." Much like the particular way in which the pairs in the Leipzig church paintings are juxtaposed, Bach's polyphonic choral opening and homophonic choral finale also have a small but striking element in common: apparently in order to signal that the

liturgy (which is not to say that he therefore must have personally agreed with them). See Martin Petzoldt, *"Texte zur Leipziger Kirchen-Musik": Zum Verständnis der Kantatentexte Johann Sebastian Bachs* (Wiesbaden: Breitkopf & Härtel, 1993), 12–19.

27. See Oehler, "Die Historie von der Zerstörung Jerusalems," 96.

28. That is to say, atypical for orchestral writing in church cantatas. Such *Zwischenspiele* were a more common feature, however, of organ accompaniment to congregational hymn singing.

TABLE 3.1 Overview of the Leipzig liturgy for the Tenth Sunday after Trinity.

Main Service

	Bells ring a half hour before service
1	Organ music
2	Motet—for example, Melchior Vulpius, *Super flumina Babylonis* (Psalm 137; sung by choir)
3	Missa (Kyrie and Gloria; sung by choir)
4	Collect (intoned at altar)
5	Epistle—1 Corinthians 12:1–11
6	Gradual Hymn (sung by congregation)
7	Gospel—Luke 19:41–48 (intoned at altar)
8	Nicene Creed (sung by choir in Latin)
9	Bach's Cantata 46 (rendered by choir with orchestra)
10	Credal hymn—"Wir glauben all an einen Gott"
11	Sermon (about one hour); confession and absolution; intercessions; notices; peace
12	Hymn
13	Lord's Prayer (intoned at altar)
14	Communion; organ or choral music and hymns until communion ended
15	Prayers
16	Benediction

Vespers

	Bells
1	Organ music
2	Motet
3	Hymn
4	Psalm (read at lectern)
5	Lord's Prayer
6	Hymn
7	Epistle—"The Destruction of Jerusalem, as it is described by Josephus, Hegesippus, and others" (read)
8	Sermon; prayers
9	Magnificat (German hymn version sung by congregation)
10	Collect
11	Benediction, followed by hymn and catechism examination

Information taken from Charles Sanford Terry, Joh. Seb. Bach: Cantata Texts, Sacred and Secular; with a Reconstruction of the Leipzig Liturgy of His Period (London: Constable, 1926).

movements are designed to be linked as a contrasting pair, these two choruses feature similar independent recorder parts with variously meandering imitative melodies in running sixteenth notes. More about this and its significance will be said later.

It is the texts of the internal recitative and aria pairs that I would first like to focus on in some detail. These pairs, too, are musically and textually contrasted in striking ways. The first recitative and aria narratively address Old Jerusalem[29] (with the story's application at the same time spiritually extending to the church), and the second pair then addresses only the church. For Bach's Leipzig listeners, it was as though they were watching a play in which, halfway through, the characters suddenly stop talking to each other and instead turn to make their further points by speaking directly to the audience.

At these recitative-and-aria pairs, Bach's libretto contains a remarkable number of key expressions also found in a printed sermon by Heinrich Müller for the Tenth Sunday after Trinity:[30] *Blitzen* (p. 908 in Müller), *Frommen* (906, 908), *Küchlein versammlet* (901, 903, 909, 910), *Lästerung* (908), *Sünder* (903, 904), *Rache* (896, 897, 904, 908), *Schafe* (895, 909), *Stab gebrochen [im] Urteil* (904), *Straffe* (896, passim), and *überhäufte Sünden* (894). Müller's sermon thus appears to be an especially useful reference for understanding Bach's libretto.

It soon becomes apparent that in narratively addressing Old Jerusalem, the tenor recitative of Cantata 46 further echoes Müller, Luther, and other writers in Bach's library by teaching not merely

---

29. Adopting the words of Lamentations 1, it was the "city of God" itself that had been mourning in the first movement; see note 112. That text (in Latin, *O vos omnes*) has often been used as if narratively on the lips of Jesus, but in Bach's Cantata 46, the opening lines of the immediately following movement clearly point to the city itself as the one that narratively had been lamenting in this case.

30. Müller, *Evangelische Schluß-Kette*, 889–919.

a critical but also a strongly contemptuous attitude toward the city and toward those of its descendants who are not turned to Jesus.

For Müller, there certainly is no mistake about the fact that the destruction of Jerusalem was a punishment from God for rejecting Jesus. He wrote (all emphasis in this and subsequent quotations is mine):

> The fire of God's wrath was ignited; [Jesus] wanted to extinguish it with his tears, and actually could have extinguished it, had the Jews not, in their stubbornness, always carted along fresh kindling.
>
> ... Josephus reports concerning Titus, the Roman general, that, when he besieged the city of Jerusalem and saw that thousands of dead bodies had been tossed over the walls in the city graves, he shall nearly have wept; [Titus then] did raise his arms to heaven, protest against the imperishable God, and say in dispirited words: "Non meum hoc opus," THIS IS NOT MY DOING. So the Lord [Jesus] wants here [in the Luke 19 pericope] to say as well: You Jews, with my tears I bear it witness—God is my witness—that I see your ruin reluctantly; but *you* plunge *yourselves* into this. Your stubbornness [literally, "stiff-neckedness"] brings the disaster on your neck [*Eure Halsstarrigkeit führt euch das Unglück über den Hals*].[31] God must punish you, since *you do not want* to be converted.[32]

Here, it should be noted, Müller (like Bach's cantata) does not specifically call attention to the biblical notion that it is God who hardens people's hearts; the precise idea, in any event, for Müller and his Lutheran colleagues would be that the sin of the Jews lies not in

31. Müller is presumably alluding to Nehemiah 13:18, *unser GOtt führete all dieses Unglück über uns und über diese Stadt?* ("our God brings all this disaster on us and on our city?").

32. Müller, *Evangelische Schluß-Kette*, both passages at 896; for similar sentiments, 906 and passim.

their stubbornness per se but in their *not wanting* to be otherwise. Later in the same sermon, Müller adds:

> A bad crow, a bad egg. The apple doesn't fall far from the tree. Godless parents seldom have upright children. What indeed did their [that is, the Jews'] fathers get as a reward? The Babylonian Captivity. And what, then, do the children have to expect? Their complete downfall. Identical sins, identical punishments. *God does not allow mockery!*[33]

Similar notions of punishment will have been clear to Bach's Leipzig congregations also from an extremely significant passage in the liturgical reading of Bugenhagen-Josephus:

> One says Titus may have been prepared to be sparing *of the Temple*, (as *of the [Jewish] religion*,) but *it was over*; God issues it that there was no sparing.[34]

Bugenhagen, incidentally, and the writers in Bach's theological library do not imagine a Christian presence in Jerusalem during the Judean revolt against Rome.[35]

---

33. Müller, *Evangelische Schluß-Kette*, 916. In the last sentence, *GOTT lässt sein nicht spotten*, Müller is presumably alluding to Galatians 6:7, *Irret euch nicht; GOtt läßt sich nicht spotten! Denn was der Mensch säet, das wird er ernten* ("Do not be deceived; God does not let himself be mocked! For whatever a man sows, that will he reap").

34. Bugenhagen, "Zerstörung der Stadt Jerusalem," 384; see also 373. Josephus, a Jewish historian, also believed that the destruction of Jerusalem was a punishment from God, not, of course, for rejecting Jesus but for sedition, tyranny, and impiety; see, for example, Josephus, *The Jewish War*, preface, §4.

35. See Bugenhagen, "Zerstörung der Stadt Jerusalem," 374–375. Luther reports that God rescued the Jerusalem Christians by having them flee before the war broke out. See Martin Luther, "Eyn Sermon von der zerstörung Jerusalem (1525)," in *D. Martin Luthers Werke: Kritische Gesamtausgabe*, vol. 17.1, edited by Georg Buchwald (Weimar: Böhlau, 1907), 384. Presumably, Luther derived this (now controversial) notion from Eusebius of Caesarea's *Historia ecclesiastica*. See

From a passage Bach marked in his Calov Bible Commentary,[36] we can document his familiarity with the notion that the destruction of Old Jerusalem represents an ongoing punishment. Concerning Leviticus 26:38, Calov wrote:

> You have to die in exile and suffering, as is what happens to quite a few of the Israelites in the 70-year Babylonian Captivity; following their final destruction and dispersion [in the year 70 with the second destruction of the Temple], the remaining Jews have to experience the same sort of thing for over 1600 years, even to this day.

Under Calov's "1600," Bach wrote "1700."[37] What exactly constitutes Jerusalem's sin that warrants this ongoing punishment is presumably so straightforward and obvious that it is not always mentioned in the printed sermons. It is in the literature of systematic theology that the matter is most likely to be discussed more specifically and thoroughly. The Lutheran theologian Christoph Scheibler wrote, for example:

> *Since the Jews Cannot Explain Away their Current Exile.*
> ... Finally, one would really like to ask a Jew what he may really suppose of himself, what the reason may be that

Eusebius, *The History of the Church from Christ to Constantine*, translated by G. A. Williamson (Baltimore: Penguin Books, 1965), 111.

36. As explained in more detail toward the beginning of chapter 1, the Calov Bible is the one theological title listed in Bach's library for which we have his own copy. It contains a large number of Bach's handwritten marginal comments and other forms of his highlighting. The volumes are now kept at Concordia Theological Seminary, St. Louis, Missouri. Facsimiles of the pages with Bach's handwritten entries are available in Howard H. Cox, ed., *The Calov Bible of J. S. Bach* (Ann Arbor: UMI Research Press, 1985).

37. Abraham Calov, *Die heilige Bibel nach S. Herrn D. Martini Lutheri Deutscher Dolmetschung und Erklärung* (Wittenberg, 1681–1682), 1:749. Neither Calov's nor Bach's arithmetic is very good here. My point is simply that it is interesting to see Bach notating anything at all for this passage.

the Lord forthwith rejects his people for such a long time and lets them be [exiled] in suffering for over 1600 years?[38] Idolatry—this is the greatest sin for which the Lord has [ever] punished his people. . . .

Now if one should take a look at the Jews of today, then one will not find such idolatry in their case. . . . *So tell me yet, my dear Jew!*: in truth, what reason could there be, that such extremely great punishment—and casting off, out of freedom into servitude—lasts so long? Idolatry is a great sin. But now this punishment is twenty times greater than the greatest punishment of the greatest idolatry. . . . Now then, a much greater sin indeed has to have been committed than any old sin there could have been among the fathers. And see, this can be no other sin than that the Messiah promised to them was sent, and yet they *did not want* to accept the same, *rather [they wanted* to] have him cut off and killed, and in the process cried out: "Away, away with this one, his blood be [Scheibler: *sey*] on us and our children," Matthew 27:23, 25.[39]

The language of these writers does at times get remarkably disdainful on the matter of not recognizing and being turned to Jesus. Müller, for example, speaks as follows concerning the story in Matthew 22 about the unworthy guests at a wedding feast:

How such things may be fulfilled in the Jews is borne witness in part by Paul[40] . . . in part by the present-day nature

---

38. In employing the expressions *Gefangenschafft* and *im Elend*, Scheibler is presumably alluding to Lamentations 1:3, *Juda ist gefangen im Elend und schwerem Dienst; sie wohnet unter den Heiden und findet keine Ruhe* ("Judah is exiled in suffering and in hard servitude; she lives among the gentiles and finds no peace").

39. Christoph Scheibler, *Aurfodina Theolog: Oder Theologische und geistliche Goldgrube* (Leipzig, 1727), 343.

40. See Acts 19:46.

of the Jews, who, living among the Christians, *want* to know nothing of Christ, and are obstinate to such an extent that one might sooner be expected to bring the Christian faith *to a stone* than to them.[41]

Turning to the following language from the tenor recitative in Cantata 46, then, one can see Bach's libretto expressing strong disdain for Old Jerusalem, in a manner that is even fiercer in its suggestion than the putative punishment from God that fell upon the city:

> *So lament* ... you wretched heap of stone and ashes! Let whole rivers of [your][42] tears flow. ... *Oh, better that you were utterly destroyed* ... heed now the flood-waves of the jealous fury that *you yourself* have drawn over you.

That this language is narratively speaking of Old Jerusalem is apparent from the following lines:

> there has befallen you an *irreparable* loss [*Verlust*] of the Most High's favor. ... You were handled like Gomorrah.[43] ... Oh, better that you were utterly destroyed than that one at present hears Christ's enemy blaspheming in you. ... *God* ... *breaks the staff* in judgment.

The word *Verlust* rarely occurs in the Luther Bibles of Bach's day, only once in the Hebrew scriptures (Psalm 144:14) and once in the New Testament (Romans 11:15). The latter verse as it

---

41. Müller, *Evangelische Schluß-Kette*, 1139. See also, for example, August Pfeiffer, *Antimelancholicus, oder Melancholey-Vertreiber* (Leipzig, 1761), 2:72–75.

42. See note 113.

43. See note 115.

appears in the Luther Bibles of Bach's day may well be relevant to Cantata 46:

> For if their[44] [that is, "Old" Israel's] loss [that is, of God the Father's favor because of unbelief in Jesus] is the reconciliation of the world, what else would that be but accepting life from the dead?[45]

If so, note that Cantata 46 would go beyond Luther's rendering of Romans by having the tenor recitative explicitly call the loss *irreparable*.[46]

Just which historical destruction of the city is being spoken of within the tenor recitative, the first (586 BCE) or the second (70 CE), is by no means always readily apparent. The import, however, of the destruction seems clear enough: "there has befallen the City of God an irreparable loss of the Most High's favor." An exacting reading would most probably suggest that Bach's tenor is at the outset declaring that Old Jerusalem was right to lament its having lost God's favor already at the first destruction of the city. Bach's setting then marks a formal division of the poetry lines 1–8 from 9–17 through instrumental V–I cadences and special figuration from the recorders at bars 9 and 20. Thus, it would appear, at bar 13, that "at present" God punishes "Jerusalem" again (now in the year 70), this time allowing the Temple to be destroyed once and for all. The present-tense verbs in the last five lines of the recitative should, it seems, so far as the narrative is concerned, be read in "historical present tense," a device employed for heightened effect, for

---

44. Calov, *Die heilige Bibel*, 6:135, specifies parenthetically "the Jews."

45. Luther Bible: *was wäre das anders, denn das Leben von den Todten nehmen.* Calov, *Die heilige Bibel*, 6:136, adds: "the life of the gentiles had thereby to be promoted . . . the Jews had to be given into death, and are rejected to eternal death."

46. In this connection, compare Bach's recitative also with Luther's comments (see note 10) about the eternal damnation of Jews on Judgment Day.

example, in the Greek of certain passages in the gospels and sometimes retained in Luther's translations, though these are typically
rendered in simple past tense in today's Bibles. So the word *jetzt*
("at present") in the sixth line from the end, as narrative, would
most likely refer to Old, ostensibly Christian-free "Jerusalem"
blaspheming in the late first century, not to the Muslim-occupied
Jerusalem of the early eighteenth century.[47] This is not to forget,
of course, the concurrent spiritual application for Bach's Lutheran
listeners of this part of the historical narrative: in this context,
the *jetzt* might be called the "sermonic, or eschatological now"
for Christian blasphemers living in eighteenth-century Saxony's
"Leipziger Jerusalem," which the city of Leipzig is called, for example, in the alto recitative from Bach's Cantata 193, *Ihr Tore zu Zion*.

Support for perhaps simply viewing the latter part of the recitative as narratively admonishing Jews of only the first century
is weakened by several considerations (in saying this, I am, again,
not forgetting about the recitative's concurrent, indeed primary,
purpose of spiritually admonishing Bach's eighteenth-century
Christian audiences). First, though this by itself is not decisive, it
is worth noting how frequently the descendants of Old Jerusalem
who are not turned to Jesus are characterized as blasphemers in
the theological literature readily available in Bach's library; that
is to say, there was some brooding within Lutheranism over what

---

47. One might understand "Christ's enemy" as the Muslims ruling Jerusalem "at
present," namely, in Bach's day. Considering the narrative and biblical contexts of
the entire recitative, however, one should much more readily and fittingly think of
first-century Jerusalem as the referent for *Christi Feind*. Consider also, for example, the wording of Philippians 3:18–19 given here at note 78; Philippians 3 is the
only place in the Luther Bibles of Bach's day where any form of the word *Christ*
and any form of the word *Feind* appear together. Significantly, Paul is here speaking strongly against various Judaizing tendencies among his rival Christian mis-
sionaries to the Gentiles. In any event, the destruction announced at the close of
Bach's recitative surely refers narratively to the devastation of the year 70; as we
shall see, no one in Bach's audience is likely to have covenantally linked to any-
where but Old Jerusalem the theologically loaded biblical allusion that is apparent
within the expression "God breaks the staff."

was perceived to be Judaism's ongoing and ever-current rejection of Jesus. Bach's recitative, then, may be understood not so much as an example of traditional (internecine) prophetic critique but of (Gentile) contempt for Old Jerusalem. And second, there is the issue of how to understand the last line of Bach's recitative: what does it mean to say that "God . . . breaks the staff in judgment"?

Before moving to the second issue, I shall briefly give a few examples of quotations from Bach's library concerning the first. Commenting on 2 John 1:9, the Calov Bible Commentary prints the following remarks of Luther:

> [We Christians know] that [the Jews] still do not have the proper God, for they *do not want* to hear his Word, . . . instead, they blaspheme and rage against it . . . they hold and worship as God *nothing but a mere dream*, indeed they acclaim lies and blasphemy as the knowledge of God. They are therefore *essentially* without God. . . . Yes, they in truth know nothing of him, and *have no sure testimony of Scripture*; instead they cast off and blaspheme the same. . . . Jews get most annoyed at us [Christians], and *shout* that we render three gods [that is, the Trinity], . . . and therefore the Jews, with their lying and blaspheming, lie to and blaspheme not us but God and Holy Scripture.[48]

This is carried still further in the following Luther quotation, which will provide a good segue to the issues surrounding Bach's recitative line about God breaking the staff in judgment. Commenting on Hosea 2:5, "And their mother is a whore, and those she has borne she fosters shamefully," Calov quotes Luther:

> Herr Luther: He calls "children of whoredom" the descendants who pursue the synagogue and the blaspheming of

48. Calov, *Die heilige Bibel*, 6:1146–1147.

God, these same who with their sins also *earn* punishment, as we see even before our eyes. The Jews *want* to be heeded just as their ancestors: they blaspheme Christ, and block all paths by which they could have been brought to the knowledge of Christ. . . . For you will find *no Jew who has taken notice* of the teaching and authority of the prophets; the Jews must consequently remain in the identical blindness, and bear the identical punishment along with their [whorish] "mother," and, in the same sins, *perish eternally* [*ewiglich verderben*].[49]

The recitative poetry of Bach's Cantata 46, too, appears to allege that those who are not now turned from the ways of the old to the new covenant are to be understood as utterly condemned, not only temporally but also eternally, namely, by asserting that "God 'breaks the staff' in judgment," an expression most likely appropriated from Zechariah 11:10 in Luther's particular rendering:

Und ich nam meinen Stab Sannft, und zubrach ihn, daß ich aufhübe meinen Bund, den ich mit allen Völckern [von Judah und Israel] gemacht hatte.[50]

49. Calov, *Die heilige Bibel*, 4:12.

50. This biblical verse is specified for this recitative line from Cantata 46 also in Ulrich Meyer, *Biblical Quotation and Allusion in the Cantata Libretti of Johann Sebastian Bach* (Lanham: Scarecrow Press, 1997), 100. Standard published translations of Bach's librettos fail to take in the biblical allusion here and thus do not quite get the line right. Z. Philip Ambrose, trans., *The Texts to Johann Sebastian Bach's Church Cantatas* (Neuhausen-Stuttgart: Hänssler-Verlag, 1984), 130, reads: "Yet heed thou still the tidal wave of passion / Which thou upon thyself dost summon, / For God, who long forbears, / The rod of judgment wields." Melvyn P. Unger, *Handbook to Bach's Sacred Cantata Texts* (Lanham: Scarecrow Press, 1996), 164: "So heed now the zeal of his watery billows, / Which though upon thyself hast drawn, / When God, after much patience, / The rod for judgment (wields)." Richard Stokes, trans., *Johann Sebastian Bach: The Complete Church and Secular Cantatas* (Ebrington: Long Barn Books, 1999), 82: "But heed now the tidal

And I took my staff Gentle, and broke it into pieces, that
I would annul my covenant, which I had made with all of the
peoples [of Judah and Israel.][51]

Already early on in his sermon for the Tenth Sunday after
Trinity, Müller makes it abundantly clear that he believes the Jews
were punished by God in the year 70 and that this was not merely
a temporary measure:

> It is invalid for one to say that the Savior may have wept
> only over the *temporal* ruin of the Jews. For he bewails the
> devastation that they *deserved* because of contempt of the
> visitation of Godly grace. This punishment was really *not
> only temporal but also eternal.* And if [his weeping shows that]
> he will not have wished them temporal punishment, much
> less [will he have wished them] eternal [punishment].[52]

And Müller is by no means alone in this. Consider, for example,
Scheibler, who even more forcefully brings matters to up to date:

> Unbelievers belong in the fiery pool of brimstone [*in den
> feurigen Schwefel-Pful*].[53] This is really the unbelievers who
> know, or *want to know, nothing* of Christ, as for example

wave of zealotry / Which you have heaped upon yourself, / Since God, after great
forbearance, / Now breaks the rod of judgement."

51. This narrowly restricted understanding of covenant with "all of the peoples" is
explained in Martin Luther, *Lectures on Zechariah (1527)*, in *Luther's Works*, vol. 20,
edited by Hilton C. Oswald, translated by Walther H. Miller (St. Louis: Concordia
Publishing House, 1973), 319; also quoted in Calov, *Die heilige Bibel*, 4:638–
639. (It is not at all clear that historical Lutheranism was right in interpreting
Zechariah's "all of the peoples" as meaning "all of the peoples *of Judah and Israel.*")

52. Müller, *Evangelische Schluß-Kette*, 898. See also "Die Konkordienformel
(1577)," in *Die Bekenntnisschriften der evangelisch-lutherischen Kirche*
(Göttingen: Vandenhoeck & Ruprecht, 1998), 1080.

53. Scheibler is alluding to Revelation 19:20, 20:10, and 21:8.

pagans, Muslims [*Türcken*], Jews, and the like.... John 3:36, 'Whoever does not believe in the Son, he will not see [eternal] life; instead, the wrath of God will remain on him.'[54]

In an extremely significant passage from his Tenth-Sunday sermon, Müller goes on to state plainly what such language as one also sees in Zechariah 11:10 would be taken to mean:

On Judgment Day ['the Day of the Lord, following *after* this life, which is our day'][55] no tears will save *you* [that is, narratively, '[Old] Jerusalem, you who are the capital city of the people of God'].[56] ... The staff is already broken;[57] the judgment is already pronounced: whoever does not believe [in Jesus],[58] he shall be condemned [*soll verdammt werden*; that is, to eternal punishment]. O, sinner, think about this.

Related ideas are also found in the Olearius Bible. Commenting on Zechariah 11:10, Olearius wrote:

54. Scheibler, *Aurfodina Theolog*, 55.

55. Müller, *Evangelische Schluß-Kette*, 904.

56. Müller, *Evangelische Schluß-Kette*, 901.

57. Müller, *Evangelische Schluß-Kette*, 904. True, Müller does not specify that he is quoting Zechariah, but then neither does he specify, for example, that he is quoting Isaiah 30:1 in speaking of *überhäufte Sünden* (894), or Matthew 23:37–39 and Luke 13:34–35 in speaking of *Küchlein versammlet* (901, 903, 909, 910).

58. As, for example, a person who remains committed solely to the beliefs and practices of Judaism (this would be someone who by definition does not believe in Jesus). In the world of Luther, Müller, and Bach, theologically speaking, Jews who turn to Jesus thereby become *Christians*. I understand Müller essentially to be saying that the religion of Judaism is condemned; the Christian question of eternal salvation for Jewish persons, however, presumably remains open, as in the Lutheran view, God may decide to take in repentant converts on or before the Day of the Lord.

Covenant. My gospel in Christ's covenant through grace
[*Gnaden-Bund*] . . . the Jews shall no longer be my people . . .
on account of their unbelief [in Jesus].[59]

Indeed, commenting on Zechariah 11 as a whole, Olearius, like
Müller, also connects the chapter specifically with the historical
destruction of Jerusalem in the first century.[60] The source for this
connection is presumably Luther himself, who opens his lecture on
Zechariah 11 with the following observations:

> Until now the prophet [Zechariah] has been preaching
> the kingdom of Christ and the power and fruit of the gos-
> pel, namely, faith among the gentiles. Here, however, he
> preaches the destruction (. . . by the Romans . . .) of the
> Jerusalem Temple and of the Jewish people [*des Jüdischen
> volcks*]. For the Jews *wanted* to keep the old kingdom and *not*
> to accept the new; and for that reason they are ruined and
> have lost both . . . they *did not want* to recognize the time of
> their visitation (Luke 19:44).[61]

And finally, commenting specifically on Zechariah's verse about
the "broken staff," Calov quotes Luther:

> Herr Luther: That is, "since they [that is, Judah/Israel] *just
> did not want* to hear me [that is, God] and my gospel, I went
> at once and, yes indeed, took it from them and turned to the
> gentiles." For such is what he [that is, God] means, when he

59. Olearius, *Biblische Erklärung*, 4.1:1143.

60. Olearius, *Biblische Erklärung*, 4.1:1141.

61. Martin Luther, "Der Prophet Sacharja ausgelegt (1527)," in *D. Martin Luthers
Werke: Kritische Gesamtausgabe*, vol. 23, edited by W. Walther (Weimar: Böhlau,
1901), 632; also quoted in Calov, *Die heilige Bibel*, 4:631. Translation adapted from
Luther, *Lectures on Zechariah*, 310.

says he will have annulled the covenant—that is, have taken and cut off [abgekürtzt] the gospel from the Jews since *it no longer concerns or reaches them*, this covenant which in truth he had made because it was to come among all the gentiles; and this covenant is broken off and cut short [verkürtzt] in truth alone upon the Jews, as Saint Paul, likewise, teaches [at Romans 9:27–28] from Isaiah 10[:22–23] of the cut-off Word, because it *does not reach to the Jews or concern them*. And in Acts 13[:46] Paul confesses that they [that is, he and his companions] have to turn to the gentiles, since the Jews *did not want* anything of the Word; and so has it happened that such covenant is annulled for the Jews, and the rod or staff cut off. And here one should note that this staff would be the gospel, which is the covenant of God among all the gentiles; but to the Jews it is taken and broken off [abgebrochen].[62]

Luther's views stand out all the more strongly in light of his commentary on his rendering of Zechariah 11:7, *Ich nam aber zween stebe zu mir. Einen hies ich Sannft, den anderen hies ich Wehe* ("And I took two staffs: one I named Gentle, the other I named Pangs"):

The law ... is a staff whose name is Painful, Distress, and Anxiety, and that is contained in the Hebrew word *hobelim*, which means much or many kinds of anxiety, such as a woman has in travail [that is, in giving birth].

---

62. Calov, *Die heilige Bibel*, 4:637. Consider also the famous sculptures of the cathedrals in Freiburg, Paris, Reims, and Strasbourg, which graphically depict the belief that the synagogue has been broken off from God's covenant, with the church taking its place. In each case, the figure of the church typically appears with staff erect, chalice in hand, and eyes open to the future; the figure of the synagogue, however, appears with *broken staff*, Torah in fallen hand, and eyes blindfolded. See James H. Charlesworth, ed., *Jews and Christians: Exploring the Past, Present, and Future* (New York: Crossroad, 1990), illustrations following p. 126. That such a metaphor has been a rich one for Christian understanding of the religion of Judaism is apparent, for example, from the title of Frank Manuel's book, *The Broken Staff: Judaism through Christian Eyes* (Cambridge: Harvard University Press, 1992).

... When [Christ] promises [the Jews] every good thing through the gospel [the staff "Gentle"], they *do not want* it; when he threatens every evil through the law [the staff "Pangs"], they despise it. What is he to do with these vipers [*solchen ottern*] except finally to break both staffs and let them go on in their unenlightenment *forever* [Luther: *immer*], without either the gospel or the law? ... [On Zechariah 11:14–15, then:] Not only the gospel is taken away but also the law. For the Jews no longer have . . . proper understanding of the law. . . . Zechariah prophesied that the gospel and the law were to be taken from the Jews because of their guilt. The Jews teach mere belly-teaching to satisfy their greed [*Sie . . . leren . . . eitel bauch lere für den geitz*].[63]

The notion that those who are not turned to the grace of Jesus shall be utterly condemned—that is, not only temporally but also eternally—is also expressed clearly and forcefully in several devotional and liturgical prayers customarily offered in Bach's day on the Tenth Sunday after Trinity in Leipzig. The *Leipziger Kirchen-Staat* provides the following prayer for the occasion:

Prayer on the 10th Sunday after Trinity.
O you compassionate Lord Jesus Christ, you do bear witness also today with your hot and bitter tears (which, out of great love and compassion, flow copiously [*mildiglich*] from your cheeks), that you have no desire for *our temporal and eternal ruin*. With your Favored Mouth [*mit deinem holdseligen Munde*][64]—by having brought forth a distressful lament on account of the contempt of [God's] visitation of grace *upon the*

63. Luther, "Der Prophet Sacharja ausgelegt," 638, 640–641; also in Calov, *Die heilige Bibel*, 4:637, 4:638–639. Translation adapted from Luther, *Lectures on Zechariah*, 316, 319–320.

64. See Ecclesiastes 10:12a, *Die Worte aus dem Munde eines Weisen sind holdselig* ("The words from the mouth of a wise person are favored").

Jews—you also let your distressed heart be divined. Ah, merciful Lord Jesus, grant that *we* may give great heed to such tears. And just as, through many drops of water, stones finally erode, so let also your tears of love render *our* hearts penitent [*Hertzen erweichen*],[65] so that *we* do not miss the time of grace and—since it is still just around the corner—the day of salvation,[66] giving you reason—constraining [you]—to laugh at the calamity of ours [*in unserm Unfall zu lachen*][67] that ensues from [God's] righteous judgment [*aus gerechtem Gerichte*],[68] when anguish and trouble [*Angst und Noth*][69] come upon us *with the evil Jews,* and we are sanctioned to wail and lament both *here* temporally *and there* eternally. Hear and govern us, dearest Lord Jesus, for the sake of your holy tears, Amen.[70]

Moreover, the Leipzig liturgy itself in Bach's day included the following collect for the Tenth Sunday after Trinity:

On the 10th Sunday after Trinity.
Merciful God, heavenly Father, we ask you fervently that through the tears of anguish of your son Jesus Christ you

65. See 2 Kings 22:19, *Darum daß dein Herz erweichet ist . . . so habe ich's auch erhöret, spricht der HErr* ("Because your heart was penitent . . . thus have I heard it, says the Lord").

66. The "day of salvation" is a biblical expression understood to refer to something taking place in the present world, as is evident from 2 Corinthians 6:1–2 (see also Isaiah 49:8).

67. See Proverbs 1:26a, *so will ich auch lachen in eurem Unfall* ("and so will I laugh at your calamity").

68. See Romans 2:5, *Du aber nach deinem verstockten und unbußfertigen Herzen häufest dir selbst den Zorn auf den Tag des Zorns und der Offenbarung des gerechten Gerichtes GOttes* ("But you by your obstinate and impenitent heart are heaping up wrath for yourself on the Day of Wrath and the revelation of God's righteous judgment").

69. See Proverbs 1:27b, *wenn über euch Angst und Not kommt* ("when anguish and trouble come upon you").

70. *Leipziger Kirchen-Staat,* 253–254.

may render our hard hearts penitent, so that *we* do not, *like the obstinate Jews*, miss the acceptable time [*die angenehme Zeit*][71] of your visitation of grace, and through our impenitence incur temporal *and eternal* punishment [*in zeitliche und ewige Straffe gerathen*], but rather be truly repentant, wake up from our sleep of security, bring you acceptable offerings in your house of prayer,[72] and receive gracious answer [to our supplication], through Jesus Christ, your son, our Lord.[73]

The contrast of an eternally cursed "old Zion" with an eternally blessed "new Zion" is likewise expressed forcefully in the first song at the section *Von der Zerstörung Jerusalems* ("On the Destruction of Jerusalem") from the hymn book listed in Bach's library as the *Wagneri Leipziger Gesangbuch*:[74]

1.

Nachdem das alte Zion sich	After the old Zion
Gewandt zum bösen thurstiglich	turned to evil brazenly[75]

71. The expression *die angenehme Zeit* is an allusion to 2 Corinthians 6:2–3 and Psalm 69:14.

72. See Isaiah 56:7, *bringen . . . in meinem Bethause, und ihre Opfer . . . sollen mir angenehm sein* ("bring . . . within my house of prayer, and their offerings . . . shall be acceptable to me"); this verse is alluded to in Luke 19:46, part of the gospel reading for the Tenth Sunday after Trinity, quoted here in the main text.

73. *Vollständiges Kirchen-Buch*, 499. All indications suggest that the prayers printed in the *Kirchen-Buch* were indeed used in Leipzig in Bach's day; my thanks to Martin Petzoldt (theology, University of Leipzig) for confirming this suspicion.

74. [Paul Wagner], ed., *Andächtiger Seelen geistliches Brand- und Gantz-Opfer—Das ist vollständiges Gesangbuch in Acht unterschiedlichen Theilen . . . Mit approbation der hochloblichen Theolog. Facult. alhier Zu GOttes Ehren und des Nechsten Erbauung herausgegeben* (Leipzig, 1697), 2:489–491. The rubric for *Nachdem das alte Zion sich* reads: "M[elodie]. Kommt her zu mir, spricht GOttes Sohn"; this tune is used, for example, at the third movement from Bach's Cantata 86, *Wahrlich, wahrlich, ich sage euch.*

75. This is an older usage of *thurstiglich/dürstiglich*, which has to do with boldness, audacity, presumption, and insolence, not with real or metaphorical want

Und wider GOttes Reich empöret,	and rebelled against God's Kingdom,
So hat Er, dem vor Sünden graut,	accordingly He, who abhors sin,
Ein neues Zion ihm gebaut,	built himself a new Zion
Und jenes alte ganz verstöret.	and utterly destroyed that old one.

2.

Sie ist dahin, die schöne Stadt,	She is no more, the beautiful city
Die alle Welt getrotzet hat,	that affronted all the world;
Sie ist zur blassen Leiche worden,	she is become a pallid corpse;
Sie hat empfangen ihren Lohn,	she—who did not shrink
Die GOttes Knechte,	from murdering God's servant,
Gottes Sohn	God's son—
Sich nicht gescheuet zu ermorden.	has received her reward.

3.

Wo vor mit Lust zu sehen war	Where before was to behold, with delight,
Der König und Propheten Schaar,	the host of kings and prophets,
Wo GOttes Feuer und Heerd gewesen,	where God's fire and hearth had been,
Da wohnet itzt der Drachen Brut,	there resides now the dragon's brood;
Da wird aus dem vergoßnen Blut Entsproßnes Distel-kraut gelesen.	there, from the shed blood, sprouted thistlewort is reaped.

of water. See, for example, the rendering of Proverbs 14:5 in the Luther Bibles of Bach's day: *Ein treuer Zeuge läuget nicht, aber ein falscher Zeuge redet dürstiglich Lügen* ("a faithful witness will not lie, but a false witness will tell lies brazenly").

4.

Sie ligt in ihrer Aschen dort	Yonder she lies in her ashes,
Jerusalem, die Ehren-pfort,	Jerusalem the triumphal arch;
Ihr Hochmut stürtzt sie in die Tieffen:	her arrogance pitches her into the depths:
Auch wird auf ihre Wüsteney	Likewise, in accordance with her example,
Des Höchsten Eyfer ohne Reu,	the zeal of the Most High will, without remorse,
Nach ihrem Beyspiel, ewig trieffen.	rain down eternally upon her wasteland.

5.

Wiewohl sie todt, so lebt sie doch	Though she is dead, she lives nonetheless
Im Nahmen und im Saamen noch,	to this day in name and in lineage,
Der als ein Fluch und Scheusal bleibet:	which persists as a curse and horror:
Ein stahren-blinder Kopf muß seyn	Cataracted unto blindness must a hardhead be,
Und härter als ein Demant-stein,	and more obdurate than a diamond stone,
Den solches nicht zur Buße treibet.	whom such a thing does not drive to repentance.

6.

Hingegen wer es nutzen kan,	In contrast, whoever can make use of it
Gehört dem neuen Zion an,	belongs to the new Zion,
Das ewig-fest im Glauben blühet:	which blossoms, eternally steadfast in faith:

Die Gnade Christi bauet dem	The grace of Christ builds for him
ein himmlisches Jerusalem,	a heavenly Jerusalem
Der stets das Irdne fallen siehet.	that ever beholds the fallen earthly Jerusalem.

This idea of eternal condemnation for those who remain committed to Judaism was expressed altogether unambiguously in the Lutheran catechism, where Luther wrote:

> These articles of the Creed, therefore, divide and distinguish us Christians from all other people on earth. All who are outside the Christian church, whether heathen, Turks, Jews, or false Christians and hypocrites, even though they believe in and worship only the one, true God [the Father], nevertheless do not know what his attitude is toward them. They cannot be confident of his love and blessing. Therefore they remain *in eternal wrath and damnation* [*in ewigem Zorn und Verdammnis bleiben*], for they do not have the Lord Christ, and, besides, they are not illuminated and blessed by the gifts of the Holy Spirit.[76]

---

76. Martin Luther, "Großer Katechismus (1529)," in *Die Bekenntnisschriften der evangelisch-lutherischen Kirche*, 661; Martin Luther, *The Large Catechism of Martin Luther*, translated by Robert H. Fischer (Philadelphia: Fortress Press, 1959), 63. In some biblical and Lutheran theological cases, the word *eternal* need not be understood literally in the sense of actually in the afterlife; according to a "realized eschatology," people may experience (a foretaste of) eternal blessing already here and now, or they may experience a similar sort of condemnation here and now (for example, as the earthly Jesus does in the synoptic Passion narratives). Neither of these present-world experiences of "eternity" would necessarily continue in the actual afterlife. In several of the citations concerning condemnation of Judaism given above, however, the more literal sense would seem to prevail. See the Luther quotation in note 10, the Müller quotation from his sermon for the Tenth Sunday after Trinity cited at notes 57 and 58, and especially the penultimate sentence of the *Leipziger Kirchen-Staat* prayer for the Tenth Sunday after Trinity cited at note 70. Consider, too, that not all such condemning of Jews or Judaism can be understood as simply standing in for the condemning of humanity in general. (And surely, I should think, even condemnations of Jews standing in for the condemning of humanity in general ought to remain ethically troubling.)

Bach's Musical Setting and Its Theological Import

Sin and the Old Covenant

Bach's opening chorus from Cantata 46 is an extremely powerful lament on the destruction of Jerusalem; though the movement travels to tonal centers far and wide, it never leaves the minor modes. For the first part of this setting of Lamentations 1:12 ("Behold, yet, and see if any sorrow be like my sorrow, which has struck me"), unsettling harmonies and chromaticisms abound while the choral lines move forward in canon, a procedure frequently employed by Bach and others when referring theologically to the Law. At the second line of text ("For the Lord has made me full of distress on the day of his fierce wrath"), the tempo speeds up, and canon gives way to permutation fugue, a manner of writing in which the same melodic lines are continually shuffled among the various voices. From a formal point of view, the exposition (bars 62–92) begins conventionally enough, with its entries of the subject centered on the pitches D and A. But immediately (at bar 93), the recorders perform a fifth entry of the subject, now centered on E. What contributes thereafter to the relentlessness of this fugue is its almost complete lack of episodic material. The subject reappears already at bar 103, and somewhat monotonously, its entries were set once again on A and D. In bar 113, however, there is a bizarre tonal fracture, as the bass line comes in on A but immediately drives the tonality through a striking harmonic catabasis to the distant key of F minor. The soprano line answers in G minor, likewise in a key that, against the norms of the genre, is not a fifth away from the tonal center of the previous entry of the subject. The third and final section containing the fugue subject appears already in bar 129, preceded by a false overlapping entry from the recorders in bar 128 and followed by a brief but vehement coda. Since the fugue section 1 has five consecutive subject entries, section 2 has four, and section 3 has only one entry, this fugue seems top- and middle-heavy;

the harmonic breach of section 2, it seems then, acts as a sort of "destruction," aptly reflecting the chorus's biblical lines concerning the Lord's fierce wrath against the city of Jerusalem.

Bach's Cantata 46 setting, throughout, musically highlights the charged import of the various expressions employed in its libretto. For a start, his tenor recitative cadences on the then-strange, and in this instance tonally rather remote, harmony of B-flat minor for the highly significant words "*an irreparable loss* of the Most High's favor," and it may be interesting also to note that the striking leap of a minor tenth between the first and second words had read before its revision in the original performing part as only a minor third.[77] Furthermore, "Gomorrah" and "Christ's enemy" and "God . . . breaks the staff in judgment" from the second section of the recitative, lines 9–17, are musically linked by melodic tritone, the *diabolus in musica* of medieval music theory; indeed, all three of these expressions appear on the very same tritone, c″ to f#″.

For these reasons, too, I would not hear the words "*God* breaks the staff in judgment" as mere generally stereotyped expression but rather, along with the other two expressions that are set here to the same c″ to f#″ tritone, as specifically charged biblical language.[78] The lexicographer Keith Spalding does note that the phrase "*den Stab* über *[jemandem] brechen*" means "to condemn someone," and he goes on to say, "When sentencing somebody to death, the

---

77. I used the photographs of the Bach manuscripts available in the Bach-Archiv, Leipzig. The Bach autograph scores and original performing parts have now been scanned for posting at http://www.bach-digital.de/. For the Cantata 46 performing parts, see http://www.bach-digital.de/receive/BachDigitalSource_source_00002403.

78. On the line about Gomorrah, see 2 Peter 2:6, *Gott hat die Städte Sodoma und Gomorra zu Aschen gemacht* ("God has made the cities of Sodom and Gomorrah into ashes"); on the line about Christ's enemies, see Philippians 3:18–19, *Denn viele wandeln . . . die Feinde des Kreuzes Christi; welcher Ende ist die Verdammnis* ("For many wander through life as enemies of the cross of Christ, whose end result is [eternal] condemnation"), together with Psalm 74:10, *GOtt, wie lange soll . . . der Feind deinen Namen so gar verlästern?* ("God, how long can the enemy be expected to blaspheme your name so entirely?").

judge broke his staff over the head of the accused, throwing the pieces before his feet." Spalding further notes that *der Stab ist gebro-chen* means "final judgement has been pronounced."[79] The former particular variety of usage shows up, for example, in Erdmann Neumeister's cantata libretto *Wer sich rächet, an dem wird sich der Herr wieder rächen,*[80] a musical setting of which was rendered on the Sixth Sunday after Trinity in 1725 at the St. Nicholas Church in Leipzig. Its first recitative reads: "Whoever wishes to take revenge himself loses God's favor and this person will personally break the staff over himself in judgment." In Bach's Cantata 46, however, it is God who breaks the staff in judgment (remember, too, the tenor's phrase "irreparable loss of the Most High's favor [*Huld*]"). For a cantata that seems likewise to link God's favor and the shepherd's staff "Gentle" of Zechariah 11, see the first recitative from Bach's church cantata *Erwünschtes Freudenlicht* (BWV 184).

On the whole, Bach's tenor recitative in Cantata 46 is extraordinary, even for him. It features a remarkable concentration of dominant and diminished-seventh chords. The four-layer texture, too, is peculiar, as it consists of an unusually disjunct vocal line accompanied by several continuo instruments on a highly punctuated bass line, upper strings with long-held notes, and two recorders relentlessly performing regular, written-out lower mordents on implied half notes. In sum, it seems that Bach's musical setting of this recitative is no unwitting, straightforward, stereotyped, or conventional affair.

The cantata narrative's musically heightened charges against Old Jerusalem do not end, however, with the recitative. There follows a ferocious aria for bass, slide trumpet, strings, and continuo, in which the singer declares to the city that its punishment was slow in coming, but after brewing from afar, at long last,

79. Keith Spalding, *An Historical Dictionary of German Figurative Usage* (Oxford: Basil Blackwell, 1952–2000), 2325.

80. Neumeister, *Geistliches Singen und Spielen* (Gotha, 1711), 353–355.

the tempest's flash breaks forth. This reflects the belief that God was angry with the city for rejecting Jesus as the long-promised Messiah and that for forty long years after Jesus's crucifixion, God simmered before finally blowing up and using the Romans to destroy the city and its Temple. This understanding of *Wetter* ("tempest") is evident also, for example, from Olearius's comments on Jeremiah 30:23 ("See, there will come with ferocity a *tempest* of the Lord; a horrible, huge thunderstorm will descend upon the head of the Godless"):

> *Tempest.* ... a sudden punishment.... in addition, some look to the destruction [of Jerusalem and its Temple] by the Romans [as prophesied in] Luke 19.[81]

Bach's aria is not so much a solo aria as a duet for bass and trumpet with accompanying strings and continuo. Parts of the movement's message are amply expressed even before the singer enters at bar 13. The string writing is set in the tradition of Monteverdi's *stile concitato*: continually repeated sixteenth notes, an Italian baroque convention for "militant" *Affects*. The trumpet's first gesture is to outline a tonic chord B-flat, D, F, B-flat, with a jarring A as a long written-out grace note preceding the top B-flat; the gesture is later, at bar 84, even transposed to F minor, with a trill on the grace note, following talk of Jerusalem's *Untergang* ("downfall"). Still more eccentric is the closing gesture of the ritornello (see bars 9 and following), a prolonged series of sixteenth-note oscillations between the second and third degrees of the scale; this is a nearly absurd-sounding gesture for the brass instruments of Bach's day.[82] Significantly, the idea

---

81. Olearius, *Biblische Erklärung*, 4.1:483.

82. Bach labeled the untransposed brass part in the first movement *Tromba. ò Corno da tirarsi*, which from a solely linguistic point of view might seem to mean either (1) "trumpet-[with-slide], or [in its stead] horn-with-slide" or (2) "['natural'] trumpet, or [in its stead] horn-with-slide." Both the first movement and the bass aria (the latter featuring a transposed brass line) would be unplayable on any

is later, at bars 49 and following, developed at length while the bass reiterates the word *unerträglich* ("unbearable").[83]

It would seem straightforward enough for Bach to have set in *stile concitato* a text narratively concerning the first-century war between Rome and Judea. But the inclusion of solo slide trumpet with its strange oscillating gestures does call for interpretation. Similarly, it is unclear what one should make of the remarkable series of written-out mordents in the preceding recitative. I hear the trumpet at the end of the ritornello in the aria as distantly but loudly echoing the recorders of the recitative. If this way of listening to the aria is sound, then the relationship of recorders to trumpet here can be imagined to mirror the notion that the Son of God's sorrow in the recitative is transformed into God the Father's explosive anger in the aria.

It is worth mentioning that in composing the aria with its odd trumpet part, Bach may have drawn on a detail from book 6 of Josephus's *The Jewish War*, a volume also in Bach's personal library[84] and one frequently cited within the sermon collections

eighteenth-century brass instrument without the slide mechanism, and so the "natural" trumpet option is out of the question; horns, on the other hand, simply were not designed in a way that could accommodate a slide. Thus, Bach's peculiar nomenclature should probably be understood as "trumpet—or [that is to say, a] brass instrument [which is not a trombone]—with slide." In short, Bach would simply be giving two names for the very same instrument, one that looked and sounded like a trumpet and one that today is called the *Zugtrompete* ("slide trumpet"). See the extraordinarily detailed discussion of Bach's various brass parts in Thomas G. MacCracken, "Die Verwendung der Blechblasinstrumente bei J. S. Bach unter besonderer Berücksichtigung der Tromba da tirarsi," *Bach-Jahrbuch* 70 (1984): 59–89.

83. Some modern editions instruct the trumpet to play *pianissimo* at this passage, but the marking does not appear in Bach's original performing part; only Bach's string lines are so marked here.

84. I used Flavius Josephus, *Historien und Bücher: Von alten Jüdischen Geschichten . . . Vom Jüdischen Krieg, und der Stadt Jerusalem, und des gantzem Lands Zerstörung* (Tübingen, 1735). This German volume went through many printings from the sixteenth to eighteenth centuries, each of them also

and biblical commentaries that Bach owned.[85] According to Josephus, the brutal attack on the Temple in Jerusalem was launched as follows:

> Two days afterward, twenty Roman soldiers ... got together, and engaged a standard bearer from the fifth legion, two knights, and one trumpeter, and went ... through the fallen rubble to the Antonia fortress, butchered the first watch (which was asleep), claimed the wall, and with the sound of the trumpet gave their enemies something to apprehend. Upon which, alarmed, the other watches awoke and quickly fled, before they could determine the number of those who were gotten up; for the fear they were in, and the sound of the trumpet [*Trompeten-Schall*], aroused such impressions in them that they thought a great band of the enemy would have to have climbed up the citadel.[86]

containing Pseudo-Hegesippus's aggressively anti-Jewish *Vom Jüdischen Krieg*. Pseudo-Hegesippus is the fourth-century Latin-writing author, not the Greek-writing Hegesippus of the second century. See Albert A. Bell, Jr., "Josephus and Pseudo-Hegesippus," in *Josephus, Judaism, and Christianity*, edited by Louis H. Feldman and Gohei Hata (Detroit: Wayne State University Press, 1987), 349–361. Editions of Josephus (in Latin) were also kept in the libraries of the St. Thomas and St. Nicholas churches; for lists of the holdings of these libraries, see Hermann von Criegern, *Katalog der Leipziger Kirchenbibliotheken* (Leipzig: Spamer, 1912). It is unknown which printing in German Bach himself had. Bach's occupation with the Tenth Sunday after Trinity is also attested by the fact that he owned a copy of Johann Jacob Rambach, *Betrachtung der Thränen und Seufzer Jesu Christi, In zweyen Predigten Am X. und XII. Sonntage nach Trinitatis, 1725 ... angestellet* (Halle, 1725).

85. For examples of these citations of Josephus, see Calov, *Die heilige Bibel*, commenting on Luke 19:44, at 6:593; Olearius, *Biblische Erklärung*, commenting on the Luke 19 pericope, at 5:543–545; Müller, *Evangelische Schluß-Kette*, sermon for the Tenth Sunday after Trinity, 896, 906, 907, 908; Luther, *Hauß-Postilla*, sermon for the Tenth Sunday after Trinity, 523.

86. Josephus, *Historien und Bücher*, 6.1.7.

This story element also appears, in a slightly different form, in the Bugenhagen summary of Josephus that was read within the vespers liturgy.[87]

Whatever the aria's concurrent spiritual application might have been, the wording of Bach's libretto and his particular treatment of the trumpet seem to narrate the historical situation of the year 70, that is, not instead, or in the narrative first instance, the Last Judgment of all sinners, including Bach's Leipzig Christians, at the Second Coming of Jesus.

Sin and the New Covenant

For the second part of Cantata 46, there appears to be a narrative change of addressee. That is to say, the cantata's second recitative-aria pair effects a move over to the "grace" side of a metaphorical law-and-grace painting. The alto sings consistently to a second-person plural *euch* and *ihr*, not to the second-person singular *deine, dich, dir,* or *du* of the tenor and bass in their earlier recitative and aria. (The distinction is not possible to capture in standard modern English, which uses *you* or *your* in both singular and plural.) Thus, whereas the tenor and bass narratively speak to an imagined Old Jerusalem, identified with Christ's enemy and with those who are to be excluded from God's covenant, the alto appears to speak directly to Bach's church audiences. The alto's addressees are, to be sure, threatened with the real possibility of punishment as harsh as that of Old Jerusalem. But where those people of narrative "Jerusalem"—those who are not ever turned from the old covenant, even at the End—shall stand utterly condemned, the alto's addressed (Christian) sinners are also described as having the true possibility of salvation, that

87. Bugenhagen, "Zerstörung der Stadt Jerusalem," 384. Pseudo-Hegesippus, *Vom Jüdischen Krieg*, 151, wrote concerning this part of the narrative: "Whereupon the trumpet was heard, sounding forth so much more horrifically [*gräßlicher*] than usual."

is, if they are properly turned to Jesus. And there is no impli-
cation, however sinful they may be, that these latter sinners
harbor "Christ's enemy" in them. Consider in this connection
the interpretation of 2 Samuel 22:44 provided in Calov's Bible
Commentary (Luther's translation of the biblical verse is in
Roman type, Calov's glosses in italics):

> *The LOrd Messiah's song of praise* [Lobgesang] *after his exalta-
> tion, particularly among the gentiles:*
> ... Vs. 44: You [that is, God the Father] deliver me [that is,
> the exalted "Lord Messiah," Jesus Christ] from the quarrel-
> some people [von dem zänckischen Volck]. *(that is, from the
> backsliding Jews [von den abtrünnigen Juden], who have become
> my [Jesus'] archenemies: from this I am delivered; indeed you
> [God the Father] are casting them out.)* [88]

From Bach's having written into the margin of his copy of Calov
the missing second half of verse 44, *und behütest mich zum Haupt
ünter den Heyden, ein Volck, das ich nicht kannte, dienet mir* ("and protect me to be the head among the gentiles; a people whom I did not
know serves me"), we know that he was closely familiar with this
passage.

Cantata 46 appears to reflect the theologically common notion
in classical Christianity that the Old Jerusalem/Israel of the synagogue and Temple has been *replaced* in God's favor by the New
Jerusalem/Israel of the Gentile church (that is, as opposed to the
idea that Jerusalem/Israel was *expanded* to include Gentiles). This
notion is given forceful expression in the Calov Bible Commentary,
for example, at Isaiah 25:2–3 (Luther's translations of the biblical
verses are in Roman type, Calov's and Luther's glosses in italics;
please note that this somewhat confusing and distracting layout

---

88. Calov, *Die heilige Bibel*, 1:1640.

closely corresponds to the manner of presentation in the Calov Bible):

vs. 2. For you render the city *(Jerusalem)* a stone heap *(Compare [Isaiah] chap. 21:9, 23:13, Revelation 14:8, 13:3 [sic])*, the secure city *(Luther: Jerusalem[89] is called this on account of its presumption [Vermessenheit] about the Temple, the law, and the worship of God, such as these things were, among them)* such that it lies in a heap; the palace of strangers *(Luther: He calls them "strangers" on account of their unbelief; there must be a mighty blindness in the Jews, that they do not ponder this exceptionally clear text.)* such that it be no longer a city, and never will be rebuilt.

vs. 3. Therefore a powerful people *(one that is gathered to you from all the world,)* will honor you *(O Lord of glory)*; the cities of mighty gentiles will honor you. *(since the gentiles from all the world will be converted to you, and will be brought to the knowledge of your name, Isaiah 11:9 [sic]. Up to here and now, says Herr Luther, a small and harsh and easy[90] people in a corner of the land of Judea have honored you; instead of them you must have a great, mighty people, namely all the gentiles; and take note here of what the worship of God of the New Testament may be: not offerings, not building of Temples, not measuring etc. [that is, "measuring by one another and keeping to one's own"],[91] but rather the praise and fear of God, without hypocrisy.)[92]*

89. Not all biblical interpreters would agree with Luther that the unspecified city in Isaiah 24–25 is Jerusalem.

90. The word *leicht* ("easy") is changed to *hartnäckicht* ("headstrong") in Calov's list of printing errors provided at the end of the last volume of his Bible Commentary, but Bach did not enter the correction here at line 35 in Calov's gloss on Isaiah.

91. See 2 Corinthians 10:12b, *dieweil sie sich bei sich selbst messen und halten allein von sich selbst, verstehen sie nichts* ("inasmuch as they measure themselves by one another and keep only to themselves, they understand nothing").

92. Calov, *Die heilige Bibel*, 3:123.

In his copy of Calov, Bach here obliterated at verse 2 Calov's word *es* in *daß es auff einem Hauffen liegt* by writing the proper Luther translation *sie* over it.[93] Bach also crossed out Calov's *ehren* ("honor") at the end of verse 3 and wrote Luther's proper rendering, *fürchten* ("fear"), in its place. Here again, Bach's close familiarity with the Bible is apparent; neither of these corrections is indicated among Calov's list of printing errors provided at the end of the last volume of his Bible Commentary.

On the notion of an Old versus a New Israel, consider also Calov's and Luther's comments on Psalm 68. Calov wrote:

> [Psalm 68:]36. God is awesome in his sanctuary; *(in his church;)* he is the God of Israel; *(of spiritual Israel [des geistlichen Israels];)* he will give to the people *(that he [that is, God the Father] had purchased with [the blood of] him [that is, Jesus], Acts 20:28; [he will give] to the holy people, those [people] of his possession [that is, the Christians], 1 Peter 2:9) power and strength. Praise be to God.*[94]

At Calov's *dem seines Eigenthums*, Bach inserted the word *Volck* between *dem* and *seines*. Bach knew that the word is similarly repeated in 1 Peter 2:9, *Ihr aber seyd das auserwehlte Geschlecht . . . das heilige Volck, das Volck des Eigenthums* ("But you [followers of Jesus] are the chosen race . . . the holy people, the people of [God's] possession"). This correction is also missing from Calov's list of printing errors.

In his lectures on the Psalms, Luther has the following to say additionally about the close of the 68th Psalm:

> Here again he calls him a "God over Israel" [*ein Gott vber Israel*][95] . . . Again, the previous verses force us to conclude

93. Both *es* and *sie* translate as "it" in English. In German, the first word is neuter and the second is feminine.

94. Calov, *Die heilige Bibel*, 2:530.

95. See 2 Samuel 7:26.

that here "Israel" must be spiritual, like what Saint Paul calls *Israel dei,* "the Israel of God," in Galatians 6[:16], not referring to physical [*leiblich*] Israel. . . . You Jews want to have God exclusively. . . . God now wants to have the sort of Israel that does not build on itself, but on him and his grace.[96]

A claim, then, that any moral or spiritual criticism of "Jerusalem" is in essence simply criticism of "us wicked Christians" will not always hold up.[97] In the case of Bach's Cantata 46, the opening lines of the second part of the work seem to reflect Luther and baroque-era Lutheranism when they narratively identify the city as *other* than the alto singer's (Christian) addressees, although the example of the city, of course, spiritually provides a good warning to the church. The different narrative emphases of Bach's two recitatives would appear to reflect Luther's notion that God's covenant with Old Israel is to be strictly distinguished from the new covenant; for the religion of Judaism, God's covenant is "annulled," and Christianity becomes sole recipient of God's promises, with it alone now constituting, at least in principle, a properly spiritual Israel.

I note here, incidentally, my puzzlement with the frequent objection from conference participants that Luther and his baroque-era followers cannot really be called theologically anti-Jewish because there was nothing special about their disdain toward Judaism; they were, so the claim goes, equally condemning of the theologies of Islam, Roman Catholicism, and so on, holding each of these attitudes for the same reasons,[98] inasmuch as Luther and his followers polemicized against

96. Luther, *Der Dritte Teil der Bücher,* 1:23r.

97. This claim is issued pretty much as a summary judgment in Petzoldt, "Zur Theologie der Kantate BWV 46," and also in Steiger, "Johann Sebastian Bachs Kantaten zum 10. Sonntag nach Trinitatis."

98. See also, for example, the anti-Catholic and anti-Islamic sentiments in Bach's Cantatas 18 (*Gleichwie der Regen und Schnee vom Himmel fällt*) and 126 (*Erhalt uns, Herr, bei deinem Wort*), the only two Bach works where such sentiments appear via explicit language.

any form of not grounding justification at the End in the unmerited gift of Jesus's imputed righteousness. But consider the following response: what should one make, for example, of those South Africans during apartheid who said that they could not properly be labeled anti-black because their passionate desire to be kept apart from the Bantu was not essentially different from their desire to be kept apart from the Indian and Pakistani populations in their country?

Let us return to the second half of Cantata 46. After the musical turbulence of Bach's bass aria, his setting of the alto recitative seems, except for a minor outburst toward the end on the word *schrecklich* ("horribly"), lackluster and downright pacific. The musical differences more specifically between Bach's tenor and alto recitatives are also extremely strong. Before, for the narrative text against the metaphorical character "Jerusalem," there was a seven-voiced texture divided into four layers of regular rhythmic activity. Now, for the text aimed even more directly against Bach's Lutheran audiences, there is a simple and rhythmically less constraining two-voice texture, evidently expected to be performed in a much freer manner. In the case of the alto recitative, Bach's original separate continuo parts transmit the vocal line, too, as useful cues; the rhythmically strict style of Bach's tenor recitative made such cues in its continuo parts unnecessary.

Bach's two arias musically contrast very strongly with each other. The *stile concitato* bass aria, in B-flat major,[99] narratively directed at "Jerusalem" of the year 70, called for lower voice and trumpet with strings and basso continuo performing in an often lower tessitura. The alto aria, in G minor, narratively directed at Bach's Lutheran audiences, calls for higher voice with two recorders and two oboes da caccia in unison (that is, a scoring without

---

99. Bach often set *stile concitato* arias in the major mode; see, for example, the bass aria from Cantata 67, *Halt im Gedächtnis Jesum Christ*; the opening duet from Cantata 60, *O Ewigkeit, du Donnerwort*; and the first duet from Cantata 80, *Ein feste Burg ist unser Gott*.

proper bass instruments) performing in an often higher tessitura. All of this makes a great deal of sense: the bass aria's poetry
focused on the threatening hellish notion that God wants to take
vengeance on those who are not turned from the ways of impenitent Old Jerusalem; the alto aria's poetry focuses on the comforting heavenly notion that Jesus wants to protect upright Christian
believers from God the Father's eternal wrath.[100]

The instrumental scoring of the alto aria—oboes and especially
recorders, familiar from bucolic or pastoral scenes in secular vocal
music of the baroque era—would lead one to expect a straightforward musical reflection of the librettist's fundamentally encourag-
ing aria poetry. But the way in which the instruments are actually
used does not sound particularly bright or rosy. Pairs of recorders
in Bach's vocal works can have various associations. They are used,
for example, for sunny pastoral themes in Cantatas 180 (*Schmücke
dich, o liebe Seele*) and 208 (*Was mir behagt, ist nur die muntre Jagd*);
for sorrow in Cantata 13 (*Meine Seufzer, meine Tränen*) and the *St.
Matthew Passion*; and for death in Cantatas 81 (*Jesus schläft, was
soll ich hoffen*), 106 (*Gottes Zeit ist die allerbeste Zeit*), 127 (*Herr Jesu
Christ, wahr' Mensch und Gott*), and 161 (*Komm, du süße Todesstunde*)
and the *Easter Oratorio* (BWV 249). Flutelike instruments have
similarly varied associations in the Bible, and Bach's death-and-
sorrow uses of recorders reflect a tradition in German baroque
music that presumably stems in part from Luther's translation
of Matthew 9:23–24, *und als [Jesus] . . . kam, und sahe die Pfeiffer
und das Getümmel des Volcks, sprach er zu ihnen: Weichet, denn das
Mägdlein ist nicht todt* ("and when [Jesus] . . . came, and saw the
pipers and the commotion of the people, he declared to them: 'go,
for the girl is not dead'"). Curiously, in the textually hopeful alto
aria from Bach's Cantata 46, the recorders adopt much more the
sorrowful manner of the recorders in Cantata 13, the *St. Matthew*

Passion, and the opening chorus of Cantata 46 than the pastoral manner in Cantatas 180 and 208.

What may be called an exquisite monotony of musical form also contributes to this alto aria's largely sorrowful tone.[101] All three segments of the ritornello (bars 1–3, 3–7, and 7–8) feature repeated use of the motive formed by the first seven notes of bar 2 in the first recorder part; and taking such ideas up to the next formal level, all four episodes (bars 8–11, 16–24, 29–37, and 45–55) feature heavy use of melodic material from the ritornello, with the first, second, and fourth episodes, in fact, featuring partial or total superimposition of ritornello segments onto the singer's motivically derivative or new melodic lines. The only break in the mood and pitch content appears at bars 45–48, where there is a striking return to the general musical effects and specific wording of the bass aria: the alto's phrase "when tempests of vengeance reward the sinners" is set with repeated notes in the oboes and nearly absurd-sounding clarion calls from the two recorders.

The musical mood of the closing movement seems even less comforting than the alto aria. Each phrase of this chorale setting features exceedingly strange interludes from the recorders alone, now four of them, with two players in unison on each of the two melodic lines.[102] In their imitative procedures and in their level of rhythmic activity (at the sixteenth note), they are similar to the likewise independent recorder lines from the opening chorus. They are not at all thematically akin to the recorder lines in the tenor recitative. In their texture (without basso continuo), they

---

101. It is normal in baroque music for the *Affect* within a movement to be basically unchanging; it is unusual, however, even in Bach, to project such sublime melancholy and to feature so little formal variation. For an aria featuring extremely similar poetry (likewise alluding to the "gathered chicks" of Matthew 23:37–39) but sounding all-out joyful, see the tenor aria from Bach's Cantata 40, *Dazu ist erschienen der Sohn Gottes*, a work set for the Second Day of Christmas.

102. See note 28.

are similar to the alto aria. There are several things, however, that make the closing movement positively unsettling. The distance between the imitative recorder entries is not at the bar, as it was in the opening chorus, but at the eighth note, and thus, between each of the chorale phrases, the sense of the meter becomes unstable. Furthermore, the movement closes with a full cadence *on* (that is, not *in*) the dominant in G minor,[103] thereby giving the movement a certain feeling of open-endedness. It may even be that the musical sounds of mourning pipers, not the verbal entreaties of the church hymn, are meant to have the very last "word": at the final bar, the recorders alone are notated with fermatas in Bach's original performing materials.

Conclusion

The official liturgical version of Bugenhagen's Josephus summary closed as follows:

> So has God punished [Old Jerusalem's] contempt and persecution [*Verachtung und Verfolgung*] of the gospel, and placed before all the world a horrible example, in order to exhort it to fear God's wrath and punishment, and to exhort it *to be converted to God and to the knowledge of Christ*: for if God has not spared even this people [that is, Old Jerusalem/Israel]—whom he had given such glorious promise [*herrliche Verheissung*], among whom there have been so many

---

103. The chorale melody here is in hypophrygian mode with A as the final. Compare Bach's tonal harmonizations for the phrygian melody of the chorale "O Haupt voll Blut und Wunden," where he provides at times tonally open-ended settings (for example, BWV 244/62), at times closed ones (BWV 244/15, 17, 62); likewise, for the chorale "Befiehl du deine Wege," compare BWV 153/5, BWV 270, and BWV 271 with BWV 244/44.

lofty, holy patriarchs and prophets, indeed this people with whom Christ is related by blood—how much more horribly will he punish other peoples, with whom out of special grace the gospel is shared [*das Evangelium mitgetheilt ist*],[104] and who nonetheless are ungrateful, despising right worship and knowledge of God, and who persecute [the gospel] with great stubbornness and cruelty, the likes of which have never before in the world taken place? That is why there may be no doubt: punishment will not be far off, and it will come to them, like it did with Jerusalem.

This *we* should ponder seriously, and take to heart, that *we* mend our ways, and *are converted to right knowledge of Christ*, Amen.[105]

Even though, without a doubt, the main point of Bach's Cantata 46, like that of the liturgical prayers and the reading of Bugenhagen-Josephus, was to call Christians to turn away from their own sin, such theological anti-Judaism as there is within the cantata must be considered fundamental to the work's messages about God's temporal and eternal wrath.

Of course, Cantata 46 cannot reasonably be expected to have accommodated twenty-first-century liberal convictions, and even so, the verbal polemic in Bach's *Schauet doch* is not particularly

104. See 1 Thessalonians 2:8, *Also hatten wir [Paulus, Silvanus und Timotheus] Herzenslust an euch und waren willig, euch mitzuteilen nicht allein das Evangelium GOttes, sondern auch unser Leben, darum daß wir euch liebgewonnen haben* ("Yes, we [Paul, Silvanus, and Timothy] had heart's-ease about you and were desirous to share with you not only the gospel of God but also our lives, this because we were won over with love for you").

105. Bugenhagen, "Zerstörung der Stadt Jerusalem," 391–392. This conclusion of Bugenhagen's is not included in some printings; see, for example, Johann Bugenhagen, "Historie von der Zerstörung der Stadt Jerusalem," in *Geistreicher Lieder-Schatz, oder Leipziger Gesang-Buch* (Leipzig, 1724), 282–291; and Johann Bugenhagen, "Historie der Zerstörung der Stadt Jerusalem," in *Leipziger Kirchen-Staat*, 275–288.

vitriolic. It could easily have been a great deal harsher. His cantata is altogether temperate, for example, compared with Luther's violence-espousing "On the Jews and Their Lies" of 1543.[106] Unlike Luther's treatise, Bach's cantata expresses no explicit brooding against real, living, contemporary Jews. Rather, without even employing the word *Jews* or *Judaism*, Bach's cantata appears simply, if more abstractly, to dismiss Old Jerusalem as temporally downfallen, *irreparably* out of God's favor, and covenantally condemned.[107]

106. Martin Luther, "On the Jews and Their Lies, 1543," in *Luther's Works,* vol. 47, *The Christian in Society IV,* edited by Franklin Sherman, translated by Martin H. Bertram (Philadelphia: Fortress Press, 1971), 123–306. Martin Luther, "Von den Juden und ihren Lügen (1543)," in *D. Martin Luthers Werke: Kritische Gesamtausgabe,* vol. 53, edited by F. Cohrs and O. Brenner (Weimar: Böhlau, 1920), 412–552; for example, at 522, lines 8–12, Luther wrote regarding Jews: "So we are even at fault for not striking them dead" (*So ists auch unser schuld, das wir . . . sie nicht todschlahen*); and at 523, lines 1–2, he recommended "that one set fire to their synagogue, or *shul* [literally, 'school'], and heap over with earth whatever will not burn" (*das man jre Synagoga oder Schule mit feuer anstecke und, was nicht verbrennen wil, mit erden uber heuffe*).

107. In this respect, Bach's cantata is rather different from his *St. John* and *St. Matthew Passions,* which in their commentary sections do not ruminate even indirectly on Judaism or on Jews and their fate. One might reasonably expect to find strong anti-Jewish sentiment especially in liturgical oratorio settings of John's Passion narrative with its continual references to "the Jews." But it seems that in Bach's Lutheran environs, Good Friday was still considered neither the time nor the place for anti-Judaism. During Holy Week, Bach and his librettists were expected to focus on the salvific import of Jesus's suffering, not on the evil of "the Jews." Consider, for example, the opening paragraph of Luther's widely disseminated sermon "A Meditation on Christ's Passion" of 1519: "Some people meditate on Christ's passion by venting their anger on the Jews. . . . That might well be a meditation on the wickedness [*Bösheyt*] of . . . the Jews, but not on the sufferings of Christ." See Martin Luther, "A Meditation on Christ's Passion, 1519," in *Luther's Works,* vol. 42, *Devotional Writings I,* edited by Martin O. Dietrich, translated by Martin H. Bertram (Philadelphia: Fortress Press, 1969), 7. For the notion that the extensive commentary sections in Bach's *St. John Passion* dramatically soften the theological anti-Judaism of John's gospel narrative, see Michael Marissen, *Lutheranism, Anti-Judaism, and Bach's St. John Passion* (New York: Oxford University Press, 1998); see also Michael Marissen, "Perspectives on the 'St. John Passion' and the Jews," *New York Times,* Sunday Arts & Leisure section, April 2, 2000 (reprinted as chapter 5 in this volume).

Thus, it would be intellectually and ethically improper to object that since the emphasis of Luther, Müller, or Bach's sermons about the destruction of Jerusalem falls on spiritual application to "us wicked Christians," there can be no real problem of theological anti-Judaism in the narrative of Bach's cantata.[108] The greater weight of disapprobation may very well fall on Bach's Christian audience. But the cantata's spiritual application depends heavily on the temporal and spiritual fear generated from the (ongoing) historical situation described in its narrative. With the "horrible example" of historical Judaism—which rejected and continues to reject Jesus and whose dispersion and despisedness, in the view of Cantata 46, continue *irreparably* forever—fear of eternal condemnation to the flames of hell is always going to be much more terrifying than even the greatest horrors of earthly destruction. And however palliating it may be to learn that the Lutheranism of Bach's milieu can allow that Jesus might mercifully save the soul also of the unbeliever in him as God's Son and Messiah with the unmerited gift of Christian faith as late as at the Final Judgment, this does not necessarily erase charges of theological anti-Judaism: the Lutheranism of Bach's heritage unambiguously and, more often than not, strongly contemptuously taught that those who ultimately are not turned from their Judaism will be appointed their portion with the unbelievers—in the End, the Jewish faith is useless.[109]

---

108. See Steiger, "Johann Sebastian Bachs Kantaten zum 10. Sonntag nach Trinitatis"; and consider Petzoldt, "Zur Theologie der Kantate BWV 46," 6: "The texts that Bach set ... for the 10th Sunday after Trinity contradict [*widerspre-chen*] the thesis advanced of Bach as projector [*Gestalter*] of Lutheran anti-Jewish polemic. ... [These texts are ones] that expressly hold and impress the eschatological warning upon the Christians."

109. In this view, as presumably in certain harsh-sounding New Testament passages (see Mark 16:16, and compare John 3:18, 3:36), there is still salvific hope for Jewish persons, because they may after all come to believe in Jesus; but there is clearly *no hope for the Jewish religion*. Reading scripture against scripture, some biblical interpreters have noted, however, that Paul's Greek text of Romans 9–11 might equally or more probably be construed as saying that at the Second Coming of Jesus, *all* Israel will be saved, that is, including the *post Christi*

If the libretto of Cantata 46 issues forth conventional warnings about sin and punishment for all sinners, together with equally conventional promises of comfort and salvation to the upright Christian, Bach's musical setting may allow the end result to send a more nuanced and less consoling message. Rather than simply reflecting the poetry it accompanies, Bach's magnificent harmony and counterpoint appear to cast a certain pall of melancholic resignation or sorrowful, apprehensive uncertainty over the poetry's assurances and entreaties in the second half of the work.

For all who wrestle with God and for any who behold and see its tidings of great sorrow, Cantata 46 may well represent Bach's art at its musically and theologically grimmest.[110]

adventum "Old Israel"; to be fully precise, Jews will be saved by the One God *as Jews*, not as last-minute Christians. (One should note, too, that using Luther's own Bible translation to defend his theology can be circular.) For this understanding, see, for example, Krister Stendahl, *Final Account: Paul's Letter to the Romans* (Philadelphia: Fortress Press, 1976), esp. 33–44. According to Stendahl, the issue at hand in Romans was the justification of Paul's Gentile converts, not of sinners in general. (Stendahl was the Lutheran bishop of Stockholm.) For incisive criticism of Stendahl's view, see Alan F. Segal, *Paul the Convert* (New Haven: Yale University Press, 1990), 276–284; but for a detailed defense of Stendahl's approach, see John G. Gager, *Reinventing Paul* (New York: Oxford University Press, 2000). Luther himself (following Augustine) took Paul's phrase "all Israel will be saved" in Romans 11:26 to mean "all of Israel who are to be saved will be saved"; see Martin Luther, *Lectures on Romans*, in *Luther's Works*, vol. 25, edited by Hilton C. Oswald, translated by Walter G. Tillmanns and Jacob A. O. Preus (St. Louis: Concordia Publishing House, 1972), 101. (Note, however, that Luther's *Lectures on Romans* were not published until the twentieth century.) Müller, *Evangelische Schluß-Kette*, 898, does allow that Jesus weeps for the Jews and wants to shed his blood for them. Note, however, that Müller, perhaps unlike Paul (but very much like the author of 1 John 2:23), apparently cannot allow the possibility that Jews might not need to come to God the Father through Jesus (that is, Jews *already have the Father*, argue many biblical interpreters today, who then go on to ask how anyone now, after a two-thousand-year perdurance of Rabbinic Judaism, can really continue to say with a straight face that Jews do not have God the Father); note, further, that Müller in this same passage suggests that a magistrate (like Luke's Jesus) declares, "I weep as a human being but condemn as a judge [*als ein Richter verdamme ich*]."

110. Depending, too, in critical part on the abilities and predilections of its performers. A recent recording on period instruments by the Amsterdam Baroque

Annotated Libretto of Bach's *Schauet doch* (BWV 46)

1. CHOR
Schauet doch und sehet,
ob irgendein Schmerz sei wie
mein Schmerz, der mich
troffen hat. Denn der Herr hat
mich voll Jammers gemacht am
Tage seines grimmigen Zorns.

1. CHORUS
Behold, yet, and see if any sorrow be like my sorrow, which
has struck me. For the Lord
has made me full of dis-
tress on the day of his fierce
wrath.[111]

2. REZITATIV (TENOR)
So klage du, zustörte
  Gottesstadt,
Du armer Stein- und
  Aschenhaufen!
Laß ganze Bäche Tränen laufen,

2. RECITATIVE (TENOR)
So lament, you destroyed City
  of God,[112]
you wretched heap of stone and
  ashes!
Let whole rivers of tears flow,[113]

Orchestra and Choir, directed by Ton Koopman (vol. 8 in a Bach cantata series for Erato Disques), sounds at the bass aria less like a storm of vengeance than a pleasant, minuet-like stroll through the gardens of Versailles; elsewhere, too, when general terror is clearly called for, Koopman provides only the occasional *horresco referens*. Though stylish and technically superb, his interpretation of Cantata 46 appears superficial and historically uninformed. For a technically and interpretively compelling performance, see vol. 11 of the series released on the BIS label by the Bach Collegium of Japan, directed by Masaaki Suzuki.

111. This is the well-known text of Lamentations 1:12, poetry originally expressing grief over the destruction of Jerusalem by God through the Babylonians in the sixth century before Jesus. As discussed in this chapter, the passage is connected in Bach's cantata also with the destruction of Jerusalem by God through the Romans in the year 70 and, it seems, with an expected eternal condemnation of those who are not turned from Christ-rejecting "Jerusalem" in God's Final Judgment at the Second Coming of Jesus.

112. The *Gottesstadt* here is, of course, Jerusalem (see Psalm 87:3), not, for example, Nineveh (at Jonah 3:3, Luther Bibles of Bach's day identify Nineveh as a "city of God"); the biblical quotation at the opening chorus concerned the city of Jerusalem.

113. The libretto's tears are those of the city of Jerusalem; see Lamentations 1:2, *Die Stadt weinet des Nachts, daß ihr die Thränen über die Backen laufen* ("The city

Weil dich betroffen hat	since there has befallen you
Ein unersetzlicher Verlust	an *irreparable* loss
Der allerhöchsten Huld,	of the Most High's favor,[114]
So du entbehren mußt	something you must do without
Durch deine Schuld.	because of your guilt.
Du wurdest wie Gomorra zugerichtet,	You were handled like Gomorrah,[115]

weeps in the night, tears flowing over her face"); see also Lamentations 2:18, and see Jeremiah 2:19, *Es ist deiner Bosheit Schuld, daß du so gestäupet wirst* ("It is by the guilt of your wickedness that you are thus flogged"). All are noted in Meyer, *Biblical Quotation*, 99.

114. From a surface reading of its German, this recitative might seem to be saying that Old Jerusalem moves from an experience of highest favor to an experience of middling or low-level favor, such that these two lines could be translated as "an irreparable loss *of the very highest favor.*" But the biblically tinged recitative is suggesting, rather, that Old Jerusalem moves from an experience of God's favor to an experience of God's disfavor; the lines should be translated as "an irreparable loss *of the Most High's favor.*" (The Most High—*elyon* in Hebrew, *hupsistos* in Greek—is a biblical term for "God.") A similar use of the word *allerhöchste* appears in Bach's Cantata 61, *Nun komm, der Heiden Heiland*, whose tenor recitative states, *O allerhöchstes Gut! Was hast du nicht an uns getan?* ("O *Most-High* possession! What have you not *done* for us?"). These lines allude in part to Sirach 3:21 in the Luther Bibles of Bach's day, *Der HERR ist der* Allerhöchste, *und thut doch große Dinge durch die Demütigen* ("the LORD is the *Most High*, and indeed *does* great things through the humble"; for Cantata 61's "What have you not *done for us,*" see also Psalm 126:3), as noted in Meyer, *Biblical Quotation*, 1. That is, Cantata 61 speaks not so much of a "very highest good" or "very highest possession" but of a "Most-High possession" or "Most-High good." (Note that the import of Luther's Sirach 3:21 differs somewhat from today's standard Bibles in English; note, too, that the text of Luther's verse 21 usually appears at verse 20 in English-language Bibles.) Cantata 46's declaring that Old Jerusalem's loss of God's favor is *irreparable* may be in some ways akin to the extremely harsh notion, promoted during the Spanish Inquisition, that not even God's miraculous grace working through Christian baptism could wash away the poisonous traits encoded in the blood of Jews (that is, regardless of their "sincerity" in wishing to convert). See the sources discussed in David Nirenberg, *Neighboring Faiths: Christianity, Islam, and Judaism in the Middle Ages and Today* (Chicago: University of Chicago Press, 2014), 120.

115. See Genesis 19:24–28, where God is reported to have completely destroyed this city on account of its wickedness; see also Isaiah 1:9.

Wiewohl nicht gar
   vernichtet.
O besser wärest du in Grund
   verstört,
Als daß man Christi Feind jetzt
   in dir lästern hört.

Du achtest Jesu Tränen nicht,
So achte nun des Eifers
   Wasserwogen,
Die du selbst über dich gezogen,

Da Gott, nach viel Geduld,

Den Stab zum Urteil bricht.

3. ARIE (BASS)
Dein Wetter zog sich auf von
   weiten,
Doch dessen Strahl bricht
   endlich ein
Und muß dir unerträglich sein,
Da überhäufte Sünden
Der Rache Blitz entzünden

Und dir den Untergang
   bereiten.

though not actually
annihilated.
Oh, better that you were
   utterly destroyed[116]
than that one at present hears
   Christ's enemy blaspheming
   in you.
You do not heed Jesus's tears;
so heed now the flood-waves of
   the jealous fury
that you yourself have drawn
   over you,
as God, after much
   forbearance,
breaks the [covenant] staff[117] in
   judgment.

3. ARIA (BASS)
Your tempest brewed from afar,

yet at long last its flash breaks
   forth
and must be unbearable to you,
as heaped-up sins
set aflame the lightning of
   vengeance
and bring about your
   downfall.

116. *Verstört* is biblical language for *zerstört* (see especially Daniel 9:26 in the Luther Bibles of Bach's day). The word *zerstört* is printed here in some modern editions of the cantata.

117. This line appears to include a significant allusion to the wording of Zechariah 11:10 in the Luther Bibles of Bach's day, something whose interpretation in baroque-era Lutheranism is discussed in detail in the main text of this

Dein Wetter zog sich auf von
weiten,
Doch dessen Strahl bricht
endlich ein.

Your tempest brewed from afar,

yet at long last its flash breaks
forth.

4. REZITATIV (ALT)
Doch bildet euch, o Sünder, ja
nicht ein,

Es sei Jerusalem allein
Vor andern Sünden voll
gewesen!
Man kann bereits von euch dies
Urteil lesen:
Weil ihr euch nicht bessert

Und täglich die Sünden
vergrößert,
So müsset ihr alle so schrecklich
umkommen.

4. RECITATIVE (ALTO)
Yet of course do not imagine,
oh [unrepentant Christian]
sinners,
that Jerusalem alone
before others may have been
rife with sins!
One can already gather this
judgment of you:
so long as[118] you do not mend
your ways
and you do increase your sins
daily,
all of you will have, in the same
manner [as Jerusalem], to
perish horribly.

5. ARIE (ALT)
Doch Jesus will auch bei
der Strafe

5. ARIA (ALTO)
Yet Jesus wants also upon
the [question of eternal]
punishment[119]

chapter: God breaks the staff in a covenant-excluding judgment in which the Jerusalem Temple is destroyed once and for all.

118. In this context, *weil* in older German is to be understood not as "because" but as "so long as" (mentioned in Petzoldt, "Zur Theologie der Kantate BWV 46," 5, n. 5); note, too, that this and the final line of the recitative form a nearly verbatim quotation of Luke 13:3 in the Luther Bibles of Bach's day.

119. Müller, *Evangelische Schluß-Kette*, 896 and passim, mentions Jesus appearing before God the Heavenly Father's *Straffe* in ultimately dealing with sinners; this

Der Frommen Schild und
Beistand sein,
Er sammlet sie als seine
Schafe,
Als seine Küchlein liebreich
ein.
Wenn Wetter der Rache die
Sünder belohnen,
Hilft er, daß Fromme sicher
wohnen.

to be the shield and support of
the upright;
he lovingly gathers them as his
sheep,
as his chicks.

When tempests of vengeance
reward the sinners,[120]
[Jesus] saves, that the upright
will live in safety.[121]

6. CHORAL
O großer Gott von Treu,

Weil vor dir niemand gilt

Als dein Sohn Jesus Christ,

6. CHORALE
Oh abounding God of
faithfulness,[122]
since before you no one is
worthy
except your son Jesus Christ,

---

particular understanding would in any event follow from catching the allusion
at lines 3–4 of the present aria to Matthew 23:37–39 or Luke 13:34–35, passages
that have traditionally been understood to speak of God's eternal judgment. See
also Hebrews 10:29.

120. Consider Luke 21:22 (where Jesus is depicted as foretelling the destruction of Jerusalem by God through the Gentiles), *Denn das sind die Tage der Rache,
daß erfüllet werde alles, was geschrieben ist* ("For these are the days of vengeance,
so all that is written [that is, in the holy scriptures] will be fulfilled"). See also
Hebrews 10:30.

121. Consider Jeremiah 23:6, *Zu desselbigen Zeit soll Juda geholfen werden, und
Israel sicher wohnen* ("At this same time Judah shall be saved, and Israel live in
safety"); verse 3 also has God saying, "I will gather [*samlen*] my flock." Lutheran
theologians understood this prophesied salvation of Judah and Israel as having
been fulfilled in a new, "*spiritual* Israel" under the kingship of Jesus (see Luther,
Lectures on Zechariah, 303); for more on "spiritual Israel," see the discussion of
Psalm 68:36 and Isaiah 25:2–3 in the main text of this chapter.

122. Some modern editions provide the reading "O großer Gott *der* Treu." The chorale line "O großer Gott *von* Treu," however, is presumably based on Exodus 34:6,
HErr GOtt, barmhertzig, und gnädig, und geduldig, und von großer Gnad und Treue

Der deinen Zorn gestillt,	who has stilled your wrath,
So sieh doch an die Wunden sein,	so look yet upon the wounds of his,
Sein Marter, Angst und schwere Pein;	his affliction, anguish and severe torment;
Um seinetwillen schone,	for his sake be tender:
Uns nicht nach Sünden lohne.	do not repay us[123] according to our sins.

("Lord God, merciful, and gracious, and patient, and of abounding grace and faithfulness"). The hymn writer could, of course, also have fulfilled the chorale's metric requirements by rendering the line as "O Gott von großer Treu," but that would have ruined the first-line parallelisms of the chorale's many stanzas ("O großer Gott von Macht," "O großer Gott von Ehr," "O großer Gott von Rath," and so on).

123. That is, us Lutheran Christians; the first word in this line, *Uns* ("us"), is given erroneously in some modern editions of the cantata as *Und* ("and"), a small detail that could considerably affect the meaning of this line and thus of the cantata (that is, changing the meaning to "and do not repay *any people* according to their sins").

Chapter 4

Bach's Cantatas and "the Jews" in the Gospel of John

The Gospel of John, unlike the other canonical gospels, consistently and explicitly denounces Jewish unbelievers in Jesus. Yet, perhaps surprisingly, the commentary movements within Bach's *St. John Passion* (BWV 245) do not really engage matters Jewish.[1] To explore Bach's construction of Judaism and Jewishness based on John, one has to turn to his church cantatas, particularly those written for Sundays whose assigned readings came from this gospel and touched, directly or indirectly, on relevant concerns, such as *Quasimodogeniti* (the First Sunday after Easter) and *Exaudi* (the Sunday after Ascension).[2] In ways that will not always be obvious

For encouragement and criticism in completing this chapter, I would like to thank Lauren Belfer, Raymond Erickson, Lars Fischer, Daniel Melamed, Robert Marshall, Michael Sommer, and Ruth Tatlow.

1. See Michael Marissen, *Lutheranism, Anti-Judaism, and Bach's St. John Passion* (New York: Oxford University Press, 1998); the commentary in the *St. John Passion* focuses on Christian guilt, as, for example, at no. 11, which asks of Jesus, "Who has struck you so?" and answers, "I, I and my sins." Regarding Bach's *St. Matthew Passion* (BWV 244), see Michael Marissen, "Blood, People, and Crowds in Matthew, Luther, and Bach," *Lutheran Quarterly* 19 (2005): 1–22 (reprinted as chapter 6 in this volume); and Johann Michael Schmidt, *Die Matthäus-Passion von Johann Sebastian Bach: Zur Geschichte ihrer religiösen und politischen Wahrnehmung und Wirkung* (Stuttgart: Kohlhammer, 2013).

2. See also Michael Marissen, "The Character and Sources of the Anti-Judaism in Bach's Cantata 46," *Harvard Theological Review* 96 (2003): 63–99 (reprinted as chapter 3 in this volume). In light of that article and this chapter, the brief

to today's listeners,[3] both the librettos and the musical settings of these cantatas, taking their cues from the distinctive language of the Gospel of John, reflect forcefully on the alleged persecution of the church (as the mystical body of Christ) by actual and metaphorical Jews both in the past and in the present.

Bach had expertise not only in music but also in scripture and its Lutheran interpretation,[4] and there can be no doubt that he was intimately familiar with the Gospel of John and its Lutheran interpretation. That said, this chapter explores not so much what Bach's heart-of-heart feelings or personal beliefs may have been but rather what his church cantatas most plausibly mean.

discussion of anti-Judaism and Bach's church cantatas in Raymond Erickson's in all other respects invaluable recent study, "The Early Enlightenment, Jews, and Bach," *Musical Quarterly* 94 (2011): 519–520, may seem overly sanguine. Note that concerning possible anti-Judaism, Erickson's essay discusses only Bach's cantatas for the Tenth Sunday after Trinity (BWV 46, 101, and 102); although his essay rightly calls attention to the altogether explicit anti-Catholic and anti-Muslim language in Bach's Cantatas 18 (*Gleichwie der Regen und Schnee vom Himmel fällt*) and 126 (*Erhalt uns, Herr, bei deinem Wort*), it strangely does not mention the directly negative references to "the Jews" and "those Jews" in Cantata 42 (*Am Abend aber desselbigen Sabbats*); see Marissen, *Lutheranism*, 52–53, 71. Eric Chafe, *J. S. Bach's Johannine Theology: The St. John Passion and the Cantatas for Spring 1725* (New York: Oxford University Press, 2014), acknowledges anti-Judaism in John and Bach but explicitly elects not to pursue the topic. Andreas Loewe, *Johann Sebastian Bach's St John Passion (BWV 245): A Theological Commentary* (Leiden: Brill, 2014), 9–10, reports that "there is no sign of anti-Judaism in [Bach's] Cantatas."

3. Conversely, some present-day listeners, I have discovered in public lecturing on Bach cantatas, imagine that the title of Bach's Cantata 163, *Nur jedem das seine!*, is anti-Jewish, as for them it preechoes the motto molded onto the gate at the Buchenwald concentration camp, *JEDEM DAS SEINE*, literally, "to each his own," which the Nazis understood as "one gets what he deserves." Cantata 163's "Only to Each His Own," however, in fact refers to the Christian obligation to pay taxes to secular authorities. The libretto of this cantata is based on specific language on the subject from Romans 13 and Matthew 22; see the Luther Bible at Matthew 22:21: *So gebet dem Käyser, was des Käysers ist, und GOTT, was GOttes ist* ("render therefore unto Caesar what is Caesar's, and unto God what is God's").

4. As explained and documented in the opening section of chapter 1 in this volume.

Jews in the Gospel of John

A key foundational text for our inquiry regarding "the Jews" in the Gospel of John and in Bach's church cantatas is John 8:31–47. Here is the passage as Bach would have known it, from Luther's translation (emphasis added):[5]

> Now then Jesus spoke to the Jews who [had] believed in Him: *"If you continue in my word, then you are my true disciples.* . . . But now you seek to kill me, a person like me who has spoken the truth to you that I have heard from God. . . . Were God your father, then you would love me; . . . Why is it that you do not know the language in which I speak?— Because you are not capable of hearing my words [Denn ihr könnet ja *meine Wort* (*sic*)[6] nicht hören]. *You are of the father the devil,* and you *want* to act according to your father's

5. Quotations from the Luther Bible are given here according to the text in Johann Olearius, *Biblische Erklärung, Darinnen, nechst dem allgemeinen Haupt-Schlüssel der gantzen heiligen Schrifft,* 5 vols. (Leipzig, 1678–1681). Bach owned a copy of this commentary Bible. Note that the biblical text of this seventeenth-century Luther Bible does not always correspond closely to what is found in modern so-called Luther Bibles, or to the readings of modern English Bibles, or to the King James Bible (despite Luther's significant influence on its wording), or to the readings of the various underlying ancient Hebrew or Greek texts; this is why I provide here literal translations of Luther's Bible into English rather than quoting from English Bibles. Luther believed it more important to convey what he thought the ancient texts *meant* than what they had *said.* Other translators who disagree with Luther's methods or results, or both, consider much of his Bible translation tendentious, both theologically and more generally.

6. Until the end of the seventeenth century, the nominative and accusative plural of *Wort* was not ordinarily inflected. The plural was introduced here (*meine Wort*) by Luther presumably to distinguish "words" as a means of communication from "the Word," that is, the divine (and incarnate) promise of salvation. "The Jews," in other words, not only failed to grasp the core message, but they did not even understand the words, the language in which the message was conveyed. As the conservative German New Testament scholar Hermann Strathmann paraphrased this thought in his commentary on the Gospel of John, "the Jews" are characterized by "an objective inability even to listen to Jesus's word. . . . Since Jesus

desire. He is *a murderer from the beginning,* and is not constituted in the truth, because the truth is not in him; *if he speaks lies, then he speaks from his own nature* [so redet er von seinem eigen], *for he is a liar, and a father of liars* [denn er ist ein Lügner, und ein Vater derselbigen].... Whoever is of God, he hears God's Word; therefore you do not hear, because *you are not of GOD.*"

Going on to read the whole of John, one will see that the gospel is predicated on a number of juxtapositions in which "the Jews" provide the negative foil for the positive attributes of what the gospel calls "the disciples" of and "the believers" in Jesus Christ:

"the Jews"	"the disciples/believers"
darkness (*Finsternis*, 1:5, 3:19, 8:12, 12:35, 12:46)[7]	light (*Licht*, 1:4–5, 1:7–9, 3:19–21, 5:35, 8:12, 9:5, 11:9–10, 12:35–36, 12:46), children of Light (*des Lichtes Kinder*, 12:36)
[children] of the devil ([*Kinder*] *von dem Teufel*, 8:44)	children of God (*Kinder Gottes*, 1:12, [11:52])
from below (*von untenher*, 8:23)	from above (*von obenher*, 8:23)

has come to destroy the works of the devil ... the children and servants of the devil have neither the ability to comprehend him nor the ability and inclination even to listen to him, let alone could they love him." Hermann Strathmann, *Das Evangelium nach Johannes* (Göttingen: Vandenhoeck und Ruprecht, 1968), 146. This commentary formed part of the prestigious commentary series *NTD* (*Das Neue Testament Deutsch*). First published in 1936, its eleventh and final print run came out in 1968 (this was a reprint of the fourth revised edition that had first appeared in 1959). Maria Neubrand quotes this passage from the second revised edition of 1954 in "Das Johannesevangelium und 'die Juden,'" *Theologie und Glaube* 99 (2009): 208.

7. It should be noted that there is a separate, more casual German term for simple physical darkness, say, at night (*Dunkelheit*). The term *Finsternis*, by contrast, is more intense and the one that would be used to refer to concepts such as "the powers of darkness," etc.

of this world (*von dieser Welt*, 8:23, [18:36])

not of this world (*nicht von dieser Welt*, 8:23, [18:36])

the law [that is, Torah] . . . through Moses (*das Gesetz . . . durch Moses*, 1:17)

grace and truth . . . through Jesus (*Gnade und Wahrheit . . . durch Jesum*, 1:17)

not to believe [in Jesus and therefore in God "the Father"] (*nicht glauben*, constant references)

to believe [in Jesus and therefore in God "the Father"] (*glauben*, constant references)

already condemned (*schon gerichtet*, 3:18)

not condemned (*nicht gerichtet*, 3:18, 5:24); [hence:] to have eternal life (*das ewige Leben haben*, constant references)

Belief in and continued acknowledgment of Jesus as God's Messiah (from the Hebrew word *mashiyach*, "anointed one"; in Greek, *Christos*) is the stated central concern of the Gospel of John (see 20:31). It portrays unbelief in Jesus Christ as the ultimate sin (see 16:9) and belief in Jesus Christ as inextricably linked to belief in God "the Father" (see 12:44). The acknowledgment of God by "the Jews" without belief in Christ, in other words, is not in fact belief in God at all, since it does not recognize the Most High as God the Father who sent his Son.

John 3:18 is a key text here, and Bach's Cantata 68, *Also hat Gott die Welt geliebt*, closes with a grim setting of this passage, verbatim: "Whoever believes in him [in Jesus], he will not be condemned; but whoever does not believe, he is already condemned [that is, will not see "eternal Life"]; for he does not believe in the name of the only begotten Son of God."

The import of John 3:18 is expanded on and clarified in 3:36 and 12:48, where the gospel says: "Whoever believes in the Son [that is, in Jesus], he has eternal life; whoever does not believe the Son, he will not see [eternal] life; instead the wrath of God remains on him. . . . Whoever despises me [Jesus] and does not receive my words, he already has his judge; the Word that I have spoken, this will condemn him on the Last Day."

All this suggests that one would be hard pressed to derive any essentially positive or even neutral perception of Jews and Judaism from the Gospel of John. The gospel moves beyond disagreement with Jewish unbelief in Jesus (which is not ethically problematic) to the teaching of contempt (which is ethically problematic: claiming that those whom it calls "Jews" are liars and murderers and *by nature* and *by volition* at that). John's anti-Judaism is not merely incidental but built into the very structure of the gospel's narrative and its import. That is to say, anti-Judaism cannot be attributed simply to traditional interpretation or misinterpretation of the gospel. The anti-Jewish sentiment is right there in the biblical text.[8]

Only after the horrors of the Shoah did the gospel's language genuinely begin to register with Christians as profoundly troubling. Against this background, many recent Christian interpreters (whether scholarly or devotional or both) have pursued vigorous strategies to avoid admitting that the gospel indeed teaches contempt for Jews and Judaism.[9] To what extent the theological anti-Judaism of the Gospel of John helped precipitate or facilitate the

8. Some interpreters emphasize that the language of John and other New Testament books is mild compared with that of other polemical writings from antiquity. See Luke T. Johnson, "The New Testament's Anti-Jewish Slander and the Conventions of Ancient Polemic," *Journal of Biblical Literature* 108 (1989): 419–441. This comparative perspective is certainly important and useful, but in the end, it cannot really get at the core problem. The Gospel of John, after all, unlike most other polemical writings from antiquity, is not an obscure historical text, consulted only occasionally by a handful of highly specialized scholars; it is, rather, a ubiquitous "living" narrative, arguably considered sacred and authoritative by billions of people.

9. A full range of interpretations is provided by the thirteen essays published in Reimund Bieringer, Didier Pollefeyt, and Frederique Vandecasteele-Vanneuville, eds., *Anti-Judaism and the Fourth Gospel* (Louisville: Westminster John Knox Press, 2001). The literature on the (possible) anti-Judaism of John is vast. Among the many other important studies are Richard Bauckham and Carl Mosser, eds., *The Gospel of John and Christian Theology* (Grand Rapids: William B. Eerdmans, 2008); Raymond E. Brown, *An Introduction to the Gospel of John* (New York: Doubleday, 2003), 157–75; William R. Farmer, *Anti-Judaism and the Gospels* (Harrisburg: Trinity Press International, 1999); and Adele

horrors of the Shoah and whether this process was inevitable are prickly questions involving much controversy. That the teaching of theological contempt is deeply problematic in its own right, though, is surely not a contentious claim, and the suggestion that this tradition of Christian anti-Judaism at the very least encouraged Gentile Christians to look the other way when their "racially" Jewish neighbors, the overwhelming majority of whom did not believe in Jesus, were deported seems eminently plausible.

Much of the controversy about possible anti-Judaism in John has hinged on the question of how most appropriately to understand the ancient Greek word *Ioudaios* (plural *Ioudaioi*). Leaving aside the titular expression *Basileus ton Ioudaion* (usually translated as "King of the Jews"), the words *Ioudaios* or *Ioudaioi* appear around seventy times in the ancient Greek texts of the Gospel of John but only once or twice in each of the other canonical gospels. It is generally accepted that in John, the words *Ioudaios* and *Ioudaioi* are used often with negative connotations, with some frequency in a neutral manner, and rarely, if ever, positively.

Many interpreters try to evade the charge of anti-Judaism by dissociating the *Ioudaioi* from the Jews, suggesting that traditional understandings, including Luther's, have misread John's expression as cultic when it ought to be read as geographical. John really meant not Jews (in the sense of worshipers of the God of Israel), so the argument goes, but Judeans (in the sense of natives of the land of Judea). According to this reading, no one today need be offended by John, because *Ioudaioi* refers narrowly to the people of a specific geographical region in antiquity, certainly not to all Jews at all times and in all places.

Yet neither history nor a plain-sense reading of John's narrative actually supports this interpretation. More than a century before Jesus, the term *Ioudaios* had already been extended to denote not

Reinhartz, *Befriending the Beloved Disciple: A Jewish Reading of the Gospel of John* (New York: Continuum, 2001).

only those people who lived in Judea or had Judean parents. A variety of historical sources demonstrate that this term could also refer to people who worshiped the God of the Temple in Jerusalem no matter where they lived or where they were born.[10] This is why it made perfect sense for John 6 to speak of Galileans—an ethnic group distinct from the people of Judea, as the first-century historian Josephus carefully notes[11]—and to call them *Ioudaioi*. Geographically, these people are Galileans; cultically, they are Jews. It likewise made sense for John 2 to refer to the purification rites of the *Ioudaioi* at a wedding in Cana, a village of Galilee (not Judea); the gospel is saying that the Galileans were practicing their own Jewish rites, not that the Galileans were practicing the rites of foreigners, namely, the Judeans. And further, when the gospel, in chapters 2, 5, 6, 7, 11, and 19, refers to the worshipers of the God of the Temple in Jerusalem as having traveled from abroad to attend the festivals of the *Ioudaioi*, the gospel is obviously referring not to the festivals of Judea but to the festivals of the Jews.[12]

Another widely endorsed means of evading the charge of anti-Judaism in John is the suggestion that when the gospel refers to "the *Ioudaioi*," it usually means the Jewish leaders and not the Jewish people in general. John was really condemning the Jewish authorities, in other words, and not ordinary Jews for rejecting Jesus. Yet a simple reading of the gospel narrative already undermines this idea. John 12:42 states that "even from among the leaders [of the Jews] *many* came to believe in Jesus." Moreover, the

10. Shaye J. D. Cohen, *The Beginnings of Jewishness: Boundaries, Varieties, Uncertainties* (Berkeley and Los Angeles: University of California Press, 1999), 69–106, is an extremely important and frequently overlooked historical study of this terminology and surrounding issues.

11. See Cohen, *The Beginnings of Jewishness*, 114, which cites Josephus, *The Jewish War*, 2.510, 4.105.

12. See especially Adele Reinhartz, "'Jews' and Jews in the Fourth Gospel," in Bieringer, Pollefeyt, and Vandecasteele-Vanneuville, *Anti-Judaism and the Fourth Gospel*, 213–227.

gospel clearly portrays the vast majority of "the people" as choosing to follow those among their leaders who did not believe in Jesus, thus rendering a distinction between the "guilt" of the leaders and the innocence of their flock meaningless.

Whom, then, *does* the Gospel of John mean by "the *Ioudaioi*"? For a start, it evidently does not mean to include any active followers of Jesus, whatever their cultic or ethnic background. In the Greek text of John, the followers of Jesus are called "the believers" nearly a hundred times, "the disciples" around seventy times, and "brothers" a couple of times.[13] Whatever their ethnicities or nationalities or cultural practices, though, the active followers of Jesus are never called *Ioudaioi*,[14] and whatever the expression "the *Ioudaioi*" might generally mean elsewhere, in John, it specifically refers only to Jews who did not yet believe, or no longer believed, in Jesus. So far as I can see, the gospel does not use the word *Ioudaioi* to refer to Jews who became followers of Jesus but otherwise remained largely observant as Jews (that is, in biblical scholarship today, these people, who ate kosher and circumcised their males, are often called Jewish Christians or Christian Jews). For the Gospel of John, those Jews who did not accept Jesus had simply settled on darkness over light, the devil over God, the forces from below over those from above, this world over the world to come, unbelief over belief, and eternal damnation over salvation. Clearly, then, Luther was entirely right in translating John's "the *Ioudaioi*" as *die Jüden* ("the Jews").[15]

13. See Paul Trebilco, *Self-Designations and Group Identity in the New Testament* (Cambridge: Cambridge University Press, 2012), 53–54, 114–117. Note that the words *christianos* (Christian) and *ekklesia* (assembly, but usually translated as "church"; rendered by Luther not as *Kirche* [church] but as *Gemeinde* [congregation/community]) do not appear in the Gospel of John. Nathanael, one of the chosen disciples of Jesus, mentioned only in John, is called (at 1:47) an "Israelite" (not a "Jew").

14. Reinhartz, " 'Jews' and Jews," 220–221.

15. For further support of this idea, see the remarkably insightful essay, Ruth Sheridan, "Issues in the Translation of οἱ Ἰουδαῖοι in the Fourth Gospel," *Journal of Biblical Literature* 132 (2013): 671–695.

What about *positive* depictions of "Jews" in the Gospel of John? Biblical interpreters have frequently argued that the gospel does also contain some fundamentally positive statements about people it calls Jews. This concerns, for instance, the "many of the Jews" mentioned in John 11:19 and 11:31–36 who showed empathy by coming to console Jesus's beloved friends Mary and Martha after the death of their brother, Lazarus. Yet the crucial point here emerges at the end of the scene, in John 11:45, when these "many of the Jews," after seeing Jesus raise Lazarus from the dead, *came to believe in Jesus*, thus ceasing, in John's scheme of things, to be Jews and becoming disciples and believers instead. The positive quality of these "many of the Jews," then, lies in their willingness to stop being Jews.

Much more significant is the frequent claim that the statement in John 4:22 that "we [Jews] understand what we worship, because salvation is from the Jews" is favorable toward Jews. I myself have suggested earlier that this verse has "extremely positive connotations."[16] Like many readers of John, I failed to pay sufficient attention to the verses surrounding this statement. John 4:21–23 reads (emphasis added):

> Jesus said to her [a woman of Samaria], "Believe me, woman, the hour is coming when you [Samaritans] will worship the Father [that is, God] neither on this mountain [Gerizim, the site of the Temple of the Samaritans] nor in Jerusalem [the site of the Temple of the Jews]. *You* [who have followed the beliefs and practices of Samaritanism] *worship what you do not understand; we* [who have followed the beliefs and practices of Judaism] *understand what we worship*, because salvation is from the Jews. *But* the hour is coming, and is now here, when the *true* worshipers will worship the Father

---

16. Marissen, *Lutheranism*, 22.

in Spirit and truth. And indeed, the Father seeks *such* [people] to worship him."

At its outset, this passage may indeed seem positive; it indicates that the Gospel of John does not reject the spiritual heritage of the pre-Christian Jewish religion. Moreover, it has Jesus explicitly self-identifying with the Jews, a people who "understand what they worship," for "salvation is from the Jews." So far, so good. Yet what follows surely gives this passage a decisive negative twist. John 4:23 clearly implies that henceforth neither Jews nor Samaritans but only those referred to by the gospel as disciples and believers qualify as *true* worshipers of God.[17] In short, salvation may be *from* the Jews, but it is *for* the Jews only if they stop being Jews and instead become believers by worshiping the Father in Spirit and truth and acknowledging the advent of God's promised Messiah in Jesus.

More than a few interpreters have also argued that the Gospel of John, whatever it may have to say about Jews, by definition cannot be anti-Jewish, for the simple reason that its author, many of the characters it portrays, and many of its original readers were in fact Jews. By the same logic, one would have to conclude that it was impossible for the British colonists who founded the United States of America to be anti-British.

Jews in Bach's Cantatas

The following discussion focuses on three cantatas in which Jews are presented through the lens of the Gospel of John in its Lutheran interpretation. These are Cantata 179, *Siehe zu, daß deine*

17. See also R. Alan Culpepper, "Anti-Judaism in the Fourth Gospel as a Theological Problem for Christian Interpreters," in Bieringer, Pollefeyt, and Vandecasteele-Vanneuville, *Anti-Judaism and the Fourth Gospel*, 74.

Gottesfurcht nicht Heuchelei sei, in which Jews feature in the form of stereotypical Pharisees; Cantata 42, Am Abend aber desselbigen Sabbats, the only cantata in which die Jüden are explicitly mentioned by name; and Cantata 44, Sie werden euch in den Bann tun, which draws on the so-called aposynagogos, the (supposed) total excommunication of Jesus's followers by the Jewish community either after or, as some would have it, even before the defeat of the Jewish uprising and the destruction of the Second Temple by the Romans in 70 CE.

The Pharisees: Cantata 179

Cantata 179 formulates a critique of lukewarm and hypocritical Christians, who it proclaims need to be "saved" from their "sins" by the "Lamb of God" (an expression that stems from John 1:29 and 1:36). Its opening chorus is a verbatim setting of Luther's translation of Sirach 1:34 (1:28–29 in the majority of modern English Bibles): "See to it that your fear of God be not hypocrisy, and do not serve God with false heart!" The immediately following recitative, set for tenor, then comments: "The Christianity of today is, unfortunately, badly appointed: most of the Christians in the world are tepid Laodiceans[18] and swelled-up Pharisees, who outwardly show themselves as upright."[19]

Here the cantata clearly buys into and reproduces the well-established stereotypical view, anchored firmly in the New Testament (though not found elsewhere in the literature of antiquity) and especially in the Gospel of Matthew, that portrays Pharisees as puffed up and hypocritical. Hence the derivation of the designation pharisaical, defined currently, for example, by Merriam-Webster as "marked by hypocritical censorious self-righteousness."

18. See Revelation 3:14–16.

19. See Matthew 23:28.

New Testament and Patristics scholar Paula Fredriksen aptly sums up this polemic based on what is in fact a caricature of the Pharisees:

> The topic 'Jesus and the Pharisees' has long functioned as a sort of shorthand for 'Grace versus Legalism,' 'Christianity versus Judaism'—and even ... 'Protestantism versus Catholicism.' ... In describing the Gospel's ancient enemy, Luther made clear the identity of its modern counterpart [that is, the Catholic Church], and so turned ancient polemic to contemporary use.[20]

Consequently, Luther "perceived and modeled" the intrareligious conflict of his era in terms of reference drawn from what was in fact a late-first-century conflict.[21] Fredriksen also notes that while few today would still condone "this Protestant conflation of Catholic/Pharisee ... the disparagement of the Pharisees continues largely unabated."[22]

Fearing the Jews, Then and Now: Cantata 42

"The Jews" feature explicitly by name in Cantata 42, where the reference is taken verbatim from John 20 and then applied emblematically to the situation of the church's ongoing persecution by rhetorical "Jews." The first recitative, a setting of John 20:19, is narrated by the tenor voice in a manner reminiscent of the heightened

20. Paula Fredriksen, *From Jesus to Christ* (New Haven: Yale University Press, 2000), 103–104; see also Charlotte Klein, *Anti-Judaism in Christian Theology*, translated by Edward Quinn (Philadelphia: Fortress Press, 1978), 67–91, a classic treatment of the problem of caricaturing the Pharisees, who many people today do not realize were heavily concerned with ethical issues and were essentially the fathers of modern Judaism.

21. Fredriksen, *From Jesus to Christ*, 104.

22. Fredriksen, *From Jesus to Christ*, 104.

intensity of the tenor Evangelist's presentation of biblical narrative in Bach's oratorios. For Bach's congregants, accustomed to the Lutheran tradition of *sola scriptura*, this would therefore have signaled the authoritative nature of this recitative's text: "But on the evening of this same sabbath, when the disciples [of Jesus] were gathered and the doors were locked out of fear of the Jews, [the resurrected] Jesus came and entered among them."[23]

The response to this passage takes the form of an exquisite and leisurely alto aria of more than ten minutes' duration, declaring that "where two and three are gathered in Jesus's precious name, there Jesus appears among them and says to this the 'amen.'"[24] Designed to comfort beleaguered followers of Jesus, this aria obviously draws on Matthew 18:20, "For where two or three are gathered in my [Jesus's] name, there I am among them."

The implications of all this for the persecuted church are forcefully spelled out by the following paired recitative and aria for bass. The recitative reads (the emphasis is added but is matched by the ferocious musical declamation, rhythmic animation, and textual repetition of the setting itself): "One can see a fine example in this, from what took place in Jerusalem; for when the disciples [of Jesus] had gathered together in the dark shadow, out of fear of those Jews, at that my Savior entered among them—as testimony that he wants to be his church's protection.[25] *So let the enemies rage!*" The bass aria

23. This narrative from the Gospel of John is heavily alluded to in the penultimate movement of *Halt im Gedächtnis Jesum Christ* (BWV 67), Bach's other surviving cantata for *Quasimodogeniti*.

24. In the canonical gospels, Jesus is often depicted as prefacing what he says with *"Amen* I say to you," typically rendered by Luther as *"Wahrlich* ich sage euch" and by the King James Bible as *"Verily* I say unto you." In the Gospel of John, and only in this gospel, to stress even further the fundamental truth of whatever Jesus says, the expression is always doubled: *"Amen, Amen,* I say to you" (this happens twenty-five times).

25. It would have gone without saying for Luther and his followers that only the true church could be *"his* [the Savior's] church" and that the Roman Catholic

then comes to the following conclusion (the added emphasis again matches that of the music's extended melisma): "Jesus is a shield to those who belong to him, when they encounter *persecution*. For them the sun must shine with the gilded caption: 'Jesus is a shield to those who belong to him, when they encounter *persecution*.'"

This notion of persecution by the Jews was well established in the traditional Lutheran reading of the Gospel of John as a whole. Just as the Jews had pursued Jesus, so they would continue to pursue the followers of Jesus, so the argument went, drawing on John 15:20–25, which has Jesus saying to his followers (emphasis added): "If they [the Jews] have *persecuted* me [see John 5:16], they will also *persecute* you.[26] . . . All this they will do to you for my name's sake. . . . Had I not come and said it to them, then they would be without sin. Yet now they cannot offer any objection to excuse their sin. . . . Had I not done my works among them . . . they would be without sin. Yet now they have seen it and yet hate both me and my father. So that the saying might be fulfilled [that is] written in *their* Law: they hate me without cause." For Cantata 42, Jews are the persecuting enemies of the disciples of Jesus, and "the Jews" of the Gospel of John are emblematic of the true church's persecuters ever since.

Bach would have encountered similar statements about Jews as the *arch*enemies of Christians in Johannes Müller's *Judaismus oder*

Church did not fall into this category; far from needing protection, it was the principal aggressor.

26. Michael S. Sommer, *Battles between Windmills: "Heresy" and "Orthodoxy" in Johannine Interpretation* (Oxford: Michael S. Sommer, 2011), 79, notes that the verb *diōkō* in John 5:16 is the ordinary Greek word for "*prosecute*" and should not be rendered here as "*persecute*." The issue at 5:16 is a legal one of Jesus's breaking the Sabbath, and it may be, then, that the use of *diōkō* again in 15:20 is meant to refer not to the persecution but to the prosecution, by the Jews, of Jesus's followers. John 15:18–25 speaks of "the world" as "hating" Jesus's followers, but it is clear from verse 25's quotation of Old Testament "law" (see Psalm 35:19 or 69:4, "they that hate me without cause") that what is especially meant in this passage is hostility from Jews in particular.

Jüdenthumb. Jews, Müller wrote, "are intensely inimical toward
Christians, so much so that Luther writes in the eighth Jena volume: 'A Christian will have, next to the devil, no more bitter and
more intense enemy than a real Jew.'"[27] Müller was quoting from
Luther's screed "On the Jews and Their Lies" (1543), which, as indicated, was included in volume 8 of the Jena edition of Luther's collected German works, though it is, of course, impossible to know for
certain whether Bach specifically read this anti-Jewish material.[28]

What is clear, however, is that Bach at the very least engaged
similar comments in his Calov Bible. This is indicated, for instance,
by Bach's marginal notation of a passage omitted at 2 Samuel
22:44, an omission not included in Calov's own list of errata.
Within Calov's chapter 22, verse 44 marks the beginning of a new
section, which in Lutheranism's radically Christocentric fashion
bears the title "The LOrd Messiah's song of praise after his exaltation, particularly among the gentiles" (*Der Lobgesang des HErrn
Messiae nach seiner Erhöhung, sonderlich unter den Heyden*). Verse 44
itself, then, reads: "You [that is, God the Father] deliver me [that
is, the exalted "Lord Messiah," Jesus Christ] from the quarrelsome
people" (*Du hilffest mir von dem zänckischen Volck*). Calov glosses this
as follows: "that is, from the backsliding Jews, who have become
my [that is, Jesus's] archenemies: from this I am delivered; indeed
you [that is, God the Father] are casting them out" (*Das ist[,] von
den abtrünnigen Juden, die meine Ertzfeinde worden sind: davon werde
ich erlöset; die werden gar von dir verstossen*). Bach entered an aster-
isk right after Calov's gloss and wrote into the margin the missing
second half of the biblical verse, "and protect me to be the head

27. Johannes Müller, *Judaismus oder Jüdenthumb—Das ist: Ausführlicher Bericht
von des Jüdischen Volckes Unglauben, Blindheit und Verstockung* (Hamburg, 1644),
1386. Bach owned both Müller's book and Luther's eight Jena volumes.

28. The passage Müller quoted can be found conveniently in Martin Luther,
"Von den Juden und ihren Lügen (1543)," in *D. Martin Luthers Werke: Kritische
Gesamtausgabe*, vol. 53, edited by F. Cohrs and O. Brenner (Weimar: Böhlau, 1920),
482, lines 8–10.

among the gentiles; a people whom I did not know serves me" (und behütest mich zum Haupt ünter den Heyden, ein Volck, das ich nicht kannte, dienet mir).[29] Since it is not obvious that any material was missing here, one sees that Bach must have read this passage about the enmity of the Jews rather attentively.

Several of my colleagues have suggested to me that Bach's own true feelings about Jews cannot have been negative, because the many annotations in his Calov Bible indicate a certain respect for the Old Testament, especially regarding King David and the music in the First Temple in Jerusalem. What I have written elsewhere about George Frideric Handel and the Old Testament applies equally to Bach, though:

> My fellow Handel admirers often assert that the compos-
> er's practice of writing oratorios on ancient Israelite sub-
> jects (for example, Israel in Egypt and Judas Maccabaeus)
> is "pro-[modern-]Jewish." What they don't realize is that
> although Handel and his contemporaries certainly did
> have a high opinion of the characters populating their Old
> Testament, this was only because Christians had already for
> many centuries thought of the righteous ancient Israelites
> as proto-Christian believers in God's expected messiah,
> Jesus of Nazareth, namely Jesus Christ. (That is to say,
> these righteous ancient Israelites were not thought of,
> as it were, as proto-Orthodox, Conservative, Reform, or
> Reconstructionist Jews.)
>
> This is why... in his oratorio Israel in Egypt, Handel can
> set the words "And [the Hebrew people's] cry came up unto
> God" to the melody of the first phrase from the Lutheran
> hymn "Christ lag in Todesbanden," a musical quotation
> that makes perfect sense from a traditional [typological]

29. See facsimile 102, in Howard H. Cox, ed., The Calov Bible of J. S. Bach (Ann Arbor: UMI Research Press, 1985).

Christian perspective but no sense from a modern Jewish perspective.

Traditional Christianity, then, often taught that in its time and place—namely, *before* the advent of Jesus—the Jewish religion was "good."[30]

Jews and "Jews" as Excommunicators and Murderers: Cantata 44

The point of departure for Cantata 42, as we saw, was John 20:19, which refers to Jesus's followers being afraid of the Jews. What was it that they supposedly feared? The narrative source explaining the ostensible grounds for this fear was John 9:22, rendered by Luther as follows: "For they [the parents of a man born blind who had been healed by Jesus] were afraid of the Jews. Because the Jews had already agreed among themselves: if someone acknowledged Him [Jesus] as Christ [that is, as God's Messiah], then he would be put under ban [that is, would be excommunicated from the synagogue]."

It is this theme, the supposed excommunication and persecution of Jews who acknowledged Jesus as Christ from and by the Jewish community, the so-called *aposynagogos*, that is at the heart of Bach's Cantata 44, *Sie werden euch in den Bann tun*. It features prominently in the gospel portion assigned to the Sunday *Exaudi* (the Sunday after Ascension), the liturgical occasion for which Bach prepared Cantata 44. In the Luther Bibles of Bach's day, this passage, John 15:26 through 16:4, reads as follows (emphasis added):

[And Jesus said to his disciples:] "When the Comforter— whom I will send to you from the Father—comes, he (the Spirit of Truth who proceeds from the Father) will bear

---

30. Michael Marissen, *Tainted Glory in Handel's Messiah* (New Haven: Yale University Press, 2014), 14–15.

witness to me. And you will also bear witness; because you have been with me from the beginning. Such things I have spoken to you so you are not offended. *They* [the Jews] *will place you under the ban; the time is coming, however, that whoever kills you will suppose he is thus doing God a service. And therefore they* [the Jews] *will do such things to you, because they recognize neither my Father nor me.* I have said such things to you so that, when the time comes, you may remember that I told you. I did not initially tell you this because I was with you."

Drawing on this passage, Bach's Cantata 44 starts with a verbatim setting of John 16:2a, "They will place you under the ban" (*Sie werden euch in den Bann tun*), for tenor and bass singers with orchestra, followed by a verbatim setting of 16:2b, "the time is coming, however, that whoever kills you will suppose he is thus doing God a service" (*es kömmt aber die Zeit, daß, wer euch tötet, wird meinen, er tue Gott einen Dienst daran*), for chorus with orchestra.[31] Here is what Bach's Calov Bible had to say about this particular verse (the italics here indicate Calov's glosses):

They *(the godless Jews)* will place you [who believe in me] under the ban *(thrust you out of their synagogues and congregations, and esteem you as cursed people, [John] chap. [9]:22, chap. 12:42)*; the time is coming, however, that whoever kills you will suppose he is thus doing God a service *(as if he were accomplishing what is commanded by GOD in the Law [of Moses], at Deuteronomy 13:6 and following verses)*. And therefore they [that is, the Jews] will do such things to you, because they recognize neither my father nor me.

---

31. Bach's other surviving cantata for *Exaudi* (BWV 183, also entitled *Sie werden euch in den Bann tun*) likewise opens with a verbatim quotation of John 16:2 but does not, so far as I can tell, go on to denounce Judaism.

In recent scholarship, the historicity of the *aposynagogos* has been fundamentally questioned. The term itself ("to [completely] put out of the synagogue"), employed three times in this gospel (at 9:22, 12:42, and 16:2), is otherwise unknown in contemporaneous or earlier texts in Greek. Many scholars doubt that anyone would have been totally banned from the Jewish community at this time simply for acknowledging Jesus as God's Messiah; elsewhere in the New Testament (in the book of Acts, for example), the apostles of Jesus are depicted as entering synagogues and the Temple without any hint that they had been excommunicated. It certainly cannot be demonstrated that anyone who acknowledged Jesus's messianic role was ever banned from a synagogue at any time before the Gospel of John was written, and what is known about the broader historical context renders any such practice highly unlikely.[32] It therefore seems rather more plausible to assume that the author of the Gospel of John did not introduce the *aposynagogos* in order to describe a historical reality that had led him to think badly of "the Jews" but in fact introduced the claim that ethnically Jewish followers of Christ had been excommunicated (rather than, say, seceding voluntarily to form their own community) to legitimize his preexisting anti-Jewish position.

Needless to say, early-modern Lutherans needed no external historical corroboration to take at face value the gospel's claim that disciples of Jesus had been excommunicated and persecuted

---

32. See Adele Reinhartz, "Introduction and Annotations: The Gospel According to John," in Amy-Jill Levine and Marc Zvi Brettler, eds., *The Jewish Annotated New Testament* (New York: Oxford University Press, 2011), 178. The once widely accepted contention, formulated in its most influential form by J. Louis Martyn in 1968, that the *aposynagogos* passages in the Gospel of John are a response to the established practice of cursing heretics as part of the regular Jewish liturgy (the so-called *birkat ha-minim*) is no longer given credence by most scholars in the field, who now assume that, to the extent that the *birkat ha-minim* was already in general use at the time, which is in any case doubtful, it would not have been directed against Christians. Versions of the *birkat ha-minim* that target Christians are clearly of a much later date. See Ruth Langer, *Cursing the Christians? A History of the Birkat Haminim* (New York: Oxford University Press, 2012), 127–129.

by Jews who did not accept Jesus as God's Messiah. For Luther and his followers, John's *aposynagogos* formed the paradigm for any form of persecution of the true church by actual or metaphorical Jews. The latter were to be found principally in the Roman church.

This Lutheran transference from the assumed earlier Jewish persecution of the initial followers of Jesus to the contemporary persecution of Protestant Christians by Rome was laid out clearly, for example, in a chapter on the subject in August Pfeiffer's *Evangelische Christen-Schule*. Before moving on to establish the contemporary relevance of the issue, Pfeiffer explained, based on a survey of later Jewish law, that "the *Jewish ban* . . . was *of three kinds,*" adding that "the scholars are not at one about which type of ban our Savior actually has in mind when he says: '*They will place you under the ban.*'"[33] He then went on to clarify:

> It is not just a question of the *Jewish ban*, but of the ban customarily applied by the Christian church. Here, then, we again set aside the *nonsensical anathema* ("fulmen brutum" [that is, futile threat]) *of the Roman Pope,* which he is in the habit of imposing not only on kings and princes but also on innocent Christian congregations. For in this he really proves himself to be *the* Antichrist, and nobody need be worried about or perturbed by such a ban. (Augustine: "Injusta vincula disrumpit justitia" [Unjust bonds justice doth break].) *What the Pope binds on earth, God looses in heaven: We might be under the Pope's ban, but the Pope is under God's ban!*[34]

Against this backdrop, it is little wonder that Bach's treatment of John 16:2 in Cantata 44 focuses on what Pfeiffer called

---

33. August Pfeiffer, "Von der *Excommunication* oder von dem Kirchen-Bann," in *Evangelische Christen-Schule* (Leipzig, 1724), 992. Bach owned this volume.

34. Pfeiffer, "Von der *Excommunication,*" 993–994.

"the Jewish ban." The choral setting of 16:2b ("the time is coming, however, that whoever kills you will suppose he is thus doing God a service") would seem to conjure up specifically the "fear of the Jews" from John 9:22, 19:38, and 20:19. Moreover, the musical rendering of "whoever *kills* you will suppose" in bars 25–31 bears a slightly cryptic but nevertheless extremely striking resemblance to some of the formidable chromaticism performed by "the Jews" in the choral setting of John 18:31b in Bach's *St. John Passion*, "we are not permitted *to kill* anyone" (*Wir dürfen niemand töten*). This music had first been rendered in Leipzig only six weeks before the Sunday for which Bach created Cantata 44.

Here the immediate response to this prediction of Jewish/ "Jewish" violence takes the form of an exquisitely melancholy da capo aria for alto singer, oboe, and continuo. Its text reads: "On earth Christians must be true disciples of Christ. Until they are blissfully overcome, torment, ban, and great anguish lie in store for them at every turn." This response clearly illustrates the transformation of the "Jewish ban" into the threat of a "ban" that confronts Christ's *true disciples* continuously, though ultimately in vain. The aria's expression "true disciples" (*wahre Jünger*) surely alludes to the turn of phrase "truly disciples of mine" (*alethos mathetai mou*) in John 8:31. This expression is found nowhere else in the Bible, and its rendering as *meine rechte Jünger* ("my true disciples") is likewise unique to Luther's Bible translation. As we saw, this very verse, John 8:31, marks the opening of the gospel's extended discourse on Jews as children of the devil, as godless, and as (inherently and by volition) mendacious and murderous.

Bach's aria expresses a sort of proleptic judgment. Yes, the true disciples of Christ experience torment and great anguish in the present world, as captured by the aria's general minor-mode melancholia and by its chromaticism at the phrase "torment, ban, and great anguish." But other musical aspects are positive and consoling. The aria features the surface rhythms of the sarabande, the noblest of the stately court dances that many of Bach's fellow

Leipzigers were being taught by resident French dance masters at the time.[35] Here another striking similarity to Bach's *St. John Passion*, rendered in Leipzig only a few weeks earlier, comes into play. There the aria "Ach, mein Sinn" set a weighed-down text to a tormented melody and corresponding harmonies but countered this with the ennobling rhythms of the sarabande.[36]

The melancholy alto aria of Cantata 44, by virtue of the relationship between its heavy mood and exalted style, thus anticipates the conceit of the last two lines of its following bass recitative, whose text reads: "The Antichrist—that great monster—seeks with sword and fire to persecute the members of Christ, because their teaching is repugnant to him. In the process he [as a rhetorical "Jew"] doubtless imagines what he does must be pleasing to God. Yet Christians are like those palm branches that, weighed down, only rise even higher." This imagery of the palm branches intentionally weighed down to stimulate their growth upward is also found, for example, in the tragedy *Papinianus* by Andreas Gryphius (1616–1664), whose main character exclaims,

35. See Meredith Little and Natalie Jenne, *Dance and the Music of J. S. Bach* (Bloomington: Indiana University Press, 2001), 3–15, 92–113, 236–250, 302–303; on Cantata 44, see 239. The sarabande, a slow triple-meter dance, is marked by four-bar phrases in which there is typically an agogic accent on the second beats in bars 1 and 3 and a point of repose on the first beat of bar 4.

36. See Marissen, *Lutheranism*, 17. Laurence Dreyfus has formulated a spirited criticism of the idea that "Ach, mein Sinn" has anything to do with sarabandes, on the grounds that the aria's apparently required tempo is too fast to project a sense of the dance and that the phrase structure does not allow for this classification. See Laurence Dreyfus, "The Triumph of 'Instrumental Melody': Aspects of Musical Poetics in Bach's *St. John Passion*," *Bach Perspectives* 8 (2011): 96–121. Elsewhere, however, Dreyfus argues that the middle movement of Bach's Sonata in G minor for gamba and keyboard (BWV 1029) successfully engages the structure of the sarabande in a meaningful way even though its given tempo, as he himself admits, is too slow to project a sense of the dance. See Laurence Dreyfus, *Bach and the Patterns of Invention* (Cambridge: Harvard University Press, 1996), 116–122. As for the question of phrase structure, baroque dance expert Meredith Little readily identifies "Ach, mein Sinn" with the sarabande. See Little and Jenne, *Dance and the Music of J. S. Bach*, 243–244.

"the noble palm rises the more one weighs it down."[37] The under-lying notion of the Christian as a growing palm tree draws on Psalm 92:13, which is rendered in the Luther Bibles of Bach's day as *der Gerechte wird grünen wie ein Palmbaum, er wird wach-sen wie ein Ceder auf Libanon* ("the righteous one will thrive like a palm tree; he will rise like a cedar on [the mountain range called] Lebanon"). Luther assumed that the unspecified tree in Psalm 1 was also a palm tree and noted, significantly, that the palm is the only tree that grows upward against every weight and pressure put upon it.[38]

What weighs down the "true disciples of Christ" in Bach's Cantata 44 is "persecution" by "the Antichrist." The *antichristos* is a mysterious, violent apocalyptic figure mentioned by name in the Bible in 1 John 2:18, 2:22, and 4:3 and also in 2 John 1:7. In Lutheran thought, "the Antichrist" was predominantly understood to be the pope, who was regularly accused of acting, in essence, like Jews, both biblical and contemporaneous.[39]

37. See Peter M. Daly, *Literature in the Light of the Emblem: Structural Parallels between the Emblem and Literature in the Sixteenth and Seventeenth Centuries* (Toronto: University of Toronto Press, 1979), 140. Daly, like Alfred Dürr, *The Cantatas of J. S. Bach: With Their Librettos in German-English Parallel Text*, trans-lated and revised by Richard D. P. Jones (Oxford: Oxford University Press, 2005), 341–342, draws on the material presented in Albrecht Schöne, *Emblematik und Drama im Zeitalter des Barock*, 3rd ed. (Munich: C. H. Beck, 1993), 72–73.

38. Martin Luther, *Operationes in Psalmos, 1519–21*, in *D. Martin Luthers Werke: Kritische Gesamtausgabe*, vol. 5, edited by Ernst Thiele (Weimar: Böhlau, 1892), 41, lines 6–7. On the egregious anti-Judaism in Luther's commentary on other parts of Psalm 1, see Marissen, "The Character and Sources" (reprinted as chapter 3 in this volume).

39. For a convenient and remarkably insightful overview of the Lutheran slur-ring of Roman Catholics as "Jews," see David Nirenberg, *Anti-Judaism: The Western Tradition* (New York: W. W. Norton, 2012), 246–268. Martin Luther, *Colloquia oder Tischreden, so von Johann Aurifaber mit Fleiß zusammen getragen* (Halle, 1743), chap. 27 (cols. 1300–1430) bears the title *Vom Antichrist oder Pabst* ("On the Antichrist or Pope"). Aurifaber's compilation went through a great many editions, one of which Bach owned. Consider, too, Philipp Jacob Spener, *Gerechter Eifer wider das Antichristische Pabstthum* (Frankfurt, 1714), a book Bach also owned.

In saying that the Antichrist "doubtless *imagines what he does* [that is, killing "the members of Christ"—the true church—"with sword and fire"] *must be pleasing to God*," this recitative text in Cantata 44 is, of course, clearly echoing the anti-Jewish polemic of John 16:2b ("whoever kills you *will suppose he is . . . doing God a service*").

That Luther had associated this threat not only with meta-phorical "Jews" such as the pope but also with contemporaneous actual Jews is evident, for example, from the widely circulated and continually reprinted "Table Talk" (*Tisch-Reden*). There Luther is quoted as saying (emphasis added): "The Jews, impersonating med-ics, deprive of life and property the Christians who take their med-ication, for *they suppose they do God a service* if only they intensely torment the Christians and secretly kill them."[40] It is clear from the formulation "for they suppose they do God a service" that Luther understood this alleged behavior on the part of contemporaneous Jews specifically as a fulfillment of the prophecy in John 16:2b.

Whether one might infer from this that Bach's Cantata 44 (and Cantata 42) could also have been meant or understood as a warning against the threat emanating from the very few Jewish families liv-ing in Leipzig at the time or from the Jews who traveled to Leipzig to attend its trade fairs is a moot point.[41] As I have been suggesting, the cantatas' principal concern is with Roman Catholicism, tarred by Lutherans with the same brush as the Jewish religion, not least for supposedly sharing what they considered Judaism's deadening focus on works-righteousness.

Some will respond to my line of reasoning by countering that contemptuous anti-Jewish language when applied not to actual Jews but to Gentiles is not truly anti-Jewish. Among other things, I have

40. Luther, *Colloquia oder Tischreden,* 2308.

41. On the very few Jews resident in Leipzig and on the many Jews attend-ing the Leipzig trade fairs, see Josef Reinhold, "Jüdischer Messebesuch und Wiederansiedlung von Juden in Leipzig im 18. und frühen 19. Jahrhundert," in *Judaica Lipsiensia: Zur Geschichte der Juden in Leipzig,* edited by Manfred Unger (Leipzig: Edition Leipzig, 1994), 12–27.

heard a great many conservative Lutheran theologians make this argument at academic conferences. Indeed, I have heard this rationale extended to the claim that the word *jew* as a verb is unproblematic when used not against Jews in particular but simply to denounce cheating or overslyness in business dealings in general. While not everyone may realize that the term *gypped* for "robbed" or "cheated" originates in the association of these transgressions with Roma and Sinti (that is, the so-called gypsies), it would surely be implausible for anyone to claim that they do not recognize the origin and connotations of the verb *jew*, regardless of the context in which it is used.

Alternatively, scholars have repeatedly suggested that a text cannot be anti-Jewish if it does not contain the words *Jew* or *Judaism*. If one follows this rather bizarre logic, none of the canonical gospels, or Bach's two surviving Passions, for that matter, could be considered pro-Christian, of course, since none of these texts contains the word *Christian* or *Christianity*.

Conclusion

Bach's substantial engagement of polemical anti-Jewish passages from the Gospel of John in his church cantatas has to all intents and purposes been missed or ignored in the vast secondary literature.[42] Doubtless, many Bach lovers, if confronted with

---

42. Some discussion of these passages took place at a conference session with the title "Antijudaismus in Bachs Passionen?" at the *Tagung der Internationalen Arbeitsgemeinschaft für theologische Bachforschung*, June 6–8, 1998, during the *Arolser Barockfestspiele* in Bad Arolsen, Germany. On this occasion, the principal speakers made the remarkable claim, over and over again, that Bach's cantatas and Passion settings cannot be "anti-Jewish" simply because they nowhere advocate the violent eradication of world Jewry. This presumably bears witness to the extent to which debates of this kind in Germany remain overdetermined by the issue of responsibility for, and complicity in, the Shoah, making it virtually impossible to acknowledge and critically assess forms of anti-Jewish resentment and polemic that fall short of outright eliminationist anti-Semitism but are, of course, more than problematic enough in their own right all the same.

the material presented here, would dismiss the relevance of this biblical language out of hand, simply on the grounds that in great classical repertories, it is "the music itself" that counts and not the words. "Beauty [or at least aesthetic magnificence] trumps all," these listeners would contend. This response is not unlike the apologetic claim that in the end, the declaration of God's boundless love for the world in the Gospel of John neutralizes its polemic against the Jews.[43] Other interpreters, of course, are more inclined to argue that the anti-Jewish polemic in the Gospel of John in fact undermines or negates its declaration of God's boundless love for the world.[44] Likewise, the aesthetic magnificence of Bach's musical settings surely makes these great cantatas *more*, not less, problematic. The notion that beauty trumps all really is too good to be true.

43. See, for example, Reimund Bieringer, Didier Pollefeyt, and Frederique Vandecasteele-Vanneuville, "Wrestling with Johannine Anti-Judaism: A Hermeneutical Framework for the Analysis of the Current Debate," in Bieringer, Pollefeyt, and Vandecasteele-Vanneuville, *Anti-Judaism and the Fourth Gospel*, 37.

44. See Reinhartz, "'Jews' and Jews," 227.

PART III

Not Taking Up Anti-Judaism in Passion Settings

Chapter 5

Bach's *St. John Passion* and "the Jews"

Among Martin Luther's best-known writings today is his screed "On the Jews and Their Lies," from 1543.[1] There Luther suggested sanctions for Jews who would not embrace his Christianity: burn their places of worship, destroy their homes, seize their prayer books and Talmudic writings, and, finally, expel them from areas of Europe. (Since the 1980s, many Lutheran church bodies have officially repudiated Luther's anti-Jewish writings.)

Now that J. S. Bach's indebtedness to Luther has come to be widely acknowledged, listeners could easily assume that Bach harbored hostility toward Jews and, accordingly, that his music projects such hostility. Throw in his engagement with the Gospel of John, with its continual harping on "the Jews" as inimical to Jesus, his followers, and truth in general, and one might reasonably wonder whether there is even room for discussion.

Indeed, the debate surrounding Bach's *St. John Passion* has grown more heated in recent decades; witness the media frenzy surrounding student objections to performances at Swarthmore College in 1995 and the picketing of the concert in which Helmuth

1. Martin Luther, "On the Jews and Their Lies, 1543," in *Luther's Works*, vol. 47, *The Christian in Society IV*, edited by Franklin Sherman, translated by Martin H. Bertram (Philadelphia: Fortress Press, 1971), 123–306; Martin Luther, "Von den Juden und ihren Lügen (1543)," in *D. Martin Luthers Werke: Kritische Gesamtausgabe*, vol. 53, edited by F. Cohrs and O. Brenner (Weimar: Böhlau, 1920), 412–552.

Rilling and the Oregon Bach Festival scheduled the work, also in 1995.

As mentioned in several earlier chapters, many music lovers maintain that Bach's librettos can simply be ignored, that his vocal music is to be valued for its timeless, so-called purely musical qualities (qualities that do, in fact, largely account for the repertory's wildly successful migration from the church to the concert hall). Devotees often go on to insist that Bach himself would have agreed with the notion that great music is best heard for its own sake.

But Bach's job in Leipzig was to be a "musical preacher" for the city's main Lutheran churches, and we can be sure that in preparing his musical setting, Bach had a thorough knowledge of the Gospel of John and its Lutheran interpretation.[2] His *St. John Passion* libretto consists of the Luther Bible's literal translation (from Greek into German) of John 18–19 in the form of recitatives and choruses, along with extensive commentary in the form of interspersed arias and hymns.

John contains many references to "the Jews," and no attentive reader can fail to notice that they are overwhelmingly negative. In this gospel, the cosmos is engaged in a battle. On one side are God the Father, Good, Heaven, Light, and Jesus and his followers. On the other side are Satan, Evil, the World, Darkness, and "the Jews" (the usual translation for John's *hoi Ioudaioi*; recent notions of rendering this more accurately as "the Judeans" or "the Jewish leaders" or "some of the Jewish leaders" are well-meaning but seem textually and contextually unwarranted).[3] Many dualisms of this sort are found in other contemporary religious writings, such as the Dead Sea Scrolls.

2. Bach's biblical and theological expertise is explained and documented in the opening section of chapter 1.

3. For a thorough, sensitive discussion, see Ruth Sheridan, "Issues in the Translation of οἱ Ἰουδαῖοι in the Fourth Gospel," *Journal of Biblical Literature* 132 (2013): 671–695.

The puzzling thing from a historical point of view is why the author of John called Jesus's opponents "the Jews" when he knew that Jesus was a Jew (4:9, 4:20–22), as were his disciples (20:19, where they are seen to observe an extension of the Sabbath; on the other hand, however, it ought to be noted that no active believers in Jesus are *called* "Jews" in the Gospel of John).[4] Furthermore, John's fundamental statement concerning Jesus as God incarnate (1:1–18) is modeled on Jewish understanding of wisdom, and his Jesus has traditionally been pictured as apocalyptic Passover lamb, securing freedom from the bondage of evil by being "lifted up."

This is a characteristic pun in John's Greek, where the concept is employed for both the crucifixion and the exaltation of Jesus. Jesus's "exaltation" on the cross, that is to say, becomes the very means by which he is lifted up to rule in glory with God the Father in heaven, as attested in a Christian reading of Isaiah 52:13 and Psalm 110:1.

In another significant bit of wordplay by John, the Jewish high priest Caiaphas unwittingly prophesies when he provides the historically most plausible reason for "the Jews" to hand Jesus over to the Romans (18:14; 11:50–52): "It would be good that one man be put to death instead of the people," this because of the social unrest the one man, Jesus, would cause during the pilgrimage festival of Passover. The gospel's word for "instead of" also means "on behalf of" or "for the benefit of." So John's Jesus dies for "the people," who, it is clear, are Jewish.

In spite of John's notion that Jesus "is the lamb of God who takes away the world's sin" (1:29) and in spite of the gospel's puns and their implications, the sad fact remains, as Samuel Sandmel observed in his valuable book about the New Testament,[5] that "in

---

4. Paul Trebilco, *Self-Designations and Group Identity in the New Testament* (Cambridge: Cambridge University Press, 2012); see also the extended discussion of this issue here in chapter 4.

5. See Samuel Sandmel, *A Jewish Understanding of the New Testament* (New York: KTAV Publishing House, 1974).

its utility for later Jew-haters, the Fourth Gospel is pre-eminent among the New Testament writings."

One approach to dealing with the difficulties of John's text has been scholarly. In this view, the anti-Jewish sentiments are to be understood in light of their historical origins.

John 9:22 claims that Jews in Jerusalem who acknowledged Jesus as God's Messiah were expelled from the synagogue. Scholars argue that the gospel's hostility reflects a late-first-century family dispute between "rabbinical" Jews and "Christian" Jews.[6]

John's polemic presented a serious problem for Judaism only when it was canonized as sacred scripture, and its Gentile readers, in a subsequently Christianized Roman Empire, came to identify with Jesus as non-Jewish. John's embattled community of Christian Jews would not have intended to issue a blanket indictment. The gospel's inveighing against "the Jews" might be seen as historically contingent and not normative, in the same way that many Christians today do not take as normative New Testament statements on slavery or the silence of women in worship gatherings.

Another suggestion has been to alter gospel texts radically in new translations intended for use in public worship.[7] This idea has met with little enthusiasm. (As anyone heading a worship committee can tell you, there is no sorrow like unto that of the liturgical reformer.)

Yet another approach, related to but more evocative and useful than the first, is to update the gospel by leaving the text intact but interpreting it theologically, reading to some degree "against the text." Whether or not they admit it, most, if not all, biblical

6. For example, Martinus C. de Boer, "The Depiction of 'the Jews' in John's Gospel: Matters of Behavior and Identity," in *Anti-Judaism and the Fourth Gospel*, edited by Reimund Bieringer, Didier Pollefeyt, and Frederique Vandecasteele-Vanneuville (Louisville: Westminster John Knox Press, 2001), 141–157.

7. For example, Norman A. Beck, *Mature Christianity in the 21st Century: The Recognition and Repudiation of the Anti-Jewish Polemic of the New Testament* (New York: Crossroad, 1994).

interpreters do just this, whenever they read the Bible, on any subject. (A striking current example is the argument that general biblical principles of love and inclusion should take priority over specific biblical passages apparently condemning homosexual activity.)

When this third approach is taken, by reading John theologically in light of the much greater emphasis on Christian sin and forgiveness that Luther found in Paul's writings in the New Testament, Bach's *St. John Passion* looks considerably less anti-Jewish than the gospel text itself. I do not mean to suggest, however, that Bach's musical output is philo-Semitic. (There are clearly anti-Jewish sentiments in his Cantatas 42, *Am Abend aber desselbigen Sabbats*, and 46, *Schauet doch und sehet*.)[8] Rather, Bach seems simply to have thought that dwelling on Jews and Judaism during Holy Week detracted from the proper application of John's narrative about Jesus's sacrificial death.

Bach's view can be inferred from the strong verbal and musical emphasis he placed on an essential point of Lutheran theology: that all humans (except Jesus), tainted by original sin, are guilty and in need of redemption, German Lutherans most of all, for they have had the benefit of a restored gospel in the vernacular and cannot claim ignorance.

Bach set John's unaltered Passion narrative to music that in no way palliates ugly aspects of the story. Where "the Jews" shout out to Pilate, "Away, away with him, crucify him!" and where the Jewish leaders exclaim soon after, "We have no king but the emperor," Bach delivered positively ferocious music.

For many composers, story elements like these occasioned still harsher commentary. Handel's *Brockes-Passion*, for example, says concerning this episode (in which Jesus is taken away to

8. See Michael Marissen, *Lutheranism, Anti-Judaism, and Bach's St. John Passion* (New York: Oxford University Press, 1998), 52–53, 71. See also Michael Marissen, "The Character and Sources of the Anti-Judaism in Bach's Cantata 46," *Harvard Theological Review* 96 (2003): 63–99 (reprinted as chapter 3 in this book); and see chapter 4 in this book.

be crucified): "Hurry, you besieged souls, leave *Achshaph's dens of murder*, come—where?—to Golgotha! Hurry toward faith's wings; fly—where?—to the skulls' hilltop; your welfare blossoms there!" (Achshaph was one of the cities the Israelites are depicted in the Bible as having wiped out in their conquest of the Promised Land of Canaan.)[9] Brockes's apparent moral: "Old Israel" should leave its murderousness behind and fly to Calvary.

The version of this poetry found in Bach's *St. John Passion* provides this commentary for the same narrative episode: "Hurry, you besieged souls, leave *your dens of torment*; hurry—where?—to Golgotha! Embrace faith's wings . . ." The concern here is not with "the Jews" at all but with Bach's fellow Christian listeners, leaving inner spiritual turmoil for the peace of the cross.

Who, then, is held accountable for Jesus's crucifixion in Bach's *St. John Passion*? The commentary hymn following Jesus's being struck by one of the attendants of "the Jews" expresses matters the most forcibly, its "I, I" referring to Bach's Lutheran congregants: "Who has struck you so? . . . I, I and my sins, which are as numerous as the grains of sand on the seashore; they have caused you the sorrow that strikes you and the grievous host of pain." Bach's Passion, in contrast to Handel's, moves the focus away from the perfidy of "the Jews" and onto the sins of Christian believers.

From our vantage point, it is easy to see that Bach's *St. John Passion* by no means comes to terms with all ecumenically or socially troubling aspects of the gospel's first-century text. Yet there are significant steps in the right direction. Crucial in this regard is the work's commentary on John 19:30, the aria "Mein teurer Heiland." With extensive melismas on the word *redemption*,

---

9. See Joshua 11:1 and 11:11–13. Curiously, in its discussion of the *Brockes-Passion*, Andreas Loewe, *Johann Sebastian Bach's St John Passion (BWV 245): A Theological Commentary* (Leiden: Brill, 2014), 247–248, has misread the city *Achsaph* (the spelling in German) of Joshua 11:1, 12:20, and 19:25 as the psalmist/musician *Asaph* of 1 Chronicles 6:39, 2 Chronicles 5:12, and Psalms 50 and 73–83. (The musician/psalmist is never referred to as *Achsaph* in Luther Bibles.)

the bass soloist asks, concerning Jesus's death, "is redemption of *all the world* here?" and proclaims the answer, "yes." (This may at first sound superecumenical, but most likely, it just means, if still generously, that—against the doctrines of Calvinism—in principle, all humanity could be saved by Jesus, in the End, as "Lutherans.")

One hopes against hope that a heightened awareness of and attentiveness to Bach's setting will give scope for seeing, in the words of the great religious scholar Jacob Neusner, "the 'St. John Passion' as occasion to identify and overcome anti-Judaism and anti-Semitism—a work of aesthetic refinement and deep religious sentiment."[10]

10. For a more detailed treatment of many of the issues mentioned here, see Marissen, *Lutheranism, Anti-Judaism, and Bach's St. John Passion.* (The Neusner comment appeared in his long blurb for that book's dust jacket.) For broader theological treatment of Bach's Passions, see especially Jaroslav Pelikan, *Bach among the Theologians* (Philadelphia: Fortress Press, 1986), 74–115; and Eric Chafe, *Tonal Allegory in the Vocal Music of J. S. Bach* (Berkeley and Los Angeles: University of California Press, 1991), 274–423.

Chapter 6

Blood, People, and Crowds
in Bach's *St. Matthew Passion*

In all of Christian scripture, probably no line has been invoked to justify theological condemnation of Jews or physical violence against Jews more frequently than the outcry for Jesus's crucifixion expressed by "all the people" in Matthew 27:25, "His blood [be] on us and on our children." This verse appears, too, of course, in J. S. Bach's *St. Matthew Passion* (BWV 244), and it is important to ask how the passage is interpreted within Bach's great choral work. Key to understanding this troubling verse are, in my view, the various terms used in Matthew's gospel to refer to groups of people mentioned in the Passion narrative (including the group that utters this remark) and the particular words used in Luther's New Testament to render these terms in German. The evidence strongly suggests that Luther's Bible intensifies whatever anti-Jewish tendencies (that is, hatred of or unreasonable prejudice against Jews or Judaism) there may be in the Greek text of Matthew, thereby significantly affecting interpretation of the expression "his blood." It is all the more significant, then, that the commentary offered by the other texts in Bach's *St. Matthew Passion*—madrigalian poetry by Bach's Leipzig contemporary Christian Friedrich Henrici ("Picander") and stanzas from Lutheran hymns by various authors—appears to

For encouragement and criticism in completing this chapter, I would like to thank Tassilo Erhardt, Daniel Melamed, and Paula Fredriksen.

work in the opposite direction, mitigating the anti-Jewish senti-ments amplified by Luther's translation of the Bible.

Laos and *Ochlos* in Matthew, *Das Volk* in Luther

In the original Greek, Matthew's gospel uses several different terms to refer to groups of people. The most common are *laos* ("people") and *ochlos* ("crowd"), each of which is often somewhat vague in its New Testament usages; thus, readers have to rely on context if they want to identify the groups more specifically. With his recent monograph on the crowds in Matthew, Robert Cousland has done an enormous service of sorting through myriad histor-ical, narrative, and theological issues.[1] The upshot of his research is that there is a strong literary tendency in Matthew to use *laos* to refer to the people of Israel (even if it does not always denote the people as a whole) and to use *ochlos* either generally for crowds or particularly for the people of Israel as opposed to their leaders. Thus, when push comes to shove, so to speak, the *ochlos* and the Jewish leaders emerge as distinct subsets of the *laos*. Seeing that Matthew finds echoes in the Hebrew Bible—through talk of the "lost sheep of the House of Israel" on the one hand and the "killers of prophets" on the other—Cousland concludes that the reason the Gospel of Matthew narratively aligns the *ochlos* with its author's understanding of the history of Jewish Israel is that the evange-list sought to win the proto-Rabbinic Jews of the first century over to his proto-Christian side, where he believed the true future for "Israel" would lie.

Cousland allows that there are anomalies for his literary scheme. He notes, for example, that "the use of *ochlos* at Matthew 9:23–25 [for a group of mourners—identified as a "crowd" at Matthew 9:23

1. J. R. C. Cousland, *The Crowds in the Gospel of Matthew* (Leiden: Brill, 2002).

but not at Mark 5:38 and Luke 8:52—making a tumult at the house of a ruler who is identified as the synagogue leader "Jairus" at Mark 5:22 and Luke 8:41 but unnamed at Matthew 9:18] would argue against any simple identification of the crowds with Israel . . . [and] at one level Matthew's understanding . . . does not depart from the [varied] view . . . [in] Mark."[2] Stomping in as a biblical-studies amateur where some experts may fear to tread, I would offer the additional observation that the use of *ochlos* at Matthew 26:47 and 26:55, this time apparently to signify a large quasi-military group sent by the Jewish leaders (that is, an *ochlos* consisting not of the general populace of Israel but of court attendants who were at the disposal of the Jewish leaders for police purposes when necessary, as in John 18:3), possibly makes for another, odd inconsistency in Cousland's word-study scheme.[3] Also, I would note that, significantly, for this gospel, the ordinary Jewish folk and their leaders appear in the end to be blended together for disapprobation (see 28:15, "and this story [that Jesus was not risen from the dead but, rather, his body had been stolen from the tomb by his disciples while the guards were sleeping] has been told among *the Jews* up to this day").[4] It appears, then, that despite Cousland's extremely stimulating and thorough study, the identity of the crowds in Matthew is still worthy of critical discussion.

2. Cousland, *The Crowds*, 93.

3. This notwithstanding the comments at Matthew 26:55b about Jesus's teaching of the *ochloi* in the Temple. Presumably, 26:47 should not be construed to mean that a large group of the commoners of Israel came with weapons they had borrowed from the chief priests and elders! Alternatively, however, it might be argued that we are supposed to read the phrase *apo ton archieron kai presbyteron tou laou* as saying that a large group "of the people [of Israel]" was "sent from" or "authorized by" their leaders. (It is worth noting that the *ochlos* is here in any event not depicted as a vigilante "mob"; whatever the *ochlos* is, it acts on legal authority.) But would chief priests and elders wish or need to authorize, and arm, a crowd of commoners to seize Jesus of Nazareth?

4. Yet another observation: are not the leaders schematically "above" the *laos* in Matthew 27:64?

For the present study on Luther's gospel translation and Bach's *St. Matthew Passion*, there is another, crucial issue surrounding possible distinctions between "crowds" and "people" in Matthew. While the overall tendency in Matthew does seem to be for *ochlos* and *laos* to connote ethnically Jewish groups, there are some narrative and historical indications that the crowds in this gospel are to be understood as partly Gentile. Concerning the narrative indications, Cousland provides a formidable discussion of the geographical references in Matthew 4:23–25, coming, however, to the following meticulously formulated conclusion on the possible presence of Gentiles:

> With one exception, the members of the crowds originate from regions that were popularly regarded as Jewish. Only the mention of the Decapolis [a grouping of ten Greek cities, with majority Gentile populations] gives grounds to the supposition that he included Gentiles in the crowds. Even in this instance, however, it is probable that he accounts the Decapolis part of Eretz Israel, given the region's one-time inclusion in the Davidic kingdom. . . .
>
> It is, of course, possible that Matthew envisages Gentiles among the crowds. Matthew's reference to the Decapolis could allow for the possibility. If so, however, this is the only point where the Gospel explicitly affords such an impression.[5]

But for further material that is consonant with the notion of a Gentile presence in the crowds specifically at Passover, I would point to a passage from Flavius Josephus's *The Jewish War*, written, like the Gospel of Matthew, toward the end of the first century.

5. Cousland, *The Crowds*, 72–73. See also the exacting formulation of W. D. Davies and Dale C. Allison, *A Critical and Exegetical Commentary on the Gospel according to Saint Matthew* (Edinburgh: T. & T. Clark, 1988–1997), 1:419: "Matthew may presuppose a Gentile presence among the crowds, but he does not emphasize this."

Josephus wrote that the greater part of those who perished in the Jewish revolt of the years 66 to 70 were of the same ethnic stock (*homophulos*) as the Jerusalemites.[6] He went on to say that the size of the multitude (*plethos*) at Passover can be determined by taking the number of lamb sacrifices and multiplying by ten; this, he noted, would not equal the full number of the multitude, however, since, for example, menstruating women and people with certain diseases could not participate in the Passover meal on account of their ritual impurities and also since it was likewise unlawful for the "*large* numbers" of visiting foreigners (*allophulois*, that is, non-Jews) to be partakers of this sacrifice.[7] Since Josephus matter-of-factly related the presence both of the ritually impure and of Gentiles in the multitudes at Passover, there is presumably nothing controversial or apologetical about the second of his two observations.

This is not to say that the Gospel of Matthew is to be read as though it was meant to be taken as a straightforward "historical" document, roughly akin to Josephus's *The Jewish War* (which, of course, has its justifying motives, too). Matthew, in comparison with its most closely related gospel, Mark, more strongly reflects a Jewish background, and this aspect of the narrative in Matthew

---

6. Flavius Josephus, *The Jewish War*, 6.421.

7. Josephus, *The Jewish War*, 6.426–427 (see also Mishnah *Pesahim* 5.3, 6.6; and Exodus 12:48; and see John 12:20, where the Gentiles ["Greeks"] attend Passover[?], and also Leviticus 22:25 and 1 Kings 8:41–43). For background on Gentiles worshiping in the Temple, see the appendix, "Gentile Participation in Worship at Jerusalem," in Emil Schürer, *The History of the Jewish People in the Age of Jesus Christ (175 B.C.–A.D. 135)*, revised and edited by Géza Vermès and Fergus Millar (Edinburgh: T. & T. Clark, 1973–1987), 2:309–313. Incidentally, the classic Whiston translation of Josephus—owing to his particular Christian bias?—erroneously assigns the "large numbers" to the entire multitude rather than to "the foreigners" (my thanks to Jonathan Price, Tel Aviv University, for helping me with this passage). Josephus cannot be referring to Gentile converts to Judaism, as proselytes *would* lawfully partake of the Passover sacrifice. Drawing on these passages in Josephus in connection with a notion of mixed crowds in the gospels has, to my knowledge, not been explored in New Testament studies.

presumably cannot simply be attributed to a greater concern on the part of its author for historical exactitude. My question is whether the gospel's naming of various groups, even if altogether theologically motivated, is so forceful and unambiguous that its earliest audiences would have identified the narrative's crowds not simply as mostly Jewish but rather as exclusively Jewish. In light of what Josephus reports, it seems that Matthew's first readers would have taken it for granted that the Passover crowds were ethnically mixed. (The presence of Gentile tourists in Jerusalem at Passover in the first century was perhaps a bit like today's large numbers of non-Catholics attending papal Easter services at the Vatican.) That is to say, while readers may concede Cousland's point that the author of Matthew has fashioned his crowds as a literary construct, it would not necessarily follow that they should reject, as Cousland does for Matthew, the notion of ethnically mixed crowds, especially at Passover.

Yet whatever the purposes might be in the Gospel of Matthew for using the words *ochlos* and *laos*, they are entirely lost in Luther's version of the gospel: Luther rendered both terms with *das Volk* (for a full listing, see table 6.1).[8] Thus, while in Matthew the *laos* might be understood to be the Jewish people and the *ochloi* to be mixed crowds of mostly Jews and some or even many Gentiles, in Luther one encounters only Jews.[9]

Now, one might object that in the vernacular of Luther's day, the word *Volk* covered a very wide semantic field that included a number of terms from the Greek New Testament. In translating both *ochlos* and *laos* as *Volk*, Luther was simply working with the limitations of the linguistic tools at hand. Table 6.1 shows, in this case, that

---

8. This significant issue has, to my knowledge, not been explored in Luther studies.

9. It is possible that Luther was simply realizing a latent tendency in the language of Matthew, as its author certainly does not project a positive view of Jews who elect not to follow Jesus. My question, however, is whether Luther might be bringing a false clarity to the text.

TABLE 6.1 Usage of *ochlos* and *laos* in Matthew.

BIBLES

E = Elberfelder

Er = Erasmus 1519

K = King James Version

L = Luther

M = passage in Matthew

N = New Revised Standard Version

NT = Greek New Testament

V = Vulgate

TERMS

C = crowd

L = *laos*

M = *Menge*

Mo = *multitudo*

Mu = multitude

O = *ochlos*

P = people

Pl = *plebs*

Po = *populus*

S = *Schar*

T = *turba*

V = *Volk*

Vm = *Volksmenge*

M	L	E	K	N	V	Er	NT	Context
1:21	V	V	P	P	Po	Po	L	Jesus will save his people
2:4	V	V	P	P	Po	Po	L	Leaders of the people
2:6	V	V	P	P	Po	Po	L	Messiah will shepherd my people Israel
4:16	V	V	P	P	Po	Po	L	People who sat in darkness
4:23	V	V	P	P	Po	Po	L	Jesus teaching in "their" synagogues, healing the people

4:25	V	Vm	Mu	C	T	T	O	Great crowds follow Jesus, from Decapolis, etc.
5:1	V	Vm	Mu	C	T	T	O	Crowds (follow Jesus, from Decapolis, etc.)
7:28	V	Vm	P	C	T	T	O	Crowds astounded at Jesus, who has authority, not as "their scribes"
8:1	V	Vm	Mu	C	T	T	O	Great crowds follow Jesus from the mountain
8:18	V	Vm	Mu	C	T	T	O	Great crowds around Jesus
9:8	V	Vm	Mu	C	T	T	O	Crowds in Jesus's own town see him healing
9:23	V	Vm	P	C	T	T	O	Crowd in a leader's house making a commotion, thinking young girl had died, but Jesus says she's only sleeping
9:25	V	Vm	P	C	T	T	O	Crowd is put outside the house
9:33	V	Vm	Mu	C	T	T		Crowds at Jesus's healing mute demoniac: "Never has anything like this been seen in Israel"
9:36	V	Vm	Mu	C	T	T	O	Jesus has compassion for crowds, who are like sheep without a shepherd
11:7	V	Vm	Mu	C	T	T	O	Jesus speaks to crowds about John the Baptist
12:15	V	Vm	Mu	C		T	O	Jesus cures many crowds following him, in fulfillment of Isaiah's prophecy of justice to and hope for the Gentiles
12:23	V	Vm	P	C	T	T	O	All the crowds amazed at Jesus's healing a mute and blind demoniac

(continued)

TABLE 6.1 Continued

M	L	E	K	N	V	Er	NT	Context
12:46	V	Vm	P	C	T	T	O	Jesus speaks to crowds of his true kindred (not his mother and brothers)
13:2a	V	Vm	Mu	C	T	T	O	Crowds gather around Jesus by the sea
13:2b	V	Vm	Mu	C	T	T	O	Whole crowd stands on the beach
13:15	V	V	P	P	Po	Po	L	This people's heart has grown dull (people here seem equated with the crowd of 13:2)
13:34	V	Vm	Mu	C	T	T	O	Jesus speaks to crowds in parables
13:36	V	Vm	Mu	C	T	T	O	Jesus leaves the crowds
14:5	V	Vm	Mu	C	Po	Mo	O	Herod fears the crowd because they regard John as a prophet
14:13	V	Vm	P	C	T	T	O	Crowds follow Jesus to a deserted place
14:14	V	Vm	Mu	C	T	T	O	Jesus has compassion for this crowd and heals their sick
14:15	V	Vm	Mu	C	T	T	O	Disciples ask Jesus to send crowds away
14:19a	V	Vm	Mu	C	T	T	O	Jesus gives food to the crowds
14:19b	V	Vm	Mu	C	T	T	O	Jesus gives food to the crowds
14:22	V	Vm	Mu	C	T	T	O	Jesus dismisses crowds
14:23	V	Vm	Mu	C	T		O	Jesus dismisses crowds
15:8	V	V	P	P	Po	Po	L	This people (the Pharisees and scribes) honors me with their lips, but . . . in vain do they worship me, teaching human precepts as doctrines

	V	Vm	Mu	C	T	T	O	
15:10	V	Vm	Mu	C	T	T	O	Jesus speaks to crowds of things that truly defile
15:30	V	Vm	Mu	C	T	T	O	Great crowds seeking Jesus's healing
15:31	V	Vm	Mu	C	T	T	O	Crowd amazed at Jesus's healing, "and they praised the God of Israel"
15:32	V	Vm	Mu	C	T	T	O	Jesus has compassion for the crowd
15:33	V	Vm	Mu	C	T	T	O	Disciples worry about food for so great a crowd
15:35	V	Vm	Mu	C	T	T	O	Jesus orders crowd to sit
15:36	V	Vm	Mu	C	Po	T	O	Disciples feed the crowds
15:39	V	Vm	Mu	C	T	T	O	Jesus sends the crowds away
17:14	V	Vm	Mu	C	T	T	O	Jesus and disciples come to the crowd
19:2	V	Vm	Mu	C	T	T	O	Large crowds follow Jesus in Judea, and he cures them
20:29	V	Vm	Mu	C	T	T	O	Large crowd follows Jesus from Jericho
20:31	V	Vm	Mu	C	T	T	O	Crowd orders blind men seeking healing to be quiet
21:8	V	Vm	Mu	C	T	T	O	Crowd spreads cloaks on the road for Jesus
21:9	V	Vm	Mu	C	Po	T	O	Crowds call to Jesus, "Hosannah"
21:11	V	Vm	Mu	C	Po	T	O	Crowds say Jesus is the prophet from Galilee
21:23	V	V	P	P	Po	Po	L	Leaders of the people
21:26	V	Vm	Mu	C	T	T	O	Leaders are afraid of the crowd, for all regarded John as a prophet

(continued)

TABLE 6.1 Continued

M	L	E	K	N	V	Er	NT	Context
21:46	V	Vm	Mu	C	T	T	O	Leaders are afraid of the crowd, for they regard Jesus as a prophet
22:33	V	Vm	Mu	C	T	T	O	Crowd astonished at Jesus's teaching
23:1	V	Vm	Mu	C	T	T	O	Jesus warns crowds and his disciples about the Pharisees
26:3	V	V	P	P	Po	Po	L	Leaders of the people
26:5	V	V	P	P	Po	Po	L	Leaders fear a riot among the people if Jesus is seized during the festival
26:47	S	M	Mu	C	T	T	O	Large crowd with weapons seek to seize Jesus
26:47	V	V	P	P	Po	Po	L	Leaders of the people
26:55	S	Vm	Mu	C	T	T	O	Crowds (with weapons, seeking to seize Jesus)
27:1	V	V	P	P	Po	Po	L	Leaders of the people
27:15	V	Vm	P	C	Po	T	O	Pilate accustomed to releasing a prisoner to the festival crowd
27:20	V	Vm	Mu	C	Po	T	O	Leaders persuade the festival crowds to ask for Barabbas but to have Jesus destroyed
27:24	V	Vm	Mu	C	Po	Po	O	Pilate washes his hands before the festival crowd
27:25	V	V	P	P	Po	Po	L	The entire people respond, "his blood [be] on us and our children"

	V	V	P	P	Pl	Pl	L
27:64							Chief priests and Pharisees ask Pilate for a guard at Jesus's tomb, so that his disciples will not be able to steal the body and say to the people, "he has been raised from the dead"

Note that Luther Bibles of Bach's day quote Matthew 4:23b almost verbatim at 9:35b, where laos is rendered as Volk; most modern Bibles do not contain this latter half verse. The plural form of ochlos appears without any qualifiers in the Greek of Matthew 5:1, 7:28, 9:8, 9:33, 9:36, 11:7, 12:46, 13:34, 13:36, 14:13, 14:15, 14:19, 14:22, 14:23, 15:36, 15:39, 21:9, 21:11, 21:46, 22:33, 23:1, 26:55, and 27:20; "many crowds" appears at 4:25, 8:1, 12:15, 13:2, 15:30, and 19:2; and "all the crowds" at 12:23 (see Cousland, Crowds in Matthew, 35, n. 19). The significance of the plural usages is unclear. But it might bolster the assumption of a mixed-crowd awareness on the part of the author of Matthew. My results here and the conclusions drawn from them will be unaffected by dealing with the only slightly different pre-nineteenth-century editions of the Luther Bible.

Luther was consistent in assuming a broad usage. We should not, in fact, expect him to do otherwise, and thus it would be altogether misguided to suspect that there is any interpretive significance in Luther's linguistic conflation of Matthew's *ochlos* and *laos*.

But is important to note that Luther did come up with unproblematic word choices to render *ochlos* when the crowds in question are clearly not the general Jewish populace. Luther gave *Schar* for the *ochlos* of believers in Jesus at Acts 1:15, *Haufe* for the great *ochlos* of Jesus's disciples at Luke 6:17, and *Schar* or *Scharen* for the *ochloi* of attendants with policing duties at Mark 14:43 and Matthew 26:47, 26:55 (see also Luke 22:47, 22:52; and John 18:3).[10] Obviously, the word *Volk* would not work in these various cases. But since *laos* and *ochlos* are not synonyms in Greek, just as *populus* and *turba* are not in Latin (that is, the language of the Vulgate Bible), why can Luther not be expected to have found another word than *Volk* to cover all or most usages of *ochlos*? For example, he did use *Menge* for large groups of people or angels in Mark 3:8; Luke 8:37; Acts 2:6, 4:32, 5:14, 6:5, 14:1, 14:4, 17:4; and Hebrews 12:22. If Luther can render *plethos* or *myrias* with *Menge*, why not also *ochlos*? The words *plethos* and *ochlos* are, in fact, closer to each other in connotation than are *laos* and *ochlos*. One might here ask, however, whether it was typical for prior German Bibles to render *ochlos* as *Volk*, such that Luther was simply following this standard usage. But as it happens, every one of the pre-Luther German Bibles did maintain a linguistic distinction between crowds and people, rendering the Vulgate's *populus* as *Volk* and rendering *turba* consistently as *Schar* (or, in some Bibles, *Gesellschaft* but in no instance ever as *Volk*).[11] Thus, Luther's

10. Almost without exception, these do read *turba* ("crowd") in the Vulgate, the Bible Luther knew from his youth. It is important to know, incidentally, that the readings in today's "Luther Bibles" often differ substantially from Luther's own version, which was still in use in Bach's day.

11. *Gesellschaft* in the Mentel Bible and the various translations derived from it, *Schar* in the Zainer Bible and its derivatives. The variant readings of these many pre-Luther German Bibles are meticulously provided in the marvelous reference work, William Kurrelmeyer, ed., *Die erste Deutsche Bibel*, 10 vols. (Tübingen: Litterarischer Verein in Stuttgart, 1904–1915).

linguistic conflation appears, in fact, to be an innovation in Bible translations.

If many pre-Luther readers of Matthew had traditionally been inclined to equate his "crowds" with "the people" anyway, this does not mean that Luther's linguistically innovative Bible thus becomes reproachless: encountering only *das Volk* for both terms, readers of Luther are now effectively *precluded* from making a distinction between Matthew's *ochloi* and *laos*.[12] Luther's rendering of *ochlos* as *Volk* could be of serious import to questions of theological anti-Judaism,[13] as the gospel narrative's key moment in the bringing about of Jesus's death involves the Jewish leaders persuading the Passover *ochloi* that they should ask Pilate to release Barabbas but *destroy Jesus* (27:20). Thus, whereas for readers of Matthew's Greek text this may arguably place blame on mixed crowds of Jews with Gentiles who have been swayed by the chief priests and elders, for readers of Luther's translation the moral responsibility for the death of Jesus can only fall on *das Volk* (that is, exclusively on "the Jews"),[14] whom Luther's readers have heard mentioned around sixty times by this point in his linguistically innovative rendering of Matthew. Luther and his ecclesiastical followers, incidentally, had

12. Luther subscribed to a theory of biblical translation in which the idea was, when deemed necessary, to provide readers not with a literal rendition but with what the translator believed to be the theologically true sense of the text; see, for example, Martin Luther, "On Translating: An Open Letter," in *Luther's Works,* vol. 35, *Word and Sacrament I,* edited by E. Theodore Bachmann, translated by Charles M. Jacobs and E. Theodore Bachmann (Philadelphia: Muhlenberg Press, 1960), 181–202. The aim of the present discussion of the crowds in Matthew is—however presumptuous this may sound—less to question Luther's methods than to question his results.

13. By "theological anti-Judaism" I mean not simply disagreement with or critique of Judaism but rather the teaching of marked contempt for or categorical dismissal of the religion of Judaism and its practitioners. The question for me is whether or to what extent a rendering of the Passion narrative in Matthew justifiably proves useful to those who wish to foster contempt for Judaism or Jews.

14. See "die Juden" at Matthew 28:19; see also Luther's rendering of Acts 10:22, *bei dem ganzen* Volk *der Juden* ("by the whole nation [*ethnos*] of the Jews"), and of John 18:35, *Bin ich ein Jude? Dein* Volk *und die Hohenpriester haben dich mir*

most likely read the above-cited passage from Josephus about the mixed multitudes at Passover. Luther himself and many sixteenth- and seventeenth-century Lutheran pastors published countless collections of sermons for a general readership in which excerpts from book 6 of Josephus's *The Jewish War* are cited.[15]

Various word choices in Luther's translation of Matthew 27 may subtly reinforce a reading of sole Jewish responsibility within the biblical narrative for inducing Pilate to crucify Jesus. In Luther's rendering, the chapter opens with all the chief priests and elders of the *Volk* (*laos* in Matthew) holding a council on how they might kill Jesus. Verse 9 then speaks of the prophet's having foretold the betrayal of Jesus for thirty pieces of silver: *Sie haben genommen dreißig Silberlinge, damit bezahlet ward der Verkaufte, welchen sie kauften von den Kindern Israel* ("They have taken thirty pieces of silver, with which the Sold One was paid for, whom they bought from

überantwortet ("Am I a Jew? Your [own] nation [*ethnos*] and the chief priests have handed you over to me"). (Considering the Gospel of John's overall intensified anti-Jewish sentiment, might it be significant that there is no mention of "crowds" in its Passion narrative?) True, the Vulgate renders Matthew's *ochlos* at 27:20, this time with *populus*, but it is important to know that the textual source Luther used in translating the gospel, Erasmus's *Novvm Testamentvm Omne* of 1519 (a Greek New Testament with Erasmus's own recension of the Latin on facing pages), specifically corrects the Vulgate's reading to *turba*; Erasmus also notes for 27:20, "And here, again, it is 'crowd,' not 'people'—*ochlos*." Since Luther consulted heavily with Philip Melanchthon, to whom Erasmus's separately bound annotations were very well known, and, moreover, since Luther also cannot have failed to notice that Erasmus's side-by-side biblical text reads *turba* with *ochlos*, it seems clear enough that he was wont to override good information that he had readily at his disposal. Heinrich Bornkamm, "Luther's Translation of the New Testament," in *Luther: A Profile*, edited by H. G. Koenigsberger (New York: Hill & Wang, 1973), 210–217, notes that Luther as a rule does (that is, in other cases than the *crowds* versus *people* issue) correct the Vulgate readings in conformity with Erasmus's suggestions. On Melanchthon and Erasmus, see Timothy J. Wengert, *Human Freedom, Christian Righteousness: Philip Melanchthon's Exegetical Dispute with Erasmus of Rotterdam* (New York: Oxford University Press, 1998).

15. Regarding such sermons for the Tenth Sunday after Trinity, see Michael Marissen, "The Character and Sources of the Anti-Judaism in Bach's Cantata 46," *Harvard Theological Review* 96 (2003): 63–99 (reprinted as chapter 3 in this book).

the children of Israel"). Already in Matthew, too, there is necessarily a conceptual link between "the people" in 27:1 and "the sons
of Israel" in 27:9.[16] But through verbal echoes brought about with
specific German word choices, Luther's text will go on to link these
two passages to verses 15, 20, 24, and 25 (that is, these are echoes
that were not produced in Matthew's Greek; see Luther's verses in
tabular format with direct translations in table 6.2).

For Luther's Passion narrative, then, as throughout his rendering of the gospel, the *ochlos* (singular in verses 15 and 24, plural
[*ochloi*] in verse 20) and the *laos* will simply turn out to be one and
the same—the Jewish populace: *das Volk*.[17]

More subtly, and probably unintentionally, Luther's text also
makes a stronger connection between verses 9 and 25 than is found in
the Greek text of Matthew 27. At verse 25, Matthew's word is *tekna*, a
term that Luther provided with a literal translation, "children" (*teknon*
means "[male or female] child," and *tekna*—here the accusative neuter
plural of *teknon*—means "male and/or female children"). At verse 9,
however, the Greek text in Matthew speaks of "[the] *sons* of Israel"
(roughly following the Greek Septuagint text of Zechariah 11:12–13),
and in this case, as with virtually all other biblical instances of "the
huioi Israel," Luther did not provide a hyperliteral rendering (that is,
he gives "the *children* of Israel," not "the *sons* of Israel"). The term
employed in Matthew, the plural of *huios,* can altogether rightly also

16. Note again, however, that there is not necessarily such a (strong) link between
the "crowds" and "the people."

17. In this, Luther is not simply following the Vulgate, as one can see from
table 6.1. Moreover, Luther's textual source, Erasmus 1519, had corrected to *turba*
or *multitudo* all but one of the (few) instances where the Vulgate had wrongly rendered *ochlos* as *populus*. And it is worth noting that in going about his task, Luther
believed he could do better than the Vulgate: his avowed intention in translating the Bible from the original languages was that he thought "that it may result
in a translation worthy of being read by Christians—I hope we shall present
our Germany with a better one than that of the Latins [that is, better than the
Vulgate]." See his letter of January 13, 1522, to Nikolaus von Amsdorf in *D. Martin
Luthers Werke: Kritische Gesamtausgabe,* series 4, vol. 2, edited by O. Clement
(Weimar: Böhlau, 1931), 423; quoted in Bornkamm, "Luther's Translation," 211.

TABLE 6.2 Verses from Luther's rendering of the Passion narrative in Matthew.

	Luther	Direct translation	Key term in Matthew
27:1	Des Morgens aber hielten alle Hohepriester und die Ältesten *des Volks* einen Rat über Jesum, daß sie ihn töteten.	When morning arrived, however, all the chief priests and the elders of *the people* held a council about Jesus, so that they might kill him.	*laos*
27:9–10	Da ist erfüllet, das gesagt ist durch den Propheten Jeremias, da er spricht: Sie haben genommen dreißig Silberlinge, damit bezahlet ward der Verkaufte, welchen sie kauften von *den Kindern Israel,* und haben sie gegeben um einen Töpfersakker, als mir der Herr befohlen hat.	And so is fulfilled what is told by the prophet Jeremiah [an adaptation of Zechariah 11:12–13; see also Jeremiah 18:2–6, 19:1–11, 32:6–15?], when he says: "They have taken thirty pieces of silver, with which the Sold One was paid for, whom they bought from *the children of Israel*, and have given them for a potter's field, as the Lord has commanded me."	*huios*
27:15	Auf das Fest aber hatte der Landpfleger Gewohnheit, *dem Volk* einen Gefangenen loszugeben, welchen sie wollten.	But during the Festival the governor was accustomed to releasing a prisoner to *the people*, whomever they wished.	*ochlos*
27:20	Aber die Hohenpriester und die Ältesten überredeten *das Volk,* daß sie um Barabbas bitten sollten und *Jesum umbrächten.*	But the chief priests and the elders persuaded *the people* that they should ask for Barabbas and *destroy Jesus.*	*ochlos*

TABLE 6.2 Continued

	Luther	Direct translation	Key term in Matthew
27:22–23	Pilatus sprach zu [dem Volk]: Was soll ich denn machen mit Jesu, von dem gesagt wird, er sei Christus? Sie sprachen alle: Laß ihn kreuzigen! Der Landpfleger sagte: Was hat er denn Übels getan? Sie schrieen aber noch mehr und sprachen: Laß ihn kreuzigen!	Pilate said to [the people]: "What, then, should I do with Jesus, of whom it is said, 'he is the Christ'?" They all said: "Have him crucified!" The governor said: "What evil thing has he done, then?" But they shouted out yet more, saying: "Have him crucified!"	[ochlos]
27:24	Da aber Pilatus sahe, daß er nichts schaffete, sondern daß ein viel größer Getümmel ward, nahm er Wasser und wusch die Hände vor dem Volk und sprach: Ich bin unschuldig an dem Blut dieses Gerechten, sehet ihr zu!	But when Pilate saw that he could do nothing—rather, that a much greater commotion was developing—he took water and washed his hands before the people and said: "I am innocent of the blood of this righteous one—you see to it!"	ochlos
27:25	Da antwortete das ganze Volk und sprach: Sein Blut komme über uns und unsre Kinder.	Then the entire people answered, saying: "His blood come over us and our children."	laos . . . teknon

be rendered as "children," since it denotes either a group of boys with girls or a group of boys exclusively. (The point is that in order to use the word *huioi*—that is, in its plural usage—there must be all boys, or some boys, in the group.) *Tekna,* however, unlike *huioi,* can be used for a group of children that is made up exclusively of females (see, for example, 1 Peter 3:6). Thus, where Matthew's chapter 27 has two different (Greek) words for the respective Jewish offspring at verses 9 and 25 (as do many standard English translations, though not the King James Bible), Luther's has only one: *Kinder* ("children"). Again, it is, of course, in no way semantically or otherwise wrong to translate both terms as "children."[18] My point is simply that only in Luther's single-word translation of Matthew's two different words can one hear the cry in verse 25 ("sein Blut komme über . . . unsere *Kinder*") as verbally echoing verse 9 ("von den *Kindern* Israel"); there is no verbal echo in the original text of Matthew.

I should mention here that while in his rendering of the biblical narrative Luther appears to place sole moral responsibility for the crucifixion with Jews, he can theologically interpret and apply his biblical narrative variously. On the one hand, for example, he can warn Christians during Holy Week to meditate on Jesus's suffering, not on the evil of "the Jews." The opening paragraph of Luther's well-known sermon "A Meditation on Christ's Passion" of 1519 reads (my emphasis):

> Some people meditate on Christ's passion by venting their anger on the Jews. . . . That might well be a meditation on the wickedness [*Bösheyt*] of . . . the Jews, but not on the sufferings of Christ. . . . You [churchgoers] should be terrified . . . by the meditation on Christ's passion. For the evildoers, the

---

18. In this case, there is a somewhat similar linguistic echo between *filiis* and *filios* in the Vulgate, one that is retained in Erasmus 1519. But to be altogether clear here, and even to risk being tiresome, I would not claim that a translation featuring the same noun for offspring at 27:9 and 27:25 should in and of itself be considered anti-Judaic; what I am suggesting is that an otherwise already

Jews, whom God has judged and driven out, were only the servants of your sin; *you are actually the one who,* as we said, by his sin killed and *crucified God's Son.*[19]

In other writings, however, he was just as likely to vilify Jews and apparently take it for granted that it was they who indeed crucified Christ. For example, in his lecture on the famous story of Jacob at Peniel in Genesis 32, Luther stated, commenting on 32:31 (my emphasis): "Without any controversy we shall say that this man [with whom Jacob wrestled] was not an angel but *our* Lord Jesus Christ, eternal God and future Man, to be crucified *by the Jews.*"[20] Commenting then on the "sciatic nerve" in the next verse, Luther wrote: "What the Hebrew word [*nasheh*] properly signifies, I do not really know. The proper name Manasseh has been derived from this word, that is, 'forgetting.' ... Certain people interpret [this word] as the "sinew of forgetfulness," as though you were able to say that [Jacob] forgot his place on account of the dislocation. But these are Jewish ideas, that is, inept and foul."[21]

somewhat anti-Judaic translation of the gospel might reasonably be seen as subtly reinforcing its polemical tendencies through such a verbal echo in this particular context.

19. Martin Luther, "A Meditation on Christ's Passion (1519)," in *Luther's Works,* vol. 42, *Devotional Writings I,* edited by Martin O. Dietrich, translated by Martin H. Bertram (Philadelphia: Fortress Press, 1969), 7–10. This sermon was reprinted in Luther's *Church Postil* and was widely circulated and studied into Bach's day; see Elke Axmacher, *"Aus Liebe will mein Heyland Sterben": Untersuchungen zum Wandel des Passionsverständnisses im frühen 18. Jahrhundert* (Neuhausen-Stuttgart: Hänssler-Verlag, 1984), 11–27.

20. Martin Luther, *Lectures on Genesis: Chapters 31–37,* in *Luther's Works,* vol. 6, edited by Jaroslav Pelikan, translated by Paul D. Pahl (St. Louis: Concordia Publishing House, 1970), 144.

21. Luther, *Lectures on Genesis,* 145.

Translation Issues Elsewhere in Luther's New Testament

Luther's apparent tendency to render ambiguous expressions in the Greek biblical text more clearly in the direction of theological anti-Judaism in his German translation is not limited to his reading of the crucifixion scene in Matthew.

To cite a key example, the Greek text of Matthew 21:43 reads: "For this reason I [Jesus] say to you ['the chief priests and the elders of the people,' Matthew 21:23] that the Kingdom of God will be taken from you and it will be given to an *ethnos* producing its fruit." Because the noun employed here to refer to the recipient of the kingdom is not plural (the *ethnei* of Matthew's *dothēsetai ethnei*, "will be given to an *ethnos*," is dative singular), there are several interpretive possibilities: the kingdom will be given to a renewed (portion of the)[22] historical *people of Israel*, or to the *church* (with a membership including people of Jewish background),[23] or to a different *nation*, or to a new *leadership* that believes in Jesus,[24] and so on. Luther, however, emended the text in Matthew by rendering the Kingdom's receiving end with a plural dative noun: *Das Reich Gottes wird von euch genommen und* den Heiden *gegeben werden, die seine Früchte bringen* ("the Kingdom of God will be taken from you and given to *the Gentiles, who* [will] bring its fruits"). Since in all other New Testament

22. Ernst Lohmeyer, *Das Evangelium des Matthäus* (Göttingen: Vandenhoeck & Ruprecht, 1962), 315.

23. See, for example, Joachim Jeremias, *Rediscovering the Parables* (New York: Scribner's, 1966), 51, 57, 63; and Georg Strecker, *Der Weg der Gerechtigkeit: Untersuchung zur Theologie des Matthäus* (Göttingen: Vandenhoeck & Ruprecht, 1971), 33. Georg Strecker, "Das Geschichtsverständnis des Matthäus," in *Das Matthäus-Evangelium*, edited by Joachim Lange (Darmstadt: Wissenschaftliche Buchgesellschaft, 1980), 347, n. 40, speaks of the *heilsgeschichtlichen Vergangenheit des jüdischen Volkes* ("obsolescence of the Jewish people in salvation history"); quoted in Davies and Allison, *A Critical and Exegetical Commentary*, 3:190, n. 81.

24. Anthony J. Saldarini, *Matthew's Christian-Jewish Community* (Chicago: University of Chicago Press, 1994), 60–61.

instances of the inflected form *ethnei*—Acts 10:35, 24:2, 24:10, 26:4; Romans 10:19—Luther has translated with the singular noun *Volk*, his rendering of *ethnei* with the plural *den Heiden* in Matthew 21 may be considered overinterpretive and, frankly, tendentious.[25] (Both the Vulgate and Erasmus 1519, unlike Luther, follow Matthew in rendering the passage with dative singular.)

In light of such a significant example, it is perhaps not surprising that Luther would (unwittingly?) conflate Matthew's *ochloi* and *laos* in a way that could augur unfavorably for the Jewish people.

"His Blood" in Bach's *St. Matthew Passion*

What, then, did Bach and his librettist Picander do with Matthew 27:25 and the matter of responsibility for the death of Jesus? I suggest that their work projects not a violent but a redemptive understanding of the verse,[26] and I conclude that fostering hostility

25. Commenting on the Greek of this verse, Davies and Allison, *A Critical and Exegetical Commentary*, 3:189, write: "If the Gentiles were in view, would we not expect the plural?" Incidentally, not one of the pre-Luther German Bibles reads "Gentiles" here. Luther frequently refers to Matthew 21:43 in his exegetical writings. See, for example, his comments on the book of Jonah in *Lectures on the Minor Prophets II*, in *Luther's Works*, vol. 19, edited by Hilton C. Oswald, translated by C. Froelich (St. Louis: Concordia Publishing House, 1974), 97–98: "That Jonah is sent from the land of the Jews into a foreign country symbolizes that the Spirit and God's Word were to be taken from the Jewish people and bestowed on the Gentiles. Thus Christ says in Matthew 21:43 . . ."

26. See also Renate Steiger, "Bach und Israel," *Musik und Kirche* 50 (1980): 20. For modern biblical scholarship arguing a redemptive interpretation of 27:25, see Raymond E. Brown, *The Death of the Messiah: A Commentary on the Passion Narratives in the Four Gospels* (New York: Doubleday, 1994), 839; and Amy-Jill Levine, *The Social and Ethnic Dimensions of Matthean Salvation History* (Lewiston: Edwin Mellen Press, 1988), 268–269. (Brown and Levine also indicate the plausibility of other, more negative interpretations.) Levine suggests a literary connection between Matthew 27:25 and the institution of the Eucharist in 26:28, and she goes on to say that "the promise made at the beginning of the gospel that Jesus would 'save his people from their sins' (1:21) is recapitulated by these same people [in 27:25]. The [*laos*] has, in very ironic circumstances, bestowed a blessing upon itself and its offspring."

toward Jews is not the subject or purpose of the commentary on the gospel's Passion narrative in Bach's *St. Matthew Passion*.[27]

It is interpretively helpful to know that an ultraliteral translation of the gospel's Greek would read, "His blood on us and our children," as there is no verb in Matthew's formula. Biblical scholar Raymond Brown notes: "It is not wrong to supply a verb ('come' or 'be'), as many translations do; but that creates the danger of misreading the phrase as a self-curse, a prophecy, or a blood-thirsty wish"[28] (which have, in fact, been the most common ways of reading the verse). The way Luther's Bible and, therefore, Bach's *St. Matthew Passion* give the passage is: "his blood *come over* us and our children." Bach would have been familiar with interpretations that took the phrase to be a self-curse,[29] and the verse is certainly taken this way, for example, in his colleague Georg Philipp Telemann's 1722 passion oratorio *Das selige Erwägen* (no. 31; my emphasis: "So you cry out, damned [*vermaledeite*] sinners, 'His blood come over us and over our children?' *You* have taken it [that is, 'his blood'] *upon yourselves* as a curse; *but for me* it will come to blessing"). But Bach's *St. Matthew Passion* reads 27:25 differently, waiting until after verse 26 (the scourging of Jesus by the Roman soldiers) to break the biblical narrative with commentary.[30] The *St. Matthew Passion*, in fact, meditates not on the responsibility of "the [Jewish]

27. This section expands on material from appendix 1 in Michael Marissen, *Lutheranism, Anti-Judaism, and Bach's St. John Passion* (New York: Oxford University Press, 1998), 72–75.

28. Brown, *The Death of the Messiah*, 837.

29. See, for example, Abraham Calov, *Die heilige Bibel nach S. Herrn D. Martini Lutheri Deutscher Dolmetschung und Erklärung* (Wittenberg, 1681–1682), 5:284 (Bach's own copy, with his numerous highlightings and marginal comments, is housed at Concordia Seminary Library, St. Louis), emphasis mine: "This was a horrible curse, through which [the Jews] have precipitately incurred and drawn upon themselves *and their entire lineage* not only temporal but also *eternal* vengeance, expulsion, and *damnation*. Of the like example, as also of such a true vengeance, among no people from the outset of the world is [there] to [be] read."

30. Steiger, "Bach und Israel," 19–20.

people" for Jesus's crucifixion[31] but on the "generously" redemptive power of "his blood." The text of the alto aria "Können Tränen meiner Wangen" reads:[32]

Können Tränen meiner Wangen	If the tears of my cheeks cannot
Nichts erlangen,	achieve anything,
O, so nehmt mein Herz hinein!	o, then take in my heart!
Aber laßt es bei den Fluten,	But let it, at the streams—
Wenn die Wunden milde bluten,	when the wounds [of Jesus] generously[33] bleed—
Auch die Opferschale sein!	also be the offering basin![34]

31. It should be noted here that, unfortunately, some translations of the *St. Matthew Passion* libretto render the closing lines from the chorus "Sind Blitze, sind Donner" as asking "hell [to] break to pieces with sudden fury the false *betrayers, that murderous race.*" Picander's text reads, "den falschen Verräter, das mördrische Blut" ("the false [or "depraved"] betrayer, that murderous blood"); that is, "the betrayer" is masculine accusative singular, referring to Jesus's disciple Judas Iscariot, and the next phrase also applies to him. *Blut,* then, here refers not to a "race" (that is, "the Jews") but simply to the character in the biblical narrative, Judas. (Compare such expressions in English as "young blood.") It should also be noted that in the aria "Ach, nun ist mein Jesus hin," the talk of Jesus being caught in "tiger-claws" refers to the bands of chief priests and elders, not to the Jewish people as a whole.

32. Translations of the *St. Matthew Passion* libretto throughout this chapter are taken from Michael Marissen, *Bach's Oratorios—The Parallel German-English Texts, with Annotations* (New York: Oxford University Press, 2008).

33. The word *milde* is here regularly translated as "gently." For the word's less well-known sense, which is much more likely the operative one in the present context, consider, for example, the wording of Psalm 37:21, "The Godless one borrows and [re]pays not; the righteous one, however, is merciful and generous [Luther: *milde*; modern Luther Bibles: *kann geben*]." On this understanding of *milde* in Bach as meaning "copiously" or "abundantly," not "calmly" or "gently," see also the theological and etymological background provided by Renate Steiger, "'Wo soll ich fliehen hin?': Das Lied und Bachs Kantate BWV 5—Theologische und musikalische Akzente in J. S. Bachs Passionen," in *"Wie freudig ist mein Herz, da Gott versöhnet ist": Die Lehre von der Versöhnung in Kantaten und Orgelchorälen von Johann Sebastian Bach,* edited by Renate Steiger (Heidelberg: [n.p.], 1995), 78–79.

34. In ancient mythology, the *Opferschale* is a basin in which the blood of the sacrificial animal is collected. Johann Christoph Adelung, *Grammatisch-kritisches*

Bach's musical setting, too, gives powerful expression to the idea that Jesus's blood-streaming chastisement is only in appearance a curse but in essence a blessing: the incessant rhythm of violent *marcato* pairs of dotted sixteenth and thirty-second notes from the recitative "Erbarm es Gott!" (which comments on the flogging Jesus received at the hands of the Roman soldiers) palpably softens by morphing into soothing *legato* pairs of dotted eighth and sixteenth notes in the aria "Können Tränen meiner Wangen."

The classic biblical commentary of the seventeenth-century orthodox Lutheran theologian Johann Olearius, a copy of which Bach owned,[35] was probably a source for Bach and Picander in producing this redemptive interpretation for the *St. Matthew Passion*.[36]

Olearius suggested that Matthew 27:25 connotes both judgment and redemption:

> *His blood; NB.* Genesis 4. Matthew 23:35. [About] this blood-guilt *NB.* Psalm 51:16; together with every curse, threat, and punishment—about this *NB.* Genesis 27:13; about this Lamentations 5:7 . . . *come over us;* about this *NB.* Genesis 27:13. [As if to say:] "Do this upon our own responsibility;

Wörterbuch der Hochdeutschen Mundart (Leipzig, 1793), 3:607. Consider, too, the offerings for the altar in the dedication of the tabernacle in Numbers 7, where twelve times a silver basin (Luther: *Schale*) is presented for use in grain offering (Luther: *Speisopfer*).

35. Johann Olearius, *Biblische Erklärung: Darinnen, nechst dem allgemeinen Haupt-Schlüssel der gantzen heiligen Schrifft* (Leipzig, 1678–1681). This reference Bible is especially useful, as it frequently also provides page references to commentaries in other books, including standard editions of Luther's complete works, several of which Bach also owned. For detailed information on the religious books in Bach's library, see Robin A. Leaver, *Bachs Theologische Bibliothek/Bach's Theological Library* (Neuhausen-Stuttgart: Hänssler-Verlag, 1985).

36. Bach and Picander possibly collaborated on the theological content of Picander's poetry in the *St. Matthew Passion*, for the libretto draws on specific wordings from the Passion sermons of Heinrich Müller that Bach had in his personal library. See Elke Axmacher, "Ein Quellenfund zum Text der Matthäus-Passion," *Bach-Jahrbuch* 64 (1978): 181–191.

we want to indemnify you. Let it come on our children and descendants. Should it happen to him unjustly, then we want to carry the guilt." At which [it is] worth remembering: . . . 2. The horrible fulfillment after 40 years [that is, the destruction of Jerusalem and its Temple in the year 70]. . . . 3. The comforting conversion of this curse into blessing. For the power of the blood of Jesus Christ comes over us, and purifies us; 1 John 1, that is to say: "Your goodness be over us," Psalm 33:22, which is redemption for the many. *NB.* Psalm 130:7.[37]

Note that Genesis 27:13 figures in Olearius's comments both on judgment and on redemption. Concerning this verse (where Rebekah replies, "the curse be on me," to her son Jacob's worry that if he goes to his blind father Isaac pretending to be his older brother Esau, he will bring on himself a curse instead of the hoped-for fatherly "Blessing from the Lord" of the firstborn), Olearius wrote: "[Rebekah said, 'Let the curse] come over me; it meet me and remain on me.' So said the Jews: 'his blood come over us,' namely the punishment of the innocent blood. Matthew 27:25. [Rebekah had] said ['the curse be on me'] to convince Jacob, for she knew assuredly that here there was not a curse to face but a blessing. So says also David, Psalm 33:22. Your goodness, Lord, be over us, as a steadfast protection, *NB.* Psalm 91:1–2, and remain over us unchangingly."[38]

At its commentary on Genesis 27:13, Bach's Calov Bible Commentary writes something similar about curses and blessings: "[Rebekah] said ['the curse be on me'] out of assured trust that it would turn out such that Jacob would receive not a curse but a beautiful fatherly blessing, at which she also could be

37. Olearius, *Biblische Erklärung*, 5:252.

38. Olearius, *Biblische Erklärung*, 1.2:208.

delighted—which ascertainment originated from God's answer [to Rebekah in Genesis] 25:23."[39]

Now, at his commentary on Psalm 33:22 ("Your goodness, Lord, be over us, as a steadfast protection"), Olearius wrote: "*Be over us truly and remain steadfast, NB. Genesis 27:13. Matthew 27:25.*"[40] That is, "goodness" in Psalm 33 and "his blood" in Matthew 27 are both said in the Luther Bible to be "over us," prompting Olearius to draw an interpretive parallel between the psalm and the gospel.

Christians take the redemptive power (that is, the goodness) of "his blood" to have been instituted by the words of Jesus in Matthew 26:27–28, words that Bach powerfully set in the *St. Matthew Passion* ("Drink from it, all [of you]; this is my blood of the new[41] covenant, which is shed for many for the forgiveness of sins"). At his commentary on Matthew 26:28, Olearius wrote: "*Blood; haima; about this 1 John 1:7. This is ratification of the new covenant through my own blood . . . thus corresponding to the sacrificial blood [of] Exodus 24:8.*"[42]

At his commentary on Exodus 24:8 ("Then Moses took the [sacrificial] blood and sprinkled the people with it, and exclaimed, 'Behold, this is the blood of the covenant that the Lord [has] made with you . . .'"), Olearius wrote: "*Blood of the covenant; Dam habberith; about this Leviticus 26 and Nehemiah 9, whose Mosaic covenant of law corresponds to the Gospel covenant of grace and the blood of Jesus Christ in the New Testament. Matthew 26. Hebrews 9:19.*"[43] That is to say, sprinkling blood over "the people" is understood by Olearius to be an act of blessing both in Exodus and in the

---

39. Calov, *Die heilige Bibel*, 1:202. The first "X" in "XXV.23" has been corrected by hand (by Bach?) in Bach's own copy.

40. Olearius, *Biblische Erklärung*, 3:208.

41. Many recent translations of Matthew read "this is my blood of the covenant." The word *new* was added to 26:28 in some early manuscripts of the gospel (the same is true for Mark 14:24) and is carried over into Luther's translation.

42. Olearius, *Biblische Erklärung*, 5:230.

43. Olearius, *Biblische Erklärung*, 1.2:496.

gospel, and thus, implicitly, the blood passages in Matthew 26 and 27 are to be linked.

To return to Bach, taking a blessing to appear behind a curse happens again toward the end of the *St. Matthew Passion*, at the aria "Ach Golgatha," whose third and fourth lines read: "the blessing and salvation of the world appears on the cross as a curse."[44] The idea of the cross as seeming curse but actual blessing is developed also in the next aria, "Sehet, Jesus hat die Hand, uns zu fassen, ausgepannt." Lutheran Passion sermon writers in Bach's personal library refer to Jesus as "the proper high priest" (*der rechte Hohepriester*), declaring that "his hands he has outstretched [*ausgespannet*] on the cross to embrace you; ... his hands he has outstretched to bless you"[45] (that is, by forming the posture of the priest in a prayer of blessing; see also the Epistle to the Hebrews, especially 7:25).

Conclusion

It might be useful in closing to present my readings of Matthew, Luther,[46] and Bach in a condensed form.

For Matthew's gospel, in the narrative itself, Jews and Gentiles ("the crowds") are together held morally responsible for the death

44. See Galatians 3:13. For similar linking of curse with blessing, see Bach's church cantatas *Herr, wie du willt, so schicks mit mir* (BWV 73) and *Jesu, der du meine Seele* (BWV 78).

45. Heinrich Müller Passion sermons, quoted in Axmacher, *Aus Liebe will mein Heyland Sterben*, 179, n. 28.

46. For an extremely spirited response to this chapter's research on Matthew and Luther, see Lothar Steiger, "Affekt und Leidenschaft in biblischer Streitkultur oder daß unsere Unfähigkeit zu streiten, z.B. dies über 'Antijudaismus' zu tun, nicht zuletzt darin seinen Grund hat, daß wir nicht mehr von der Hermeneutica sacra der Frühen Neuzeit wissen, weshalb die folgende Erörterung hier zu orten ist—Eine freundliche Entgegnung auf Michael Marissen, 'Blood, People, and Crowds in Matthew's Gospel, Luther's New Testament, and Bach's St. Matthew Passion Libretto,'" in *Passion, Affekt und Leidenschaft in der Frühen Neuzeit*, edited by Johann Anselm Steiger (Wiesbaden: Harrassowitz Verlag, 2005), 2:585–590.

of Jesus (27:20, 27:24), the Kingdom of God passes to some new or renewed entity (21:43), and "the [Jewish] people" are depicted as crying out "his blood [be] on us and our children" (27:25, one verse after Pilate has declared himself innocent before the festival "crowd"), presumably because Matthew wishes to point to the violence heaped upon Jews in the year 70, the generation of "the people's" children or grandchildren, when the Jewish Temple was destroyed.[47]

Within Luther's linguistically innovative translation of the gospel narrative itself, however, only Jews will and *can* be held morally responsible for the death of Jesus.[48] Against Matthew's distinction between "the crowds" and "the people," for Luther it is the same *Volk* of 27:20 that cries out a blood curse upon itself in 27:25; the Kingdom of God passes from Jews to non-Jews, "the gentiles"; and "the [Jewish] people" do indeed curse themselves for all time *post Christi adventum* (because, Luther believed, they have become a God-forsaken group who should naturally expect continual persecution if they do not convert to Christianity).[49]

<hr>

47. Here perhaps a contextual reference ought to be made to the Great Commission of Matthew 28:16–20, where Jesus says, "go and make disciples of all nations." New Testament interpreters are divided on whether Matthew's world mission excludes or includes Jews (for bibliography, see Davies and Allison, *A Critical and Exegetical Commentary*, 3:684, n. 39). Luther certainly did not give up on an idea of converting "ethnic Israel," but in both his earlier and his later writings, he was extremely contemptuous of the religion of Judaism. He (and many of his followers) had no doubt that God via the Romans destroyed the Jerusalem Temple not only to punish Jews for rejecting Jesus but also to abrogate their covenant with God and to bring definitively to an end the validity of their religion. See the discussion and extensive documentation of these issues, for example, in Marissen, "The Character and Sources" (reprinted here as chapter 3).

48. Perhaps it should be mentioned here that Luther and the New Testament authors apparently see no inconsistency between concomitant claims about human responsibility and about God's will; for example, people can be held responsible for Jesus's death even if the crucifixion was in truth the will of God.

49. A theme in many of Luther's writings but most prominently, of course, in his "On the Jews and Their Lies, 1543," in *Luther's Works*, vol. 47, *The Christian in Society IV*, edited by Franklin Sherman, translated by Martin H. Bertram (Philadelphia: Fortress Press, 1971), 123–306.

For Bach's *St. Matthew Passion* (whose narrative portions come verbatim from the Luther Bible), the biblical story itself depicts Jews as morally responsible for the death of Jesus, while in the commentary portions, Christians alone are chastised for their guilt in having caused Jesus's death; there is no mention of the passing of God's Kingdom; and it emerges from the commentary that "the [Jewish] people" are understood ironically to have called upon themselves and their children a blessing effected by the redemptive blood of Jesus.

Given the historical evidence, it does not appear that the kind of interpretation of the gospel projected by the words and music of Bach's *St. Matthew Passion* can be said to have any reasonable connection with the physically violent or determined eternal-damnation strains of anti-Jewish sentiment often associated (whether rightly or wrongly) with Matthew's Passion narrative. What remains unclear, however, is just how "generous" listeners may believe the redeeming blood of Jesus proclaimed in Bach's aria "Können Tränen meiner Wangen" to be. While the Pauline idea of justification only by grace through faith surely applies for Gentiles, does the same necessarily hold true, according to Bach's *St. Matthew Passion*, for the salvation of so-called Old Israel?[50] Are

50. For recent biblical criticism suggesting that according to historically informed reading of Paul, the same actually does not hold true for Jews, see John G. Gager, *Reinventing Paul* (New York: Oxford University Press, 2000); and Krister Stendahl, *Final Account: Paul's Letter to the Romans* (Philadelphia: Fortress Press, 1976), esp. 33–44. Stendahl argues that the issue at hand in the book of Romans was the justification of Paul's Gentile converts, not of sinners in general. (Stendahl was the Lutheran bishop of Stockholm; that is to say, one does not have to agree with Brother Martin to be a good Lutheran.) Luther himself (following Augustine), however, took Paul's key phrase "all Israel will be saved" in Romans 11:26 to mean that "all among Israel who are to be saved will be saved"; see Martin Luther, *Lectures on Romans, Luther's Works*, vol. 25, edited by Hilton C. Oswald, translated by Walter G. Tillmanns and Jacob A. O. Preus (St. Louis: Concordia Publishing House, 1972), 101; that is, Luther's Paul appears to be saying that *"not* all Israel will be saved." (Luther's *Lectures on Romans* were not published until the twentieth century.)

listeners rightly to understand the *St. Matthew Passion* as construing salvation altogether inclusively when, for example, in Bach's recitative no. 22, the text states (my emphasis):

Der Heiland fällt vor seinem Vater nieder;	The Savior falls down before his Father;
Dadurch erhebt er mich *und alle* Von unserm Falle	thereby he lifts me *and everyone* from our Fall
Hinauf zu Gottes Gnade wieder.	up to God's grace again.

As with the conclusions on the *St. John Passion*, as discussed in chapter 5, this *St. Matthew Passion* recitative may at first sound superecumenical, but most likely, it just means, if still generously, that—against the doctrines of Calvinism—in principle, all humanity could be saved by Jesus, in the End, as "Lutherans."

In any event, if the hope behind a redemptive understanding of Matthew 27:25 is that *all* the children of Israel will accept the saving power of Jesus's blood, this could still give the passage a "violent" effect: would not such a confession mark the death of "Judaism"?[51]

---

51. See Amy-Jill Levine, "Matthew, Mark, and Luke: Good News or Bad?" in *Jesus, Judaism & Christian Anti-Judaism: Reading the New Testament after the Holocaust*, edited by Paula Fredriksen and Adele Reinhartz (Louisville: Westminster John Knox Press, 2002), 92. As far as I can see, the validity of Levine's point here about possible "anti-Jewish" effects even in a redemptive reading of Matthew 27:25 is in no way weakened by acknowledging that Jewish identity was rather more fluid in the first century than it is today (that is, many early "Christians" would not have identified themselves as "not Jewish").

PART IV

Religious Expression
in Secular Chamber Music

Chapter 7

The Theological Character
of Bach's *Musical Offering*

The cross alone is our theology.
MARTIN LUTHER, commentary on Psalm 5:12

The cross of Christ is our glory.
HEINRICH MÜLLER, Apostolische Schluß-Kette

The complicated transmission problems of the print of J. S. Bach's *Musical Offering* (BWV 1079), dedicated in 1747 to King Frederick II ("the Great") of Brandenburg-Prussia, have occasioned an enormous amount of scholarly speculation about the way the collection was put together and the possible significance of its ordering. Substantial progress on the first question was made more than

For encouragement and criticism in completing this chapter, I would like to thank Gregory Butler, Eric Chafe, Eugene Helm, Robert Marshall, Daniel Melamed, Joshua Rifkin, David Schulenberg, and Jeanne Swack.

Regarding the first epigraph for this chapter, see Alister E. McGrath, *Luther's Theology of the Cross: Martin Luther's Theological Breakthrough* (Oxford: Basil Blackwell, 1985), 1, 152, 167, 169. Luther's commentary on Psalm 5 appeared in vol. 3 of the sixteenth-century Wittenberg Edition of his collected works (various printings), which, according to Robin A. Leaver, *Bachs Theologische Bibliothek/ Bach's Theological Library* (Neuhausen-Stuttgart: Hänssler-Verlag, 1983), 64, formed part of Bach's extensive theological library. Regarding the second epigraph, see the front-matter engraving for Heinrich Müller, *Apostolische Schluß-Kette* (Frankfurt, 1687), where the author is shown holding an an open book and pointing to its extra-large-print words *Crux Christi nostra Gloria*. According to Leaver, *Bachs Theologische Bibliothek*, 109, Bach owned a quarto copy of this *Schluß-Kette*, a book on the epistle readings in the Lutheran liturgy.

forty years ago in research by Christoph Wolff, who published new findings based on a close examination of the technical features in each of the (incomplete) surviving exemplars of Bach's print.[1] Wolff demonstrated that none of the previously suggested orderings for the *Musical Offering* could be supported by the early documents. He proposed a new ordering of the various fascicles of Bach's print but suggested that it probably had little, if any, significance for thinking about or performing the collection.

Wolff assumed that Bach's print had been produced entirely by Johann Georg Schübler. His reconstruction was consequently called into question by Wolfgang Wiemer's discovery that two members of the Schübler family of Zella had worked as the engravers in preparing the print.[2] In light of Wiemer's research, I have argued elsewhere that Bach probably arranged the various pieces in the *Musical Offering* by genre (two fugues, sonata, ten canons) and that the final engraving product from the Schübler brothers essentially reflected this arrangement.[3] Close study of the print, along with evidence from secondary manuscripts of the collection and contemporary letters describing it, suggests that the layout of the complete print corresponded to the description found in a 1747

1. Christoph Wolff, "Der Terminus 'Ricercar' in Bachs Musikalischem Opfer," *Bach-Jahrbuch* 53 (1967): 70–81 (updated in Christoph Wolff, *Bach: Essays on His Life and Music* [Cambridge: Harvard University Press, 1991], chap. 25); Christoph Wolff, "New Research on Bach's *Musical Offering*," *Musical Quarterly* 57 (1971): 379–408 (updated in Wolff, *Bach: Essays*, chap. 18); Christoph Wolff, *Kritischer Bericht* for Johann Sebastian Bach, *Neue Ausgabe sämtlicher Werke* ["*Neue Bach-Ausgabe*"], series VIII, vol. 1, *Kanons/Musikalisches Opfer* (Kassel: Bärenreiter, 1976); Christoph Wolff, "Überlegungen zum 'Thema Regium,'" *Bach-Jahrbuch* 59 (1973): 33–38 (updated in Wolff, *Bach: Essays*, chap. 25).

2. Wolfgang Wiemer, *Die wiederhergestellte Ordnung in Johann Sebastian Bachs Kunst der Fuge* (Wiesbaden: Breitkopf & Härtel, 1977), 40–43. Newer research shows that the print represents the engraving work of *three* Schübler brothers; see Gregory Butler, "The Printing History of J. S. Bach's *Musical Offering*: New Interpretations," *Journal of Musicology* 19 (2002): 306–331.

3. Michael Marissen, "More Source-Critical Research on J. S. Bach's *Musical Offering*," *Bach* 25, no. 1 (1994): 11–27.

Leipzig newspaper advertisement: "[The *Musical Offering*] consists of 1.) two fugues, one with three, the other with six obbligato parts; 2.) a sonata for transverse flute, violin, and continuo; 3.) diverse canons, among which [*wobey*] is a *fuga canonica*."[4]

In this chapter, I propose that the *Musical Offering* assumes an increasingly theological character as it moves from genre to genre (fugues, sonata, canons). This interpretation conflicts with previous views of the collection, the majority of which locate themselves on a continuum between two extreme positions. The first, advanced most forcefully by Friedrich Blume and still widely accepted among scholars, holds that this music—in particular, its canons—is "abstract": it explores "pure" issues of form, was not really meant to be performed, and is nonreferential.[5] The other, advanced by Ursula Kirkendale and widely accepted among performers, holds that the music is loaded with significance: it was meant, as declared in Bach's preface, to glorify its dedicatee, and accordingly, the collection was organized in such a way that it takes on the classical form and content of a detailed rhetorical argument.[6] Blume's view has been partly discredited, as some scholars, for example, have taken seriously the clear performance indications in the print: the sonata is printed in separate parts rather than in score; Canons 2 and 8 specify scorings; Canons 2–3, 6, and 8–10 provide articulation markings; and Canons 2, 4, and 6–9 provide trills.[7] Kirkendale's

4. The advertisement was unknown to scholars before the 1970s, when it was published in Wolff, "New Research," 399.

5. See Friedrich Blume, "J. S. Bach," in *Musik in Geschichte und Gegenwart*, vol. 1, *Aachen–Blumner*, edited by Friedrich Blume (Kassel: Bärenreiter, 1949–1951), 962–1047.

6. Ursula Kirkendale, "The Source for Bach's *Musical Offering*: The *Institutio Oratoria* of Quintilian," *Journal of the American Musicological Society* 33 (1980): 88–141.

7. Wolff, *Kritischer Bericht*, 118. Wolff goes on to show that the various contrapuntal lines in the canons with unspecified scorings correspond to normal eighteenth-century flute, violin, and keyboard ranges (119–121). Throughout this chapter, the numbering of Bach's canons corresponds to that employed in the *Neue Bach-Ausgabe*.

view has been questioned, too, but her critics have focused more on the form of her argument than on its general import, pointing out that the proportions of a rhetorical oration are completely distorted in the suggested sequence for Bach's movements.[8]

Like Kirkendale, I believe Bach's music does carry referential meanings. But in light of the collection's strange prefatory language and rubrics, predominantly old-fashioned musical style, and often almost funereal *Affect* (especially and most significantly in Canon 4, as we shall see), Bach's stated intention of glorifying Frederick the Great appears incomprehensible if "glorification" is understood in the conventional manner. Bach's music seems here to project a rather different notion of glory. Far from elevating or shedding radiance and splendor on Frederick, the *Musical Offering* promotes a biblical-Lutheran understanding of glory, one that Frederick cannot have found sympathetic: the idea of "glorification through abasement," a view tied up with Luther's "theology of the cross" as opposed to the "theology of glory." In the end, then, Bach's collection could act as a sort of general argument not just for different forms and styles of music—Bach's high baroque, "learned" counterpoint rather than the galant homophony and occasional galant counterpoint of the Prussian court—but for decidedly different world-and-life views from those promoted by French-Enlightenment thinkers such as Frederick.[9] This music is an homage to God.[10]

---

8. See Wolff, *Bach: Essays*, 421–423. Kirkendale's interpretation, which accepts a nineteenth-century ordering of the collection, also suffers from seriously implausible observations on source-critical matters (consider, for example, her stating, at p. 127, that "with two [keyboard] instruments it would be possible . . . to play [the canons] easily [*sic!*] from the original abbreviated notation"); see Marissen, "More Source-Critical Research," 26.

9. Regarding this sort of conflict of Weltanschauung more broadly, see Rémy Gilbert Saisselin, *The Enlightenment against the Baroque: Economics and Aesthetics in the Eighteenth Century* (Berkeley and Los Angeles: University of California Press, 1992).

10. Martin Geck, *Johann Sebastian Bach: Life and Work*, translated by John Hargraves (Orlando: Harcourt, 2006), 639, is dismissive: "There is little reason

Contexts

Before exploring musical details of the *Musical Offering* and their contribution to the collection's increasingly theological character, it is worth considering some of the historical background for the meeting of Bach and Frederick. The private appearance on May 7, 1747, of J. S. Bach, church musician in Saxony, at the court of Frederick the Great, King in Prussia,[11] is the most extensively documented event in Bach's otherwise unglamorous career. The full story has been told many times, and therefore only the most relevant aspects of it will be mentioned here.[12] The normal evening concert at the Prussian court involved a series of sonatas for flute and continuo performed by Frederick and one of his accompanists (C. P. E. Bach among them) or flute concertos performed by Frederick and a group of his chamber musicians. The music was

to assume, with Michael Marissen, that the *Musical Offering* is actually dedicated to God. It is more a confidently completed piece of journeyman work—an unlooked-for commission, as difficult as it was important." Surely, however, any construal of Bach's staggering accomplishments in the *Musical Offering* as journeywork or daywork (Martin Geck, *Bach: Leben und Werk* [Reinbek: Rowohlt, 2000], 701: "selbstbewusste Tagesarbeit"), even in Bach's own eyes, should seem rather hard to credit. Also, this music cannot have been, for Bach, an unexpected or unlooked-for incoming project or commission (Geck: "ein unvermutet hereingekommener . . . Auftrag"). As we shall see, it is well documented that Bach gave himself the assignment of composing on the Royal Theme (note the primary sources I cite here in notes 16 and 18).

11. After 1701, in return for certain military and political favors, the Holy Roman Emperor granted the Electors of Brandenburg (who did not actually rule a "kingdom") permission to use the title "King *in* Prussia." In 1772, Frederick the Great adopted the title "King *of* Prussia."

12. For the entire story, see especially Hans T. David, *J. S. Bach's Musical Offering* (New York: G. Schirmer, 1945), 3–15; and Wolff, *Kritischer Bericht*, 101–110. A full study of Frederick and Bach, one that is remarkably insightful—and enviably readable—is James R. Gaines, *Evening in the Palace of Reason: Bach Meets Frederick the Great in the Age of Enlightenment* (New York: Harper Perennial, 2005); I was most delighted to read in Gaines's acknowledgments (314–318) that the present essay "inspired and provides an underpinning for this book."

almost invariably composed by Frederick himself or by Johann Joachim Quantz, his teacher and flute maker.[13] The recitals were extremely strict affairs. One had to be specifically invited by the king (the audience was small, the chamber musicians typically being the only persons present who were not from the aristocracy), and, on pain of reprimand (possibly violent in the case of the musicians), nobody except Quantz was permitted to react in any way to the king's performances.[14] Frederick's last-minute reconfiguring of one of these evening concerts by inviting Bach to take over, then, should be considered socially remarkable.

Bach was well known in professional musical circles throughout the German-speaking areas of Europe not only for his abilities in composition and keyboard playing but also for his improvisations. Frederick must have been primarily, perhaps exclusively, interested in the latter, for Bach's concert apparently involved only a series of improvisations, that is, not a series of Bach's compositions. At one point during the evening, Frederick provided Bach with a difficult theme on which to improvise a fugue. The audience and Frederick were astonished by Bach's performance, but Bach himself was dissatisfied with his improvised fugue.[15] He reportedly made known then and there that he intended "to set [Frederick's theme] down on paper in a *regular* [*ordentlichen*] fugue and have it

13. Karl Friedrich Zelter, *Karl Friedrich Christian Fasch* (Berlin, 1801), 14, 49.

14. Regarding the atmosphere of Frederick's concerts, see Ernest Eugene Helm, *Music at the Court of Frederick the Great* (Norman: University of Oklahoma Press, 1960), 28–39. See also Sabine Henze-Döhring, *Friedrich der Große: Musiker und Monarch* (Munich: C. H. Beck, 2012).

15. The leading German newspapers reported that everyone present was filled with amazement at Bach's improvisation; see Werner Neumann and Hans-Joachim Schulze, eds., *Bach-Dokumente II* (Kassel: Bärenreiter, 1969), no. 554; and Christoph Wolff, ed., *The New Bach Reader* (New York: W. W. Norton, 1998), 224. Jacob Adlung, *Anleitung zu der Musikalischen Gelahrtheit* (Erfurt, 1758), described the experience as "still fresh in people's minds" (more than ten years later); see Hans-Joachim Schulze, ed., *Bach-Dokumente III* (Kassel: Bärenreiter, 1972), no. 693.

engraved in copper."[16] Considering the typically severe atmosphere of Frederick's chamber concerts, one has to wonder what sort of impression such an announcement, however politely expressed, would have made. For a start, it contradicts the king's own opinion of Bach's performance; moreover, it points up the higher value of thinking through and reflecting on the demands of fugue; and, finally, it suggests the value of publishing results for others to study and contemplate.[17] In his preface to the print, Bach was fairly explicit about all of this:

> Your Majesty's Self deigned to play to me a theme for a fugue upon the clavier, and at the same time charged me most graciously to carry it out in Your Majesty's Most August Presence. To obey Your Majesty's command was my most humble duty. I noticed very soon, however, that for lack of necessary preparation, the execution of the task did not fare as well as such an excellent theme demanded. I resolved therefore and promptly pledged myself to work out this right Royal theme more fully [or "more closely to perfection," *vollkommener auszuarbeiten*] and then make it known to the world. This resolve has now been carried out as well as possible.[18]

16. See the newspaper report in Neumann and Schulze, *Bach-Dokumente II*, no. 554; and Wolff, *The New Bach Reader*, 224.

17. In this connection, it is worth noting that Frederick did not permit Quantz to publish his music composed for the Prussian court concerts, because these pieces were to be written and preserved only for the entertainment of the king. See Charles Burney, *The Present State of Music in Germany, the Netherlands and United Provinces* (London, 1775), 2:153.

18. Wolff, *The New Bach Reader*, 226–228; facsimile in Christoph Wolff, ed., *Johann Sebastian Bach: Musicalisches Opfer BWV 1079* (Leipzig: Peters, 1977). This wording is also reproduced in David, *J. S. Bach's Musical Offering*, 6–7; in *Neue Bach-Ausgabe*, series VIII, vol. 1, 12–13; and in Werner Neumann and Hans-Joachim Schulze, eds., *Bach-Dokumente I* (Kassel: Bärenreiter, 1963), no. 173.

Bach's entering Frederick's chamber music rooms must really have constituted a meeting of two clashing worlds.[19] Bach was sixty-two years old. Frederick was thirty-five (that is, younger than Bach's oldest children). Bach was middle-class, had been married twice, and had fathered twenty children. Frederick was, of course, aristocratic, had a politically arranged marriage, and had no children (a homosexual or bisexual, he did not spend much time with his wife, and he did not live with her). Bach was an orthodox Lutheran, deeply interested in music and theology, who spoke and wrote German and was probably not fully comfortable with French. Frederick was strongly anti-Christian (though politically tolerant),[20] deeply interested in French Enlightenment philosophy and poetry, and, above all, in personal control of political power. He spoke and wrote in French and was apparently not fully comfortable with German. When Johann Christoph Gottsched once remarked to him that German poets could not expect to get any encouragement so long as the German language was too little understood and French too much understood among the nobility and at the courts, Frederick replied: "That is true, for from my youth I have read not a single German book, and I speak the language like a coachman; now, however, I am an old fellow of 46, and have no more time for it."[21]

Bach's and Frederick's stated views on the functions of music could hardly have been more different. Bach believed the primary

19. The contrasting characterizations that follow have partly been drawn from Adalbert Schütz, "Zur Deutung des Musikalischen Opfers (Joh. Seb. Bach und Friedrich der Große)," *Wort und Dienst: Jahrbuch der Theologischen Schule Bethel* 6 (1959): 170–179.

20. Regarding his views on Christianity, see Frederick II, King of Prussia, *Briefe über die Religion*, edited by Rudolf Neuwinger (Berlin: Nordland, 1941); and Frederick II, King of Prussia, *Theologische Streitschriften*, edited by Rudolf Neuwinger (Berlin: Nordland, 1939).

21. Letter of October 22, 1757, from Gottsched to Cölestin Christian Flottwell; see Gustav Mendelssohn Bartholdy, *Der König: Friedrich der Große in seinen Briefen und Erlassen* (Ebenhausen bei München: Langewiesche-Brandt, 1912), 314–318.

purpose of music was to honor God and refresh people's minds or spirits and that music was a craft involving concentrated effort for composers, performers, and listeners. In his teachings on continuo playing, Bach remarked: "[The basso continuo makes] a well-sounding harmony to the Glory of God and to the sanctioned enjoyment of the spirit [*zulässiger Ergötzung*[22] *des Gemüths*]; the aim and final reason, as of all music, so of the thorough bass, should be none else but the Glory of God and the refreshing of the mind."[23] Frederick believed the primary purpose of music was to entertain and divert, that music should be straightforwardly pleasant and uncomplicated, and that it should not require concentrated effort on the part of composers, performers, and listeners. While playing the flute before cabinet meetings, Frederick focused his thoughts on other things and came up with answers to difficult political problems. His flute apparently played this sort of role also on the battlefield.[24] Comparing the relative merits of various artistic and intellectual pursuits, Frederick remarked early in his career to Ulrich, Count von Suhm: "We have divided our activities [at court] into two categories. The one is useful, the other agreeable. Studying philosophy and the history of languages are among the useful; the agreeable include music, the comedies and tragedies which we

22. In modern German, *Ergötzen* has largely taken on the meaning "to amuse" or "to entertain," but in eighteenth-century usage, it meant "to bring about palpable joy"; see Johann Christoph Adelung, *Grammatisch-kritisches Wörterbuch der Hochdeutschen Mundart* (Leipzig, 1793), col. 1894. Adelung provides several examples for its usage, mostly from the Bible, none of which has to do with entertainment or diversion. The word is used in this more edifying sense each time it appears in Bach's church cantatas.

23. Printed in Philipp Spitta, *Johann Sebastian Bach* (Leipzig, 1873–1880), 2:916. This represents Bach's wording of thoughts expressed in Friedrich Erhardt Niedt, *Musicalische Handleitung* (Hamburg, 1710–1717, rev. ed. 1721).

24. Georg Thouret, *Friedrich der Große als Musikfreund und Musiker* (Leipzig, 1898), 134, citing an unspecified letter from Frederick to Jean le Rond d'Alembert. Thouret's report seems to fit perfectly with the contents of Frederick's voluminous correspondence with d'Alembert, but I have not succeeded in locating Thouret's source.

stage, the masquerades and the gifts that we give each other. But the serious occupations always take precedence over the others."[25]

Against this background, then, what sort of collection did Bach compose, publish, and dedicate to Frederick? It was a fairly mixed bag of musical items: a series of two fugues, a sonata, and ten canons, all based on the king's theme. The more usual practice at the time was to dedicate pieces (typically six of them) in the same genre. For example, C. P. E. Bach dedicated the six keyboard sonatas now known as the Prussian Sonatas (H. 24–29/Wq 48) to Frederick in the early 1740s. It was also the more usual practice to dedicate pieces known to be more ideally in line with the tastes of the dedicatee. It is difficult to imagine a stronger contrast in the 1740s than that between the strict style (*gelehrte Stil*, "learned" counterpoint) of most of Bach's *Musical Offering* and the typically galant style (thin-textured homophony with singing melodies and relatively unobtrusive basses) of most of the hundreds of sonatas and concertos by Quantz and Frederick that were performed night after night at the Prussian court.

All things considered, it seems unlikely that Frederick had any real interest in studying or performing the relentlessly strict counterpoint encountered in Bach's *Musical Offering*. His personal copy evidently passed out of his library during his lifetime; this same exemplar at one time belonged to Johann Philipp Kirnberger, who died three years before Frederick.[26] Hoping to prove to Baron van Swieten that Bach's musical understanding was unmatched, in 1774 (almost thirty years after the fact), Frederick sang aloud the

25. Letter of October 23, 1736; Mendelssohn Bartholdy, *Der König*, 73; translated in Robert B. Asprey, *Frederick the Great* (New York: Ticknor & Fields, 1986), 111.

26. Wolff, *Kritischer Bericht*, 61. The possible significance of this has been passed over unmentioned, even in the most substantial and insightful recent literature, for example, David Yearsley, "The Autocratic Regimes of *A Musical Offering*," in *Bach and the Meanings of Counterpoint* (Cambridge: Cambridge University Press, 2002), 128–172; and Mary Oleskiewicz, "The Trio in Bach's Musical Offering: A Salute to Frederick's Tastes and Quantz's Flutes?" *Bach Perspectives* 4 (1999): 79–110.

chromatic fugue subject he had given to Bach, who on the spot, according to Frederick, had made of it a fugue in four parts, then in five parts, and finally in eight parts![27] As enthusiastic as Frederick's assessment is, it appears nonetheless to be fully in line with his un-Bachian tastes. Frederick was evidently interested in the power of fugue as "spectacle"; he may very well have found it an entertaining and exciting diversion to witness Bach improvise completely unpremeditated fugues on a difficult subject (more entertaining, say, than he would have found variations on a theme, something less harrowing because it requires less skill). Frederick was evidently not much interested, however, in fugue as composition. He gave Carl Heinrich Graun the order in the 1740s not to write French overtures, reportedly in part because of his distaste for their fugal sections, and among his more than 120 surviving sonatas, there is only one movement in fugal style (the third movement from his Sonata no. 2 in C minor for Flute and Continuo, a pleasant one and a half minutes of simple galant counterpoint);[28] none of Frederick's compositions is in the stricter, learned style.

Citing obscure nineteenth-century research by Georg Thouret, some scholars have reported that Frederick was, in fact, a great

27. See Schulze, *Bach-Dokumente III*, no. 790; and Wolff, *The New Bach Reader*, 366–367.

28. Regarding Frederick's fugal composition, see Warren Kirkendale, *Fugue and Fugato in Rococo and Classical Chamber Music* (Durham: Duke University Press, 1979), 311; and Oleskiewicz, "The Trio in Bach's Musical Offering," 83–85. Earlier literature had reported that Quantz's more than one hundred sonatas composed for Frederick are all three-movement works in galant style without fugues. See Kirkendale, *Fugue and Fugato*, 310; and Charlotte Gwen Crockett, "The Berlin Flute Sonatas of Johann Joachim Quantz" (Ph.D. diss., University of Texas at Austin, 1982), 55–56. In further and closer research, however, Oleskiewicz, "The Trio in Bach's Musical Offering," 80, 103, n. 4, notes that Quantz did, in fact, write some fugal flute sonatas and concertos for Frederick. Regarding Graun's overtures, see Helm, *Music at the Court of Frederick the Great*, 144 (but see also 200). Oleskiewicz, "The Trio in Bach's Musical Offering," 80, 104, n. 13, notes, however, that Frederick disliked French music in general and that the French overture was no longer in vogue. Oleskiewicz provides extremely important corrections on musical style and on instruments and their technique, but she does not enter

lover of learned composition.[29] The reliability of Thouret's material needs to be considered carefully in context, however, since his essay is engaged in a rather ugly diatribe against what he calls "Italian superficiality and French insipidity" as compared with the "beauty, truth, and nobility" of "authentic German" music.

In addition to Frederick's not keeping his copy of the *Musical Offering*, it may also be worth noting that there is no evidence that Frederick ever acknowledged or rewarded Bach's efforts. In this case, Bach may well have had the experience of what Voltaire came to call "working for the King of Prussia," that is, to work for nothing.

Fugues

Bach's Three-Part Fugue has come under a great deal of criticism, especially from Hans T. David, who found serious shortcomings in it, suggesting that it probably represents exactly or approximately

into the broader cultural issues possibly raised by Bach's *Musical Offering*. In any event, I should think that Quantz's (marvelous) Berlin fugues and canons, unlike most of Bach's *Musical Offering*, sound (in their general melodiousness and pleasant *Affects*) very much more "galant" than "learned."

29. See Andreas Holschneider, "Johann Sebastian Bach in Berlin," in *Preußen, Dein Spree-Athen: Beiträge zu Literatur, Theater und Musik in Berlin*, edited by Hellmut Kühn (Reinbek: Rowohlt, 1981), 140, quoting Georg Thouret, "Die Musik am preußischen Hofe im 18. Jahrhundert," *Hohenzollern-Jarhbuch* 1 (1897): 56; see also Wolff, *Kritischer Bericht*, 105. Thouret does not specify the nature of his source for Frederick's views (contrary to Wolff), but he must have gotten them from Zelter, *Karl Friedrich Christian Fasch*. Zelter (p. 48) relates an incident of Fasch's improvising a third entry into the accompaniment of a canonic passage from a flute sonata composed and performed by Frederick. Reacting to this improvisation, Frederick reportedly said (which is what Thouret quotes; my emphasis): "It always makes me glad when I find that music is concerned with the faculty of understanding; when *a beautiful piece of music* sounds learned, this is as *pleasant* to me as when I would hear *clever conversation* at table." (That is, Frederick is quoted as saying not "when a piece of music" but "when a *beautiful* piece of music.")

what Bach had improvised for Frederick.[30] David's dissatisfaction with the fugue centers on its lack of balance and symmetry, properties David did find for the rest of the *Musical Offering*—or at least in his symmetrical reconstruction of the collection. In light of source-critical research by Wolff and others, David's reconstruction could no longer be considered plausible, but writers have continued nonetheless to share David's sense of stylistic unease with the Three-Part Fugue.

Wolff accounted for the stylistic peculiarities of the piece by investigating alternative meanings of the word *ricercar*.[31] In Bach's time, the term could refer to an improvisation (typically noncontrapuntal) in which one "searches out" themes or tests the tuning and probes the key. Principally, though, *ricercar* was employed in its other sense, for strict and highly elaborate fugues. Wolff suggested that in the *Musical Offering* print, Bach used the term for both a free three-part fugue and a strict six-part fugue not carelessly but with the idea of exploring the two different types of ricercar.

Perhaps, though, this does not do justice to Bach's achievement in these pieces, particularly in the case of the Three-Part Fugue. Regarding the notion that the Three-Part Fugue represents Bach's actual or approximate improvisation for Frederick, recall that Bach had declared himself to be dissatisfied with his improvised fugue and resolved on account of the "lack of necessary preparation [that the] excellent theme demanded" to "write down on paper a regular [*ordentliche*] fugue." He also declared his printed results to have been worked out "as well as possible." In light of these biographical and the earlier mentioned musical considerations, it becomes

30. David, *J. S. Bach's Musical Offering*, 8, 30, 35, 44, 63, 134, 143, 147, 151, 152. Similar statements were made by Spitta, *Johann Sebastian Bach*, 2:673; and, more strongly, by Albert Schweitzer, *J. S. Bach* (Leipzig: Breitkopf & Härtel, 1908), 398. See also Christoph Wolff, *The New Grove Bach Family* (New York: W. W. Norton, 1983), 109.

31. Wolff, *Bach: Essays*, 329–331.

much more difficult to reconcile Bach's printed Three-Part Fugue exactly (or even approximately) with the notion of improvisation. Furthermore, some of the most formulaic music within Bach's two ricercars occurs not in the Three-Part but rather in the Six-Part Fugue. The latter contains sequential episodic passages in which the fugue subject is alluded to remotely if at all (bars 29–39, 79–83); the episodic passages in the Three-Part Fugue, in contrast, are continually marked by the learned procedures for which Bach was so well known (combination of two cells from the initial counter-subject in bars 18–22; combination of the subject's head and tail in bars 31–37, 115–118; stretto on the tail—simultaneously in diminution—in bars 122–124; stretto on a prominent secondary motive in bars 150–151; and a close point of imitation on the initial countersubject in bars 161–165). In other words, although there is undoubtedly a strict/free or severe/loose contrast between these two fugues in general mood, it is not so readily apparent that there is such a contrast in form or contrapuntal procedure.

In fact, taking a lead from Bach's enthusiastic disciple Friedrich Wilhelm Marpurg, we could actually exchange the strict/free des-ignations and apply the former to the Three-Part Fugue and the latter to the Six-Part Fugue. Marpurg says that there are two kinds of "regular fugue": "strict or free." In strict fugues, the episodes frequently allude to or quote from parts of the subject and its ini-tial counterpoint by means of division, augmentation, diminution, and contrary motion. If such a piece is worked out at length and introduces all kinds of contrapuntal artifices, it can be called by the Italian name of *ricercare* or *ricercata*.[32] Marpurg notes that Bach's fugues typically conform to this style. In free fugues, the episodes mostly present material that may be related to but is not derived

---

32. Friedrich Wilhelm Marpurg, *Abhandlung von der Fuge* (Berlin, 1753), 1:18–20; Schulze, *Bach-Dokumente III*, no. 655; Wolff, *The New Bach Reader*, 359. The quota-tion from Marpurg in Wolff, *Bach: Essays*, 330, needs to be reconsidered in light of this wider context.

from the subject and its initial counterpoint. Marpurg notes that the fugues of Handel typically conform to this style. On the basis of Marpurg's discussion, then, Bach's Six-Part Fugue would more likely have been labeled "free" and the Three-Part Fugue "strict."

Nonetheless, throughout the Three-Part Fugue, Bach cultivated some elements of the galant style: thinner textures, triplet figuration within music that is otherwise duple at each metric level, and "sighing" appoggiaturas.[33] Wolff focuses on the galant passages to show the breadth of Bach's stylistic interests and to make the compelling argument that this fugue is well served in performance on the fortepiano. Bach was no doubt interested in exploiting the capabilities of the relatively new instrument, but he could certainly have used much more effective means than inserting a few galant-style passages into an extended, strict high-baroque fugue. In addition to broad compositional or specific organological explanations, perhaps these passages, undeniably conspicuous, need further interpretation.

Each of the passages in question features rapid modulatory sequential movement in the flat direction. In bars 38–42, the music moves from C minor to E-flat minor (transposed at bars 87–91, where it reaches A-flat minor), and in bars 109–118 from G minor to E-flat minor/major. Bach rarely travels so many steps away from the home key in his instrumental works. In that repertory, he mostly sticks to the tonic, dominant, and subdominant keys and their relatives, what Bach's contemporary Johann David Heinichen called the "ambitus" of the key.[34] In his choruses and arias, Bach much more frequently visits keys outside the ambitus, almost invariably for textual reasons. Distant tonal movement in the flat direction in Bach's church cantatas frequently expresses ideas concerning death,

---

33. Wolff, *Bach: Essays*, 254–255.

34. See Eric Chafe, *Tonal Allegory in the Vocal Music of J. S. Bach* (Berkeley and Los Angeles: University of California Press, 1991), 65–72. Whether Bach knew Heinichen's term is unknown.

spiritual decay, lament, suffering, vanity, emptiness, and the like.[35] This tonal procedure and its expressive associations are found also in at least one nonliturgical keyboard work, the *Capriccio sopra la lontananza del fratello dilettissimo* (BWV 992), where, in the section entitled "Is a setting-forth of various casualties that could befall him abroad," the music moves rapidly in the flat direction, well outside the ambitus, to B-flat minor. In the Three-Part Fugue from the *Musical Offering*, the rapid movement toward the flattest extremes of the tonal circle (E-flat minor and A-flat minor) right where the music changes from high-baroque to galant textures appears to suggest negative associations with the lighter style. So although the Three-Part Fugue has galant elements, they are undercut by a tonal device that reinforces the piece's strict qualities.

Sonata

Whereas keyboard fugues can hardly have been expected to conform to the tastes typically cultivated at Frederick's court concerts, a sonata would seem, on the face of it, to be much more promising. Yet here, too, Bach's music is aesthetically somewhat at odds with its dedicatee. First of all, Bach's sonata ought ideally to have been, like the vast majority of Frederick's and Quantz's contemporary sonatas, a galant-style work for solo flute with unobtrusive continuo or obbligato keyboard. In a performance of Bach's sonata for a Prussian court soirée, though, the flutist would not occupy visually or musically the central position, because the piece is a trio sonata in the learned contrapuntal style for flute, violin, and continuo.[36] Also, a

35. Many of these are discussed in Chafe, *Tonal Allegory*. Bach's cantatas also feature tonal arrivals outside the ambitus in the sharp direction, associated with matters such as joy, forgiveness, life, redemption, and so on.

36. Although Bach published the dedication sonata as a trio sonata, he apparently also at one point envisioned, but immediately abandoned, a performance

sonata conforming to Prussian court taste would follow Giuseppe Tartini's model with three movements: Slow, Fast, Fast(er). Nearly all of Quantz's more than one hundred sonatas for the Prussian court are galant-style pieces in three movements, marked Slow, Fast, Fast, except for six of them that are Fast, Slow, Fast. Bach's sonata has four movements in the configuration Slow, Fast Fugue, Slow, Fast Fugue, and thus, it would have been classified as a "church sonata" (*sonata da chiesa*), not a galant "chamber sonata" (*sonata da camera*).[37]

Whether or not Frederick would have classified sonatas as *da chiesa* or *da camera*, he evidently associated various sorts of contrapuntal music with the church, and according to Charles Burney, he had a strong distaste for all music that "smells of the church." Reporting on a conversation with Johann Friedrich Agricola about some of his church compositions, Burney wrote: "he said that it was a style of writing which was but little cultivated at Berlin, as the King will not hear it. . . . [H]is Prussian majesty carries his prejudice against this kind of music so far, that when he hears of any composer having written an anthem, or oratorio, he fancies his taste is contaminated by it, and says, of his other productions, every moment, *Oh! this smells of the church.*"[38] It is not surprising, therefore, that among the hundreds of surviving sonatas from Frederick's library there are so few that could be classified as sonatas *da chiesa*.

(in Leipzig?) of this piece for solo instrument and obbligato keyboard; see Wolff, *Kritischer Bericht*, 74–75.

37. Sonatas were categorized this way by eighteenth-century French writers from Sebastien de Brossard to Jean-Jacques Rousseau. Bach was evidently aware of the *da camera* and *da chiesa* designations, as his musical library included pieces listed as such. See Kirsten Beißwenger, *Johann Sebastian Bachs Notenbibliothek* (Kassel: Bärenreiter, 1992). Bach was presumably familiar with the contrapuntal, four-movement Sonata in G minor labeled *Sonata da chiesa* in the *Zweiundzwanzigste Lection* of Georg Philipp Telemann's *Der getreue Music-Meister* (Hamburg, 1728), a collection in which Bach's *Canon à 4* (BWV 1074) was published.

38. Burney, *The Present State of Music*, 91–92; emphasis in original. Zelter, *Karl Friedrich Christian Fasch*, 46, also reports, from his conversations with Fasch, that Frederick's dislike for church music was well known and that he once said at the opera, "the music smells of the church [*schmeckt nach der Kirche*]!"

Bach's trio sonata, with its contrapuntal "smell of the church," could be called anti-galant. This goes well beyond its surface texture. Consider, for example, Bach's treatment of galant mannerisms in the Andante, passages today widely regarded as representing Bach's concessions toward Frederick's taste.[39] These excerpts can actually be considered among the least pro-galant in the sonata. The movement does indeed open with a textbook galant-style, balanced period with parallel thirds and sixths in the upper voices and with appoggiaturas marking the phrase endings. But the gesture is immediately undermined by isolating and weirdly sequencing its various elements into overlapping phrases of irregular length; in other words, one might say the galant is "baroqued." Simultaneously, the music moves rapidly outside the ambitus to B-flat minor in the first half of the movement and E-flat minor in the second half; see the absurdly extended, parody-like sequential passage of isolated appoggiaturas at bars 20–28. As already mentioned, traveling outside the ambitus is rare in Bach's instrumental music but more common in his church music, where such movement in the flat direction is associated with negative topics in his texts. Bach's sonata employs this tonal procedure right at the point where galant gestures have been most clearly set up, interpreting and contradicting, rather than supporting, the galant melodic style—again, a highly "baroque," parodying approach, similar to that taken in the isolated galant passages in the Three-Part Fugue.[40]

39. See, for example, David, *J. S. Bach's Musical Offering*, 123; Alfred Dürr, *Im Mittelpunkt Bach* (Kassel: Bärenreiter, 1988), 55; Gerhard Herz, *Essays on J. S. Bach* (Ann Arbor: UMI Research Press, 1985), 177; Holschneider, "Johann Sebastian Bach in Berlin," 141; Kirkendale, "The Source for Bach's *Musical Offering*," 122; Hans-Joachim Schulze, "Johann Sebastian Bachs 'Musikalisches Opfer'—Bemerkungen zu seiner Geschichte und Aufführungspraxis," in *Zur Aufführungspraxis und Interpretation der Musik von Johann Sebastian Bach und Georg Friedrich Händel*, edited by Eitelfriedrich Thom (Blankenburg/Michaelstein: Kultur- und Forschungsstätte Michaelstein, 1985), 11–15; and Wolff, *Kritischer Bericht*, 105.

40. Oleskiewicz, "The Trio in Bach's Musical Offering," 87, points out that some of Quantz's flute sonatas can also modulate to very distant keys and that others

In the trio sonata, there are also subtler sorts of conflicts with galant sensibilities. Consider the stylistic mixtures and contradictions in the first Allegro, whose opening takes on the features of a French bourrée.[41] In bourrées, the first phrase is eight beats in length, preceded by an upbeat. Beat seven and the first half of beat eight constitute the primary repose, or "thesis," whereas beat three and the first half of beat four provide a preliminary resting point, or secondary thesis; beats one and two, the second half of beat four, beats five and six, and the second half of beat eight involve motion, or "arsis."[42] The eight quarter-note beats of Bach's bars 1–4 accommodate this arsic-thetic description of dance steps. The description does not map onto Bach's second phrase (also four bars in length), however, which is organized by falling sequences, each two beats in duration. The third phrase is only two bars long, and it brings the movement to its first thetic arrival on the tonic.

At the point where the traits of the French bourrée begin to fall apart (bars 5 and following), the music begins clearly to show features of Italian concerto ritornellos. Bach's concerto-style works (including many arias and some sonatas) show a predilection for a Vivaldian ritornello type containing three clearly differentiated internal divisions, now known as the *Fortspinnungstypus*. In the Vivaldian ritornello most often cultivated by Bach, the first segment (*Vordersatz*) grounds the tonality with primarily tonic and

can feature sequences on a sighing gesture. My point about the Bach trio, however, is that these two things are *combined* in a particular way that may sound like (grim) *parodying*. Oleskiewicz notes that Quantz's Sonata in G minor (QV 1:114) "features passages not unlike that of the Andante from Bach's Trio Sonata," but I confess that the two pieces do not sound much alike to me; the Quantz does not sound at all like parodying.

41. For the properties of the various dances in Bach's time, see Meredith Little and Natalie Jenne, *Dance and the Music of J. S. Bach* (Bloomington: Indiana University Press, 2001).

42. This "arsic-thetic" terminology of the ancient Greeks is adopted by Little and Jenne, *Dance and the Music of J. S. Bach*, 16.

dominant harmonies, ending on either the tonic or (more typically) the dominant. The second segment (*Fortspinnung*) is sequential, often marked with root movement by fifths. And the third segment (*Epilog*), whether involving further sequencing or other procedures, brings the ritornello to a satisfying close by way of a cadential gesture in the tonic.[43] This description maps neatly onto Bach's bars 1–10 of the sonata Allegro, where bars 1–4 are *Vordersatz*, bars 5–8 are *Fortspinnung*, and bars 9–10 are *Epilog*. Because the ten bars are tonally closed (that is, begin and end in the tonic) and their subsequent quotations are immediately surrounded by episodic material, the section acts like a concerto ritornello. The movement could therefore also be considered what German contemporaries called a *Sonate auf Concertenart* ("sonata in concerto style").[44]

The mixture of genres becomes more complex at bar 11, however, as the flute joins in, performing the entire ritornello a fifth higher, after which the ensemble moves on with episodic material derived from the three segments of the opening. In other words, this bourrée-style, concerto-style sonata movement turns out to be a fugue, one that Marpurg would have considered a "strict" fugue. At the first middle entry (some 25 bars later!), Bach piled on yet another genre reference. The new slow-moving bass line, presented with rhythmically more active counterpoints above it, corresponds to baroque cantus-firmus technique. This bass line is experienced less as a new countersubject than as a distinct melody that virtually overwhelms the fugue subject. The cantus firmus turns out, of course, to be the Royal Theme provided by Frederick.

Enlightenment thinkers would not necessarily have had anything against mixing features of so many genres in one work.

43. On formulating these categories primarily in terms of harmonic properties rather than thematic ones, see Laurence Dreyfus, *Bach and the Patterns of Invention* (Cambridge: Harvard University Press, 1996).

44. See Jeanne Swack, "On the Origins of the *Sonate auf Concertenart*," *Journal of the American Musicological Society* 46 (1993): 369–414.

Aestheticians did speak frequently and forcefully of the need for clarity in the representation of styles and genres,[45] and one straightforward way to effect this was to avoid combining them. But such mixtures were certainly tolerated and even encouraged so long as they were "agreeable" (that is, did not obscure or contradict one another). That is why eighteenth-century German composers could speak of the merits of combining certain elements of the French and Italian styles in their galant chamber music.[46]

They might have experienced some problems, however, with the mixture of styles in Bach's sonata. It is not difficult to imagine that strict fugue and cantus-firmus technique—the references closest to the surface of this music—would have been perceived as contributing to the piece's severity. The concerto and bourrée references, however, are in conflict with this *Affect.* Concertos, with their wayward episodes for soloists, are obviously much less strict than fugues and cantus-firmus pieces. But more to the point, bourrées were especially prized in the eighteenth century for their carefree character. In 1739, Johann Mattheson described its essential characteristics as: "*contentment; pleasantness* reigns; and as a result bourrées are so to speak somewhat *unconcerned, tranquil,* easy going, leisurely, and yet not at all unpleasant."[47] This was evidently also Bach's basic understanding of the bourrée, for the texts of nearly all his cantata movements written in bourrée style speak straightforwardly of carefree, joyful, and sunny matters.[48] These

45. See Ernst Cassirer, *The Philosophy of the Enlightenment* (Princeton: Princeton University Press, 1951), 275–360.

46. For insightful discussions of these and related issues, see Dreyfus, *Bach and the Patterns of Invention.*

47. Cited in Little and Jenne, *Dance and the Music of J. S. Bach,* 226, n. 2; Johann Mattheson, *Der Vollkommene Capellmeister* (Hamburg, 1739), 226 (emphasis in original).

48. See Doris Finke-Hecklinger, *Tanzcharaktere in Johann Sebastian Bachs Vokalmusik* (Trossingen: Hohner, 1970), 29–31, 135, 140–142.

associations with the bourrée conflict with the fugal and cantus-firmus styles in Bach's sonata.

The "disagreement" in this sonata movement is not limited to problems of surface *Affects*. The Royal Theme nearly drowns out the counterpoint in all the middle entries of this da capo fugue. The Royal Theme is nine bars long, whereas the fugue subject is ten. The Royal Theme therefore enters in the second bar of the middle entries. In other words, the new counterpoint seems like the principal voice of the fugue even though its entrance does not coincide with the beginning of the expositions. If the Royal Theme destroys the sense of what constitutes the subject in this fugue, it also, more subtly, obfuscates the bourrée dance steps that had been clearly accommodated at the outset by the contours of the subject's *Vordersatz*; whereas the third strand in the middle entries supports the arsic-thetic properties of the bourrée dance steps in the *Vordersatz* segments, the Royal Theme obscures them, for its arses appear on the bourrée's theses (see, for example, the first beats in bars 47 and 49).

The remaining movements of the sonata also mix various genres with opposing *Affects*. The Largo features slow-moving repeated notes in the bass (here outlining the head of the Royal Theme!), a common trait in (relaxed) galant sonatas, while the upper voices move more actively, their rhythm being organized according to the properties of the (socially formidable) French sarabande, the most difficult and sophisticated of baroque dance steps (basically outmoded by the 1740s). At the same time, this highly formal dance takes on some of the syntax of the more wayward Italian concerto style without fully conforming to its tonal procedures (*Vordersatz*, bars 1–8; *Fortspinnung*, bars 9–13; *Epilog*, bars 13–16; in the B section, there are episodes and returns of segments from the A section). The second Allegro features a highly ornamented variation of the Royal Theme as the severe chromatic subject for a dancelike but strict fugue.

Canons

If the fugues and sonata do not seem altogether closely to match Frederick's tastes and interests, Bach's often severely learned canons (contrasting with the galant canon writing of Quantz and others) must almost surely have represented an affront to Frederick's aesthetic ideals of musical composition. Enlightenment writers on music considered canons to be the most learned form of counterpoint. Many of them, not surprisingly, had little good to say about this sort of writing, calling it unnatural, unmelodious, excessively artificial, eye-oriented rather than ear-oriented, and so forth.[49] Canons were considered completely at odds with the desire for freedom of expression in music. Mattheson went so far as to label the canon with its binding rules as a "Dictator," in relation to whom "delectable variety stands completely to the wayside."[50]

Bach does not appear to have been interested in canon primarily as a form in which to demonstrate his compositional wares. He employs canon and other forms of learned counterpoint throughout his career, most commonly in his church music, on account of their association with the positive *moral* and *ethical* aspects of the first section of the Bible, "the Law" (as opposed—in Lutheranism and in much of Christianity more broadly—to this section of the Bible's purportedly negative aspects, namely, its *ceremonial* and *ritual* laws, associated with Judaism). This is, of course, the original meaning of the word *canon*: "rule," "measuring stick," or "law." Canon and other forms of learned counterpoint in Bach's music are often tied up somehow with the number ten, by reference to

49. For a survey of eighteenth-century German writers on this topic, see Peter Schleuning, *Geschichte der Musik in Deutschland—Das 18. Jahrhundert* (Reinbek: Rohwolt, 1984), 338–347.

50. Johann Mattheson, *Critica Musica* (Hamburg, 1722), 1:341, nn. (a) and (c); quoted in Schleuning, *Geschichte der Musik*, 342.

biblical law (encapsulated in the Ten Commandments). For example, ten movements (every third one) from the thirty *Goldberg Variations* are pieces of strict counterpoint (a series of canons, at the unison through ninth, followed by a quodlibet). There are ten imitative expositions in the opening chorus of the cantata *Du sollt Gott, deinen Herren, lieben* (BWV 77), whose text is based on the New Testament summary of the Law and whose accompaniment includes ten trumpet entries of phrases from the chorale "Dies sind die heilgen zehn Gebot" ("These are the holy Ten Commandments"), five of them in canon with the continuo.[51] And there are ten canons in the *Musical Offering*.

In this context, it becomes clearer how the *Musical Offering*, viewed as a whole,[52] takes on an increasingly theological character: learned contrapuntal keyboard ricercars and a learned contrapuntal sonata *da chiesa*, both employing tonal procedures uncommon in Bach's instrumental music but more familiar from his church cantatas, move to a series of ten mostly austere canons.[53]

---

51. See Herz, *Essays on J. S. Bach*, 205–217.

52. The issue of whether a collection is best performed as a whole can be separate from whether there is any value in thinking about a collection as a whole. There are instances of Bach's writing whole works that were certainly not performed at one sitting; for example, he carefully numbered the various sections in the *Christmas Oratorio* and the *Mass in B minor*. This point was made by John Butt, *Bach: Mass in B Minor* (Cambridge: Cambridge University Press, 1991), 21.

53. Warren Kirkendale, "On the Rhetorical Interpretation of the Ricercar and J. S. Bach's *Musical Offering*," *Studi Musicali* 26 (1997): 357, contends that the notion here of a series of ten canons unrelieved by other intervening styles of music would be unthinkable for Bach, as it betrays a lack of musical-artistic sensibility and an unawareness of the basic principles of rhetoric. But see, for example, the *Verschiedene Canones über die ersteren acht Fundamental-Noten vorheriger Arie* ("Various Canons on the First Eight Bass Notes of the Preceding Aria") that Bach wrote as a series into the end of his personal copy of a print of the *Goldberg Variations*; these fifteen consecutive canons (numbered 1 through 14 by Bach, with two versions of number 10) are musically less varied than the ten canons in the *Musical Offering*.

What understanding of the Law is Bach likely to have had, and to what purpose would the *Musical Offering* refer to the Law? Luther taught that the Law has two functions, the one "civil" and the other "spiritual" or "theological." The first function concerns public peace and order in the present world, and it operates through God-instituted offices of government, parents, and teachers. Humans are able to fulfill these laws and therefore also God's Law in its civil sense. The Law has another function, however, insofar as it is not understood in its political sense but in its spiritual sense, which Luther said is its true and genuine meaning. Humanity, after the Fall into sin, simply cannot fulfill the Law in its spiritual or theological sense, because doing so demands a pure heart, perfect obedience, and perfect fear and love of God—all unattainable conditions. This Law is not satisfied by outward fulfillment, since after the Fall, humans are essentially sinful (that is, they are tainted by "original sin"), no matter what their actual behavior. Here the function of the Law is to make people feel its power, recognize their sin, experience God's wrath, and be led to repentance (all of this is expressed clearly in the concluding verses of Luther's chorale "Dies sind die heilgen zehn Gebot"). The Law, however, is not God's entire word. The gospel (that is, "good news") stands alongside it. Law and gospel, according to Luther, have opposite functions, even though each contains aspects of the other. The Law condemns and makes people conscious of their inherent sinfulness, whereas the gospel preaches forgiveness of sins through Christ. The Law leads into death; the gospel proclaims eternal life (that is, "salvation") by Christ's redemption. The Law places humans under the wrath of God (what Luther calls God's "alien work"); the gospel brings grace (God's "proper work").

Bach's ten canons in the *Musical Offering* are possibly tied up with Luther's understanding of the theological function of the Law. This seems most clear from the canons that Bach provided with inscriptions. The heading above Canon 9 reads "Quaerendo invenietis," and there can hardly be any doubt that Bach is alluding to

Matthew 7 or Luke 11: *Quaerite, et invenietis* ("Seek, and you will find"). That Bach attached great importance to the notion of seeking in the *Musical Offering* is also evident from his use of the term *ricercar* (which means "to search/seek out") for the opening fugues and from his inscription "Regis Iussu Cantio Et Reliqua Canonica Arte Resoluta," spelling out RICERCAR for the canons.[54]

What humans ultimately seek, to the Lutheran mind, is salvation. Luther taught that justification cannot be attained through good works but only through faith, something itself not humanly attained but received as a gift from God. For Luther, the minimum condition for justification appears to be a recognition of one's need for grace and an appeal to God's merciful bestowal of it. This is indicated, as Reformation scholar Alister McGrath has pointed out, by Luther's numerous discussions of faith and humility but also by the extremely frequent use in his writings of verbs such as "cry out," "ask," "seek," and "knock."[55] Bach's heading for Canon 9, "Seek, and you will find," should probably not be understood only (or even primarily?) as a practical musical matter, an invitation for the reader to solve the puzzle of the second voice's entry. Rather, in the context of canonic reference to the Law, this inscription, quoted from the Bible, can also be further understood as a reminder of the theological function of the Law: recognition of sin and the need for receiving God's grace. Abraham Calov's Bible with Lutheran commentaries (Wittenberg, 1681–1682), Bach's copy of which survives

54. In Frederick's copy, however, this acrostic appears at the opposite side, which is otherwise blank, of the first page of the Three-Part Fugue. Bach's full title admits so many possible translations that it is difficult to know what it means. His inscription may also have something to do with Proverbs 25:2, which reads in the Luther Bibles of Bach's day, *Es ist GOttes Ehre, eine Sache verbergen; aber der Könige Ehre ists, eine Sache erforschen* ("It is the honor of God to conceal a matter, but it is the honor of kings to search out a matter"); my thanks to Michael Carasik for this suggestion.

55. Alister E. McGrath, *Luther's Theology of the Cross: Martin Luther's Theological Breakthrough* (Oxford: Basil Blackwell, 1985), 89.

(as is explained in more detail toward the beginning of chapter 1), also interprets Matthew's "Seek, and you will find" in terms of the need for receiving the gift of faith from God.

Two other canons are marked with inscriptions only in Frederick's copy of the collection. Canon 4 here reads, "As the notes increase, so may the fortune of the king," and Canon 5 reads, "As the notes ascend, so may the glory of the king." These two canons were clearly meant to be linked, for "king" (*Regis*) appears only once, between the two canons and, uniquely, in bold script, to serve as the last word for both of the inscriptions.[56] These two canons show a remarkable opposition between their *Affect* and their external signs of glory.[57] In the first, the dichotomy appears between the usual significance of the majestic French overture rhythms and the unmistakably melancholy tone,[58] and in the second, it appears between the evidently all-encompassing modulations and their deliberate registral finiteness.[59] Chafe concludes that Bach seems here to highlight what Walter Benjamin called the "disproportion between the unlimited hierarchical dignity with which [the monarch] is divinely invested and the humble estate of his humanity."[60]

I would like to underscore and augment Chafe's observations by focusing on a few more aspects of Canon 4 and the wording of

56. Fortune and glory were commonly linked; this is true, for example, for the character *Schicksal* in Bach's secular cantata *Angenehmes Wiederau* (BWV 30a).

57. Noted in Chafe, *Tonal Allegory*, 22–23, 213–215.

58. Chafe, *Tonal Allegory*, 23. In the absence of any prior discussion, my students have invariably experienced these two canons as having negative *Affect*, no matter how the pieces are performed.

59. Chafe's view here contradicts Douglas R. Hofstadter, who suggests that Bach relished the idea that Canon 5 could theoretically modulate upward ad infinitum to glorify the king; see Douglas R. Hofstadter, *Gödel, Escher, Bach* (New York: Basic Books, 1979), 10.

60. Chafe, *Tonal Allegory*, 23; Walter Benjamin, *The Origin of German Tragic Drama*, translated by John Osborne (London: Verso, 1977), 70.

Bach's preface to the collection. Consider first Bach's preface, which has not figured prominently in interpretive discussions of the *Musical Offering*. It is possibly somewhat peculiar that Bach sent to Frederick a printed German preface. Courtesy, in the original sense of the word, might ideally have called for a dedication in French. It is true that the work, although dedicated to Frederick, was published with a wider audience in mind. But Quantz's *Versuch einer Anweisung die Flöte traversiere zu spielen* (Berlin, 1752), likewise dedicated to Frederick and also intended for a wider audience, was published in two editions, one in German and the other in French. As mentioned earlier,[61] Frederick was apparently not altogether comfortable with the German language. At any rate, he certainly made himself clear about what he thought of German as a vehicle for intellectual discourse in his scathing essay of 1780, *De la littérature allemande*.[62] Not surprisingly, he saw to it that the *Societät der Wissenschaften* in Berlin continued publishing its proceedings in French after such groups elsewhere in the German states had decided on the vernacular.[63]

Several phrases in Bach's German preface suggest a heavily theological tone for Bach's collection. The opening sentence reads: *Ew. Majestät weyhe hiermit in tiefster Unterthänigkeit ein Musicalisches Opfer . . .* ("To your Majesty, [I] consecrate herewith, in deepest submission, a Musical Offering . . ."). Compare this wording with the similar but more conventional language of the opening sentence in the preface from Quantz's flute book, lacking the significant word

---

61. See the quotation cited in note 21.

62. I have relied on Frederick II, King of Prussia, "An Essay on German Literature: Its Defects, Their Causes, and the Means by Which They May Be Corrected," in Frederick II, King of Prussia, *Posthumous Works*, translated by Thomas Holcroft (London, 1789), 13:397–457. For a discussion of Frederick's essay and its broader contexts, particularly social ones, see Norbert Elias, *The History of Manners* (New York: Pantheon, 1978), 10–15.

63. See Eric A. Blackall, *The Emergence of German as a Literary Language 1700–75* (Ithaca: Cornell University Press, 1978), 109–111.

Opfer and using *widmen* for Bach's *weyhen: Eurer Königlichen Majestät darf ich hiermit, in tiefster Unterthänigkeit, gegenwärtige Blätter widmen* . . . ("To your Royal Majesty, may I herewith dedicate, in deepest submission, these pages . . ."). On Bach's title page, the word *Opfer* ("offering," "sacrifice") is set dramatically larger than the rest of the text, suggesting that his choice of wording is significant. The expression "musical *offering*" may not seem so meaningful in and of itself; Bach's student Lorenz Christoph Mizler, for example, refers to serenading as a *"musicalisches Opfer."*[64] Linking *weyhen* with *Opfer* in a published collection of instrumental music in the late 1740s, however, must have sounded strange.[65] For Bach to write *"consecrate* an *offering"* makes his dedication "smell of the church" right from the outset. The religious import of Bach's language is also clear from similar expressions in his Calov Bible. Consider the following excerpt from Exodus 29 (text in parentheses is Calov's commentary): "v. 37 Seven days you shall make atonement for the altar and [Bach inserted the missing word *weihen,* 'consecrate'] it (in the consecration [*Heiligung*] of the altar which occurred then for the first time so that in its use no sin would be committed and so that the gift of the altar itself would be consecrated [*geheiliget würde*]. . . . Also in memory: God did not want offerings [*das Opfer*] brought to Him in any other place but that which was consecrated [*geweihet war*])."[66]

Toward the end of his preface, Bach used some peculiar language that seems especially significant and possibly extra-heavily theological: "This resolve [to work out the Royal Theme] . . . has none other than this irreproachable intent, to glorify . . . the fame

64. Lorenz Christoph Mizler, *Musikalische Bibliothek* (Leipzig, 1752), 3:607; cited in Kirkendale, "The Source for Bach's *Musical Offering,*" 136, n. 152.

65. My thanks to Emery Snyder (Princeton University), a specialist in eighteenth-century German literature, for confirming this suspicion.

66. Translated in Howard H. Cox, ed., *The Calov Bible of J. S. Bach* (Ann Arbor: UMI Research Press, 1985), 406.

of a monarch [*den Ruhm eines Monarchen zu verherrlichen*]." Both *rühmen* and *verherrlichen* mean "to glorify," and neither one of these words by itself would seem particularly significant. But to use them together, the one as the object of the other, would in the 1740s have seemed linguistically odd in a secular dedication, especially one to Frederick the Great.[67] When Bach's text speaks of "glorifying the glory" of the king, it presumably refers to different notions of glory.

For help on this question, we can turn to the texts of Bach's surviving vocal works. The only instance there of "glorifying glory" is found in the opening chorus from the first, third, and fourth versions of the *St. John Passion* (BWV 245). The text reads (my emphasis): "Lord [*Herr*], our ruler [*Herrscher*], whose glory [*Ruhm*] is glorious [*herrlich*] in all the lands, show us through your Passion that you, the true son of God, have at all times, *even in the most serious abasement*, been glorified [*verherrlicht*]!" Like Bach's preface to the *Musical Offering*, this text links *Ruhm* with *verherrlichen*. The wording "*Ruhm* . . . *verherrlicht*" in the *St. John Passion* was presumably adopted deliberately, for the libretto otherwise quotes Psalm 8, a well-known psalm, whose text speaks of the glory of God's *Name* ("name"), not the glory of God's *Ruhm*.

The *St. John Passion* chorus reflects very clearly one of the central ideas in Lutheran theology, the notion that Christ's glorification as the king of humanity centers on his suffering on the cross. This is obviously not the place for a detailed consideration

67. My thanks again to Professor Snyder for confirming this suspicion. To give Bach's phrase in English as "to extol the fame" might seem on the face of it to be simpler and to make more sense, but, leaving aside the question of this translation's accuracy, we would need to consider how likely it is that Bach would want to extol fame (on this point, see the quotation cited in note 70). Yearsley, "The Autocratic Regimes," argues that theological language per se can *respect* monarchism, and I entirely agree. The issue, though, is not the presence of theological language per se but the presence of the run of *this particular* theological language. There is no concern here, so far as I can see, about monarchism per se; Bach's language may be questioning Frederick's (unwelcome) personal world-and-life views, not the (welcome) impersonal fact of his royal "office."

of Luther's "theology of the cross."[68] The upshot is that the only place God's glory is revealed to humans is, paradoxically, hidden in Christ's suffering on the cross and that this, in turn, provides a model for how humans ought to live.[69] This is why Bach's church cantatas can speak so often of finding joy in suffering; it is also clear from a perusal of Bach's markings in his Calov Bible that the practical applications of the theology of the cross in one's daily life were of great importance to him. For Lutherans, true knowledge of God and a right ethical attitude were not separate matters but one and the same. Seeking knowledge of God through philosophical speculation was considered to be in the same category as seeking salvation through good works. Both exalt humans to the level of God, and both use the same standard for God and for people's relationship to God: glory and power.

Regarding human notions of glory, consider also the following passage of commentary that Bach underlined in his Calov Bible: "As soon as a little success comes to us human beings, from that moment on we want the honor [*Ehre*], and soon pride [*Ehrgeitz*] overtakes us, making us believe that I have done that myself and that the nation and the people owe me their debt and we reach for the glory [*Ruhm*] that belongs solely and purely to God."[70]

Frederick, by contrast, wrote frequently and forcefully in favor of a view very much opposed to Bach's. Consider the following example, from his remarks in a letter of September 26, 1770, to

---

68. For detailed treatments, see McGrath, *Luther's Theology of the Cross*; and Walther von Loewenich, *Luther's Theology of the Cross* (Minneapolis: Augsburg Publishing House, 1976).

69. McGrath, *Luther's Theology of the Cross*, 176–181, 191, points out that twentieth-century scholars came too strongly to emphasize Luther's notion of God's hiddenness (with the devastation of war in Europe, was God *really* there?). Luther believed, however, that God's glory is *revealed* within or behind its opposite, "hidden" in the cross and suffering. McGrath does not mean to suggest that the theology of the cross was anything less than central to Lutheran theology (hence the subtitle of his study: *Martin Luther's Theological Breakthrough*).

70. Translated in Cox, *The Calov Bible*, 424.

d'Alembert: "Talents no doubt ought to be distinguished, especially when they rise to supereminence. Great minds labour only for fame, and it would be treating them severely to let them always hope for, yet never enjoy, the thing of which they are in search. The penalties annexed to all ranks of mankind can only be softened by this balm, a little of which is necessary, even to the greatest men."[71]

The theology of the cross, in contrast to Frederick's views, recognizes God in Christ's suffering and sees humans as being called to suffer, ultimately allowing God to work in them instead of seeking glory through their own acts. It is in this sense that the theology of the cross is a theology of faith; God's hidden "proper work" of grace that justifies people (the gospel) is a gift tied up with God's manifest "alien work" of wrath (the Law) that makes people recognize their worthlessness and sinfulness. And so, like the Law, glory might be said to have two senses, the one essentially spiritual and the other more worldly. Bach captured this in the St. John Passion and in the preface to the Musical Offering by using for the one verherrlichen (literally, to glorify in the sense of "to make Godlike," to suffer) and for the other rühmen (to glorify in the sense of "to make known").

Bach musically represented the spiritual glorification of worldly glory in a particularly striking and straightforward way in Canon 4 from the Musical Offering. Here the bass line points to the French overture with its traditional baroque associations of majesty and glory (see also the "Contrapunctus 6 a 4 in Stylo Francese" in Bach's print of the Art of Fugue). The realization of the canon, however, calls for augmentation and contrary motion. In its realization, the line becomes deregalized, because at half speed, the dotted rhythms can no longer give the impression of the French overture.[72] In other words, the obvious worldly glory of the original line is spiritually glorified by the canonic realization. The music,

71. Frederick II, King of Prussia, Posthumous Works, translated by Thomas Holcroft (London, 1789), 11:192–193.

72. Some performers (for example, on the well-known 1970s recording directed by Gustav Leonhardt, released on various labels and formats) assimilate overdotting

in this interpretation, hardly needs an inscription to make its point clear to a Lutheran audience. The inscription provided only in Frederick's copy, "As the notes increase, so may the fortune of the king," in this context has a rather different meaning from what is usually suggested (namely, "Vive le roi!").[73] The melancholy *Affect* and the deregalized canonic solution link regal fortune (worldly works, glory) not to splendor, might, and fame but to the theology of the cross.

Conclusion

The general message of the *Musical Offering* as interpreted here would probably not have been lost on a well-versed intellectual such as Frederick (if he even bothered to consider in any detail Bach's music and its inscriptions); and it is unlikely that Bach would have shied away from making bold statements before a king. In his Calov Bible, Bach highlighted a passage of commentary that reads: "[A preacher] need not guard his mouth nor take into view gracious

---

in the augmented voice with overdotting in the bass, so that performed thirty-second notes of the original voice become thirty-second notes in the augmented voice, too. Bernhard Kistler-Liebendörfer, *Quaerendo invenietis: Versuch über J. S. Bachs Musikalisches Opfer* (Frankfurt: Fischer, 1985), 14, also recommends this solution. One of the main reasons Kistler-Liebendörfer argues for assimilated double-dotting (and, presumably, why Leonhardt employed it) is that it softens the dissonances in a realization featuring an augmentation of the entire bass line. Bach must have meant only the first half of the bass line to be featured in the augmented realization, however, since, as few performers will have noticed from their modern editions, augmenting the entire line necessarily involves changing the 1747 print's melodic readings and rhythms. The realization works unproblematically when only the first half of the printed bass line is augmented (a solution encountered in Bach's own realizations of other augmentation canons; for the details, see Wolff, *Kritischer Bericht*, 114). I would argue that no matter which canonic realization is employed, assimilated overdotting should not be adopted, because it goes against the letter and the spirit of the augmentation and its rubric.

73. See, for example, Kirkendale, "The Source for Bach's *Musical Offering*," 107, 110; Lothar Hoffmann-Erbrecht, "Von der Urentsprechung zum Symbol: Versuch

or wrathful lords or noblemen, nor consider money, wealth, honor, or power, shame, poverty, or harm; he need not think any further than that he says what his office demands."[74] The many printed copies of the *Musical Offering* instructed not only Frederick, however, but also Bach's fellow German musicians and friends in the ways of severe learned counterpoint (as opposed to the ways of galant homophony or galant fugues and canons) and of the theology of the cross.[75] Bach, it seems, believed that in his compositional ventures, he was fulfilling the commandment of the gospel's summary of the Law ("love God, and love your neighbor as yourself"). According to Bach's understanding of the Law, loving one's neighbors implies imparting one's God-given knowledge to them. His preface to a series of organ chorales reads: *Orgel-Büchlein* . . .

einer Systematisierung musikalischer Sinnbilder," in *Bachiana et alia Musicologica: Festschrift Alfred Dürr zum 65. Geburtstag*, edited by Wolfgang Rehm (Kassel: Bärenreiter, 1983), 118; and Yearsley, "The Autocratic Regimes." The notion of this counterpoint's funereal mood *in combination* with its deregalizing augmentation working powerfully against a conventional glorification of Frederick are passed over unmentioned by Oleskiewicz, "The Trio in Bach's Musical Offering"; and by Yearsley, "The Autocratic Regimes," 172, who suggests (my emphasis) that "In the inscription to [this canon], Bach *warmly* acknowledges the monarchic program of the piece."

74. Cox, *The Calov Bible*, 444. Yearsley, "The Autocratic Regimes," registers great skepticism about the notion that Bach might be inclined to make bold statements before a king; the supporting contextual evidence, however, from Bach's highlighting of Calov is not mentioned. For more concerning the Calov Bible and connections between Bach's instrumental music and his practical understanding of theology, see Michael Marissen, *The Social and Religious Designs of J. S. Bach's Brandenburg Concertos* (Princeton: Princeton University Press, 1995).

75. Perhaps even the apparently conflicting formats of oblong and upright papers in the print of the *Musical Offering* play visually into this notion of the cross. This is not so far-fetched as it might initially sound. Consider that Bach highlighted in his Calov Bible a verse and its commentary describing how Old Testament priests took offerings [*Opfer*] and waved them back, forth, up, and down before the Lord. The commentary, remarkably, specifies that they did this "to form the cross of Jesus." See Cox, *The Calov Bible*, 406 (see also the second paragraph of 407). For another view of Bach's collection, see Joel Sheveloff, *J. S. Bach's Musical Offering: An Eighteenth-Century Conundrum* (Lewiston: Edwin Mellen Press, 2014).

Dem Höchsten Gott allein' zu Ehren, / Dem Nechsten, draus sich zu belehren ("Little Organ-Book [BWV 599–644] . . . To the Most High God alone unto Honor;[76] / To the neighbor, from which to instruct himself").[77]

Ultimately, the *Musical Offering* instructs Bach's fellow humans and, like all of his music, was designed primarily to honor God.

---

76. See Romans 9:21, *Hat nicht ein Töpfer Macht aus einem Klumpen zu machen ein Gefäß zu Ehren, und das andere zu Unehren?* ("Has not a potter power to make out of one lump [of clay] one jar unto Honor, and the second [jar] unto Dishonor?") The biblical "neighbor"—the Hebrew *rea* of Leviticus 19 and the Greek *plésion* of Matthew 5, 19, and 22, as well as Mark 12 and Luke 10—was rendered in the Luther Bibles by the word *Nächste* (which is the more standard spelling of Bach's *Nechste*), not *Nachbar.*

77. The couplet has often been cited in English as "In Praise of the Almighty's will / and for my neighbor's greater skill." This, however, is not what the lines mean.

WORKS CITED

Primary Literature

Adelung, Johann Christoph. *Grammatisch-kritisches Wörterbuch der Hochdeutschen Mundart.* Leipzig, 1793.

Adlung, Jacob. *Anleitung zu der Musikalischen Gelahrtheit.* Erfurt, 1758.

Bach, J. S. *Kantate 12: Weinen, Klagen,* edited by Arnold Schering. Zurich: Eulenberg, 1926.

Bach, J. S. *Weinen, Klagen, Sorgen, Zagen BWV 12,* edited by Ulrich Leisinger. Stuttgart: Carus, 1996.

Die Bekenntnisschriften der evangelisch-lutherischen Kirche. Göttingen: Vandenhoeck & Ruprecht, 1998.

Bugenhagen, Johann. "Historie der Zerstörung der Stadt Jerusalem." In *Leipziger Kirchen-Staat: Das ist Deutlicher Unterricht vom Gottes-Dienst in Leipzig,* 275–288. Leipzig, 1710.

Bugenhagen, Johann. "Historie von der Zerstörung der Stadt Jerusalem." In *Geistreicher Lieder-Schatz, oder Leipziger Gesang-Buch,* 282–291. Leipzig, 1724.

Bugenhagen, Johann. "Zerstörung der Stadt Jerusalem, wie sie von Josepho, Egesippo, und andern beschrieben worden." In *Vollständiges Kirchen-Buch,* 369–392. Leipzig, 1731.

Burney, Charles. *The Present State of Music in Germany, the Netherlands and United Provinces.* London, 1775.

Calov, Abraham. *Die heilige Bibel nach S. Herrn D. Martini Lutheri Deutscher Dolmetschung und Erklärung.* Wittenberg, 1681–1682.

Eusebius. *The History of the Church from Christ to Constantine,* translated by G. A. Williamson. Baltimore: Penguin Books, 1965.

Frederick II, King of Prussia [Friedrich der Große]. *Briefe über die Religion*, edited by Rudolf Neuwinger. Berlin: Nordland, 1941.

Frederick II, King of Prussia [Friedrich der Große]. "An Essay on German Literature: Its Defects, Their Causes, and the Means by Which They May Ce Corrected." In Frederick II, King of Prussia, *Posthumous Works*, vol. 13, translated by Thomas Holcroft, 397–457. London, 1789.

Frederick II, King of Prussia [Friedrich der Große]. *Posthumous Works*, vol. 11, translated by Thomas Holcroft. London, 1789.

Frederick II, King of Prussia [Friedrich der Große]. *Theologische Streitschriften*, edited by Rudolf Neuwinger. Berlin: Nordland, 1939.

Gerhard, Johann. *Erklährung der Historien des Leidens vnnd Sterbens vnsers HErrn Christi Jesu (1611)*, edited by Johann Anselm Steiger. Stuttgart-Bad Cannstatt: Frommann-Holzboog, 2002.

Josephus. *Historien und Bücher: Von alten Jüdischen Geschichten ... Vom Jüdischen Krieg, und der Stadt Jerusalem, und des gantzem Lands Zerstörung*. Tübingen, 1735.

Josephus. *The Jewish War*, translated by G. A. Williamson, revised by E. Mary Smallwood. New York: Penguin Books, 1981.

Kirchen-Buch für die Chur-Sächsischen Länder. Leipzig, 17[2]1.

"Die Konkordienformel (1577)." In *Die Bekenntnisschriften der evangelisch-lutherischen Kirche*, 737–1100. Göttingen: Vandenhoeck & Ruprecht, 1998.

Lehms, Georg Christian. *Gottgefälliges Kirchen-Opffer*. Darmstadt, 1711.

Leipziger Kirchen-Staat: Das ist Deutlicher Unterricht vom Gottes-Dienst in Leipzig. Leipzig, 1710.

Luther, Martin. "Abbildung des Pabsttums (1545)." In *D. Martin Luthers Werke: Kritische Gesamtausgabe*, vol. 54, edited by O. Clemen and J. Luther, 346–373. Weimar: Böhlau, 1928.

Luther, Martin. "Am Fünfften Sontag nach der Trifeltigkeyt— Evangelion Luce 5." In *D. Martin Luthers Werke: Kritische Gesamtausgabe*, vol. 52, *Hauspostille*, edited by Georg Buchwald, 394–404. Weimar: Böhlau, 1915.

Luther, Martin. *Colloquia oder Tischreden, so von Johann Aurifaber mit Fleiß zusammen getragen*. Halle, 1743.

Luther, Martin. *Der Dritte Teil der Bücher ... Lutheri, darin zusamen gebracht sind Christliche vnd tröstliche erklerung vnd auslegung der fürnemesten Psalmen*. Wittenberg, 1550.

Luther, Martin. "Eyn Sermon von der zerstörung Jerusalem (1525)." In *D. Martin Luthers Werke: Kritische Gesamtausgabe*, vol. 17.1, edited by Georg Buchwald, 380–399. Weimar: Böhlau, 1907.

Luther, Martin. "Fifth Sunday after Trinity." In *Dr. Martin Luther's House-Postil*, vol. 3, edited by Matthias Loy, translated by E. Schmid, 115–132. Columbus: J. A. Schulze, 1869–1884.

Luther, Martin. "Großer Katechismus (1529)." In *Die Bekenntnisschriften der evangelisch-lutherischen Kirche*, 543–733. Göttingen: Vandenhoeck & Ruprecht, 1998.

Luther, Martin. *Hauß-Postilla, Über die Sonntags- und fürnehmsten Fest-Evangelien durchs gantze Jahr.* Leipzig, 1692.

Luther, Martin. *The Large Catechism of Martin Luther*, translated by Robert H. Fischer. Philadelphia: Fortress Press, 1959.

Luther, Martin. *Lectures on Genesis: Chapters 31–37.* Vol. 6 of *Luther's Works*, edited by Jaroslav Pelikan, translated by Paul D. Pahl. St. Louis: Concordia Publishing House, 1970.

Luther, Martin. *Lectures on Romans.* Vol. 25 of *Luther's Works*, edited by Hilton C. Oswald, translated by Walter G. Tillmanns and Jacob A. O. Preus. St. Louis: Concordia Publishing House, 1972.

Luther, Martin. *Lectures on the Minor Prophets II.* Vol. 19 of *Luther's Works*, edited by Hilton C. Oswald, translated by C. Froelich. St. Louis: Concordia Publishing House, 1974.

Luther, Martin. *Lectures on Zechariah (1527).* Vol. 20 *Luther's Works*, edited by Hilton C. Oswald, translated by Walther H. Miller. St. Louis: Concordia Publishing House, 1973.

Luther, Martin. "Luther an Amsdorf, Wartburg, 13. Januar 1522." In *D. Martin Luthers Werke: Kritische Gesamtausgabe*, series 4, vol. 2, 422–24, edited by O. Clemen. Weimar: Böhlau, 1931.

Luther, Martin. "A Meditation on Christ's Passion (1519)." In *Luther's Works*, vol. 42, *Devotional Writings I*, edited by Martin O. Dietrich, translated by Martin H. Bertram, 3–14. Philadelphia: Fortress Press, 1969.

Luther, Martin. "On the Jews and Their Lies, 1543." In *Luther's Works*, vol. 47, *The Christian in Society IV*, edited by Franklin Sherman, translated by Martin H. Bertram, 123–306. Philadelphia: Fortress Press, 1971.

Luther, Martin. "On Translating: An Open Letter." In *Luther's Works*, vol. 35, *Word and Sacrament I*, edited by E. Theodore Bachmann, translated by Charles M. Jacobs and E. Theodore Bachmann, 181–202. Philadelphia: Muhlenberg Press, 1960.

Luther, Martin. *Operationes in Psalmos, 1519–21*. Vol. 5 of *D. Martin Luthers Werke: Kritische Gesamtausgabe*, edited by Ernst Thiele. Weimar: Böhlau, 1892.

Luther, Martin. "Der Prophet Sacharja ausgelegt (1527)." In *D. Martin Luthers Werke: Kritische Gesamtausgabe*, vol. 23, edited by W. Walther, 477–664. Weimar: Böhlau, 1901.

Luther, Martin. "Von den Juden und ihren Lügen (1543)." In *D. Martin Luthers Werke: Kritische Gesamtausgabe*, vol. 53, edited by F. Cohrs and O. Brenner, 412–552. Weimar: Böhlau, 1920.

Luther, Martin. "Wie das Gesetz und Euangelion recht grundlich zu unterscheiden sind . . . nach der Jenaer Gesamtausgabe (1532)." In *D. Martin Luthers Werke: Kritische Gesamtausgabe*, vol. 36, edited by Georg Buchwald, 24–42. Weimar: Böhlau, 1909.

Marpurg, Friedrich Wilhelm. *Abhandlung von der Fuge*. Berlin, 1753.

Mattheson, Johann. *Critica Musica*. Hamburg, 1722.

Mattheson, Johann. *Der Vollkommene Capellmeister*. Hamburg, 1739.

Mizler, Lorenz Christoph. *Musikalische Bibliothek*. Leipzig, 1752.

Müller, Heinrich. *Apostolische Schluß-Kette . . . Gründliche Auslegung der gewöhnlichen Sonn- und Fest-Tags-Episteln*. Frankfurt, 1687.

Müller, Heinrich. *Evangelische Schluß-Kette . . . Gründliche Außlegung der gewöhnlichen Sonntags-Evangelien*. Frankfurt, 1672.

Müller, Heinrich. *Gräber der Heiligen, Mit Christlichen Leich-Predigten*. Frankfurt, 1685.

Müller, Johannes. *Judaismus oder Jüdenthumb—Das ist: Ausführlicher Bericht von des Jüdischen Volckes Unglauben, Blindheit und Verstockung*. Hamburg, 1644.

Neumann, Werner, ed. *Sämtliche von Johann Sebastian Bach vertonte Texte*. Leipzig: VEB Deutscher Verlag für Musik, 1974.

Neumann, Werner, and Hans-Joachim Schulze, eds. *Bach-Dokumente I*. Kassel: Bärenreiter, 1963.

Neumann, Werner, and Hans-Joachim Schulze, eds. *Bach-Dokumente II*. Kassel: Bärenreiter, 1969.

Neumeister, Erdmann. *Geistliches Singen und Spielen*. Gotha, 1711.

Niedt, Friedrich Erhardt. *Musicalische Handleitung*. Hamburg, 1710–1717, rev. ed. 1721.

Olearius, Johann. *Biblische Erklärung, Darinnen, nechst dem allgemeinen Haupt-Schlüssel der gantzen heiligen Schrifft*. Leipzig, 1678–1681.

Pfeiffer, August. *Antimelancholicus, oder Melancholey-Vertreiber.* Leipzig, 1761.

Pfeiffer, August. "Von der *Excommunication* oder von dem Kirchen-Bann." In his *Evangelische Christen-Schule,* 988–1001. Leipzig, 1724.

Quantz, Johann Joachim. *Versuch einer Anweisung die Flöte traversiere zu spielen.* Berlin, 1752.

Rambach, Johann Jacob. *Betrachtung der Thränen und Seufzer Jesu Christi, In zweyen Predigten Am X. und XII. Sonntage nach Trinitatis, 1725 . . . angestellet.* Halle, 1725.

Rost, Johann Christoph. *Nachricht, Wie es, in der Kirchen zu St. Thom: allhier, mit dem Gottes Dienst . . . pfleget gehalten zu werden.* Manuscript, 1716–[1739], Archiv der ev.-luth. Thomas-Matthäi-Gemeinde Leipzig, no call number.

Scheibler, Christoph. *Aurfodina Theolog: Oder Theologische und geistliche Goldgrube.* Leipzig, 1727.

Schulze, Hans-Joachim, ed. *Bach-Dokumente III.* Kassel: Bärenreiter, 1972.

Spener, Philipp Jacob. *Gerechter Eifer wider das Antichristische Pabstthum.* Frankfurt, 1714.

Stepner, Salomon. *Inscriptiones Lipsiensis: . . . Verzeichniß allerhand denckwürdiger Vberschrifften, Grab- und Gedächtniß-Mahle in Leipzig.* Leipzig, 1675.

Telemann, Georg Philipp. *Der getreue Music-Meister.* Hamburg, 1728.

Vollständiges Kirchen-Buch. Leipzig, 1731.

[Wagner, Paul], ed. *Andächtiger Seelen geistliches Brand- und Gantz-Opfer—Das ist vollständiges Gesangbuch in Acht unterschiedlichen Theilen . . . Mit approbation der hochloblichen Theolog. Facult. alhier Zu GOttes Ehren und des Nechsten Erbauung herausgegeben.* Leipzig, 1697.

Wolff, Christoph, ed. *Johann Sebastian Bach: Musicalisches Opfer BWV 1079* [facsimile of Bach's original print]. Leipzig: Peters, 1977.

Wolff, Christoph, ed. *The New Bach Reader.* New York: W. W. Norton, 1998.

Zelter, Karl Friedrich. *Karl Friedrich Christian Fasch.* Berlin, 1801.

Secondary Literature

Ambrose, Z. Philip, trans. *The Texts to Johann Sebastian Bach's Church Cantatas.* Neuhausen-Stuttgart: Hänssler-Verlag, 1984.

Asprey, Robert B. *Frederick the Great*. New York: Ticknor & Fields, 1986.

Axmacher, Elke. *"Aus Liebe will mein Heiland sterben": Untersuchungen zum Wandel des Passionsverständnisses im frühen 18. Jahrhundert*. Neuhausen-Stuttgart: Hänssler-Verlag, 1984.

Axmacher, Elke. "Ein Quellenfund zum Text der Matthäus-Passion." *Bach-Jahrbuch* 64 (1978): 181–191.

Bauckham, Richard, and Carl Mosser, eds. *The Gospel of John and Christian Theology*. Grand Rapids: William B. Eerdmans, 2008.

Beck, Norman A. *Mature Christianity in the 21st Century: The Recognition and Repudiation of the Anti-Jewish Polemic of the New Testament*. New York: Crossroad, 1994.

Begbie, Jeremy. *Music, Modernity, and God: Essays in Listening*. New York: Oxford University Press, 2013.

Beißwenger, Kirsten. *Johann Sebastian Bachs Notenbibliothek*. Kassel: Bärenreiter, 1992.

Bell, Jr., Albert A. "Josephus and Pseudo-Hegesippus." In *Josephus, Judaism, and Christianity*, edited by Louis H. Feldman and Gohei Hata, 349–361. Detroit: Wayne State University Press, 1987.

Benjamin, Walter. *The Origin of German Tragic Drama*, translated by John Osborne. London: Verso, 1977.

Bieringer, Reimund, Didier Pollefeyt, and Frederique Vandecasteele-Vanneuville. "Wrestling with Johannine Anti-Judaism: A Hermeneutical Framework for the Analysis of the Current Debate." In *Anti-Judaism and the Fourth Gospel*, edited by Reimund Bieringer, Didier Pollefeyt, and Frederique Vandecasteele-Vanneuville, 3–37. Louisville: Westminster John Knox Press, 2001.

Bieringer, Reimund, Didier Pollefeyt, and Frederique Vandecasteele-Vanneuville, eds. *Anti-Judaism and the Fourth Gospel*. Louisville: Westminster John Knox Press, 2001.

Blackall, Eric A. *The Emergence of German as a Literary Language 1700–75*. Ithaca: Cornell University Press, 1978.

Blume, Friedrich. "Antwort von Friedrich Blume." *Musik und Kirche* 32 (1962): 153–156.

Blume, Friedrich. "J. S. Bach." In *Musik in Geschichte und Gegenwart*, vol. 1, *Aachen–Blumner*, edited by Friedrich Blume, 962–1047. Kassel: Bärenreiter, 1949–1951.

Blume, Friedrich. "Outlines of a New Picture of Bach." *Music and Letters* 44 (1963): 214–227.

Blume, Friedrich. "Umrisse eines neuen Bach-Bildes." *Musica* 16 (1962): 169–176.

Boer, Martinus C. de. "The Depiction of 'the Jews' in John's Gospel: Matters of Behavior and Identity." In *Anti-Judaism and the Fourth Gospel*, edited by Reimund Bieringer, Didier Pollefeyt, and Frederique Vandecasteele-Vanneuville, 141–157. Louisville: Westminster John Knox Press, 2001.

Bornkamm, Heinrich. "Luther's Translation of the New Testament." In *Luther: A Profile*, edited by H. G. Koenigsberger, 210–217. New York: Hill & Wang, 1973.

Brainard, Paul. "Bach as Theologian?" In *Reflections on the Sacred: A Musicological Perspective*, edited by Paul Brainard, 1–7. New Haven: Yale Institute of Sacred Music, 1994.

Brown, Raymond E. *The Death of the Messiah: A Commentary on the Passion Narratives in the Four Gospels.* New York: Doubleday, 1994.

Brown, Raymond E. *An Introduction to the Gospel of John.* New York: Doubleday, 2003.

Butler, Gregory. "The Printing History of J. S. Bach's *Musical Offering*: New Interpretations." *Journal of Musicology* 19 (2002): 306–331.

Butt, John. *Bach: Mass in B Minor.* Cambridge: Cambridge University Press, 1991.

Butt, John. "Bach's Metaphysics of Music." In *The Cambridge Companion to Bach*, edited by John Butt, 46–59. Cambridge: Cambridge University Press, 1997.

Butt, John. "'A Mind Unconscious That It Is Calculating'? Bach and the Rationalist Philosophy of Wolff, Leibniz and Spinoza." In *The Cambridge Companion to Bach*, edited by John Butt, 60–71. Cambridge: Cambridge University Press, 1997.

Cassirer, Ernst. *The Philosophy of the Enlightenment.* Princeton: Princeton University Press, 1951.

Chafe, Eric. *J. S. Bach's Johannine Theology: The St. John Passion and the Cantatas for Spring 1725.* New York: Oxford University Press, 2014.

Chafe, Eric. *Tonal Allegory in the Vocal Music of J. S. Bach.* Berkeley and Los Angeles: University of California Press, 1991.

Charlesworth, James H., ed. *Jews and Christians: Exploring the Past, Present, and Future.* New York: Crossroad, 1990.

Cohen, Shaye J. D. *The Beginnings of Jewishness: Boundaries, Varieties, Uncertainties.* Berkeley and Los Angeles: University of California Press, 1999.

Cousland, J. R. C. *The Crowds in the Gospel of Matthew.* Leiden: Brill, 2002.

Cox, Howard H., ed. *The Calov Bible of J. S. Bach.* Ann Arbor: UMI Research Press, 1985.

Criegern, Hermann von. *Katalog der Leipziger Kirchenbibliotheken.* Leipzig: Spamer, 1912.

Crockett, Charlotte Gwen. "The Berlin Flute Sonatas of Johann Joachim Quantz." Ph.D. diss., University of Texas at Austin, 1982.

Culpepper, R. Alan. "Anti-Judaism in the Fourth Gospel as a Theological Problem for Christian Interpreters." In *Anti-Judaism and the Fourth Gospel,* edited by Reimund Bieringer, Didier Pollefeyt, and Frederique Vandecasteele-Vanneuville, 61–82. Louisville: Westminster John Knox Press, 2001.

Daly, Peter M. *Literature in the Light of the Emblem: Structural Parallels between the Emblem and Literature in the Sixteenth and Seventeenth Centuries.* Toronto: University of Toronto Press, 1979.

David, Hans T. *J. S. Bach's Musical Offering.* New York: G. Schirmer, 1945.

Davies, W. D., and Dale C. Allison. *A Critical and Exegetical Commentary on the Gospel according to Saint Matthew.* Edinburgh: T. & T. Clark, 1988–1997.

Detmers, Achim. *Reformation und Judentum: Israel-Lehren und Einstellungen zum Judentum von Luther bis zum frühen Calvin.* Stuttgart: Kohlhammer, 2001.

Dreyfus, Laurence. *Bach and the Patterns of Invention.* Cambridge: Harvard University Press, 1996.

Dreyfus, Laurence. "The Triumph of 'Instrumental Melody': Aspects of Musical Poetics in Bach's *St. John Passion.*" *Bach Perspectives* 8 (2011): 96–121.

Drinker, Henry S. *Texts of the Choral Works of Johann Sebastian Bach in English Translation.* New York: Association of American Colleges, Arts Program, 1942–1943.

Dürr, Alfred. *The Cantatas of J. S. Bach: With Their Librettos in German-English Parallel Text,* translated and revised by Richard D. P. Jones. Oxford and New York: Oxford University Press, 2005.

Dürr, Alfred. *Im Mittelpunkt Bach.* Kassel: Bärenreiter, 1988.

Dürr, Alfred. *Die Kantaten von Johann Sebastian Bach.* Munich and Kassel: Deutscher Taschenbuch Verlag and Bärenreiter, 1985.

Dürr, Alfred. *Kritischer Bericht* for Johann Sebastian Bach, *Neue Ausgabe sämtlicher Werke*, series I, vol. 9, *Kantaten zum 1. Ostertag*. Kassel: Bärenreiter, 1986.

Dürr, Alfred. "Zum Wandel des Bach-Bildes: Zu Friedrich Blumes Mainzer Vortrag." *Musik und Kirche* 32 (1962): 145–152.

Elias, Norbert. *The History of Manners*. New York: Pantheon, 1978.

Erickson, Raymond. "The Early Enlightenment, Jews, and Bach." *Musical Quarterly* 94 (2011): 518–547.

Erickson, Raymond, ed. *The Worlds of Johann Sebastian Bach*. Milwaukee: Amadeus Press, 2009.

Farmer, William R. *Anti-Judaism and the Gospels*. Harrisburg: Trinity Press International, 1999.

Finke-Hecklinger, Doris. *Tanzcharaktere in Johann Sebastian Bachs Vokalmusik*. Trossingen: Hohner, 1970.

Foerster, Richard. "Die Bildnisse von Johann Hess und Cranachs 'Gesetz und Gnade.'" *Jahrbuch des Schlesischen Museums für Kunstgewerbe und Altertümer* 5 (1909): 117–143, 205–206.

Franklin, Don O. "Konvention und Invention in Kantate 46: Johann Sebastian Bachs Kantate für den 10. Sonntag nach Trinitatis." In *Hof- und Kirchenmusik in der Barockzeit: Hymnologische, Theologische und Musikgeschichtliche Aspekte*, edited by Friedhelm Brusniak and Renate Steiger, 181–205. Sinzig: Studio, 1999.

Fredriksen, Paula. *From Jesus to Christ*. New Haven: Yale University Press, 2000.

Fredriksen, Paula. "The Holy City in Christian Thought." In *City of the Great King: Jerusalem from David to the Present*, edited by Nitza Rosovsky, 74–92. Cambridge: Harvard University Press, 1996.

Gager, John G. *Reinventing Paul*. New York: Oxford University Press, 2000.

Gaines, James R. *Evening in the Palace of Reason: Bach Meets Frederick the Great in the Age of Enlightenment*. New York: Harper Perennial, 2005.

Geck, Martin. *Bach: Leben und Werk*. Reinbek: Rowohlt, 2000.

Geck, Martin. *Johann Sebastian Bach: Life and Work*, translated by John Hargraves. Orlando: Harcourt, 2006.

Guratzsch, Herwig, ed. *Vergessene altdeutsche Gemälde: 1815 auf dem Dachboden der Leipziger Nikolaikirche gefunden*. Heidelberg: Braus, 1997.

Haselböck, Lucia. *Bach Textlexikon: Ein Wörterbuch der religiösen Sprachbilder im Vokalwerk von Johann Sebastian Bach*. Kassel: Bärenreiter, 2004.

Helm, Ernest Eugene. *Music at the Court of Frederick the Great.*
Norman: University of Oklahoma Press, 1960.

Helms, Marianne. *Kritischer Bericht* for Johann Sebastian Bach, *Neue Ausgabe sämtlicher Werke,* series I, vol. 5, *Kantaten zum Epiphaniasfest bis zum 2. Sonntag nach Epiphanias.* Kassel: Bärenreiter, 1976.

Hengel, Martin. *Judaism and Hellenism: Studies in Their Encounter in Palestine during the Early Hellenistic Period,* translated by John Bowden. Philadelphia: Fortress Press, 1974.

Henze-Döhring, Sabine. *Friedrich der Große: Musiker und Monarch.* Munich: C. H. Beck, 2012.

Herz, Gerhard. *Essays on J. S. Bach.* Ann Arbor: UMI Reseach Press, 1985.

Herz, Gerhard. "Toward a New Image of Bach." *Bach* 1, no. 4 (1970): 9–27, and *Bach* 2, no. 1 (1971): 7–28.

Hoffmann-Erbrecht, Lothar. "Von der Urentsprechung zum Symbol: Versuch einer Systematisierung musikalischer Sinnbilder." In *Bachiana et alia Musicologica: Festschrift Alfred Dürr zum 65. Geburtstag,* edited by Wolfgang Rehm, 116–125. Kassel: Bärenreiter, 1983.

Hofstadter, Douglas R. *Gödel, Escher, Bach.* New York: Basic Books, 1979.

Holschneider, Andreas. "Johann Sebastian Bach in Berlin." In *Preußen, Dein Spree-Athen: Beiträge zu Literatur, Theater und Musik in Berlin,* edited by Hellmut Kühn, 135–145. Reinbek: Rowohlt, 1981.

Irwin, Joyce L. "Johann Sebastian Bach: A Musician, Not a Theologian." In *Neither Voice nor Heart Alone: German Lutheran Theology of Music in the Age of the Baroque,* 141–152. New York: Peter Lang, 1993.

Jeremias, Joachim. *Rediscovering the Parables.* New York: Scribner's, 1966.

Johnson, Luke T. "The New Testament's Anti-Jewish Slander and the Conventions of Ancient Polemic." *Journal of Biblical Literature* 108 (1989): 419–441.

Kirkendale, Ursula. "The Source for Bach's *Musical Offering*: The *Institutio Oratoria* of Quintilian." *Journal of the American Musicological Society* 33 (1980): 88–141.

Kirkendale, Warren. *Fugue and Fugato in Rococo and Classical Chamber Music.* Durham: Duke University Press, 1979.

Kirkendale, Warren. "On the Rhetorical Interpretation of the Ricercar and J. S. Bach's *Musical Offering.*" *Studi Musicali* 26 (1997): 331–376.

Kistler-Liebendörfer, Bernhard. *Quaerendo invenietis: Versuch über J. S. Bachs Musikalisches Opfer.* Frankfurt: Fischer, 1985.

Klein, Charlotte. *Anti-Judaism in Christian Theology,* translated by Edward Quinn. Philadelphia: Fortress Press, 1978.

Kunzle, David. "World Upside Down: The Iconography of a European Broadsheet Type." In *The Reversible World: Symbolic Inversion in Art and Society,* edited by Barbara A. Hancock, 39–94. Ithaca: Cornell University Press, 1978.

Kuper, Michael. "Zur Topographie der verkehrten Welt." In *Zur Semiotik der Inversion,* 10–18. Berlin: Verlag für Wissenschaft und Bildung, 1993.

Kurrelmeyer, William, ed. *Die erste Deutsche Bibel.* Tübingen: Litterarischer Verein in Stuttgart, 1904–1915.

Kusko, Bruce. "Proton Milloprobe Analysis of the Hand-Penned Annotations in Bach's Calov Bible." In *The Calov Bible of J. S. Bach,* edited by Howard H. Cox, 31–106. Ann Arbor: UMI Research Press, 1985.

Landesamt für Denkmalpflege Sachsen, ed. *Die Bau- und Kunstdenkmäler von Sachsen: Stadt Leipzig, Die Sakralbauten.* Munich and Berlin: Deutscher Kunstverlag, 1995.

Langer, Ruth. *Cursing the Christians? A History of the Birkat Haminim.* New York: Oxford University Press, 2012.

Leaver, Robin A. *Bachs Theologische Bibliothek/Bach's Theological Library.* Neuhausen-Stuttgart: Hänssler-Verlag, 1985.

Leaver, Robin A. "Bach's Understanding and Use of the Epistles and Gospels of the Church Year." *Bach* 6, no. 4 (1975): 4–13.

Leaver, Robin A. *J. S. Bach and Scripture: Glosses from the Calov Bible Commentary.* St. Louis: Concordia Publishing House, 1985.

Leaver, Robin A. *Luther on Justification.* St. Louis: Concordia Publishing House, 1975.

Lemper, Ernst-Heinz. *Die Thomaskirche zu Leipzig: Die Kirche Johann Sebastian Bachs als Denkmal deutscher Baukunst.* Leipzig: Koehler & Amelang, 1954.

Levine, Amy-Jill. "Matthew, Mark, and Luke: Good News or Bad?" In *Jesus, Judaism & Christian Anti-Judaism: Reading the New Testament after the Holocaust,* edited by Paula Fredriksen and Adele Reinhartz, 77–98. Louisville: Westminster John Knox Press, 2002.

Levine, Amy-Jill. *The Social and Ethnic Dimensions of Matthean Salvation History.* Lewiston: Edwin Mellen Press, 1988.

Levine, Amy-Jill, and Marc Zvi Brettler, eds. *The Jewish Annotated New Testament*. New York: Oxford University Press, 2011.

Little, Meredith, and Natalie Jenne. *Dance and the Music of J. S. Bach*. Bloomington: Indiana University Press, 2001.

Loewe, Andreas. *Johann Sebastian Bach's St John Passion (BWV 245): A Theological Commentary*. Leiden: Brill, 2014.

Loewenich, Walther von. *Luther's Theology of the Cross*. Minneapolis: Augsburg Publishing House, 1976.

Lohmeyer, Ernst. *Das Evangelium des Matthäus*. Göttingen: Vandenhoeck & Ruprecht, 1962.

MacCracken, Thomas G. "Die Verwendung der Blechblasinstrumente bei J. S. Bach unter besonderer Berücksichtigung der Tromba da tirarsi." *Bach-Jahrbuch* 70 (1984): 59–89.

Manuel, Frank. *The Broken Staff: Judaism through Christian Eyes*. Cambridge: Harvard University Press, 1992.

Marissen, Michael. *Bach's Oratorios—The Parallel German-English Texts, with Annotations*. New York: Oxford University Press, 2008.

Marissen, Michael. "Blood, People, and Crowds in Matthew, Luther, and Bach." *Lutheran Quarterly* 19 (2005): 1–22.

Marissen, Michael. "The Character and Sources of the Anti-Judaism in Bach's Cantata 46." *Harvard Theological Review* 96 (2003): 63–99.

Marissen, Michael. *Lutheranism, Anti-Judaism, and Bach's St. John Passion*. New York: Oxford University Press, 1998.

Marissen, Michael. "More Source-Critical Research on J. S. Bach's *Musical Offering*." *Bach* 25, no. 1 (1994): 11–27.

Marissen, Michael. "Perspectives on the 'St. John Passion' and the Jews." *New York Times*, Sunday Arts & Leisure section, April 2, 2000.

Marissen, Michael. *The Social and Religious Designs of J. S. Bach's Brandenburg Concertos*. Princeton: Princeton University Press, 1995.

Marissen, Michael. *Tainted Glory in Handel's Messiah*. New Haven: Yale University Press, 2014.

Marissen, Michael. "The Theological Character of J. S. Bach's *Musical Offering*." In *Bach-Studies 2*, edited by Daniel R. Melamed, 85–106. Cambridge: Cambridge University Press, 1995.

Marschall, Rick. *Johann Sebastian Bach*. Nashville: Thomas Nelson, 2011.

McGrath, Alister E. *Iustitia Dei: A History of the Christian Doctrine of Justification*. Cambridge: Cambridge University Press, 1998.

McGrath, Alister E. *Luther's Theology of the Cross: Martin Luther's Theological Breakthrough*. Oxford: Basil Blackwell, 1985.

Melamed, Daniel R., and Michael Marissen. *An Introduction to Bach Studies*. New York: Oxford University Press, 1998.

Mendelssohn Bartholdy, Gustav. *Der König: Friedrich der Große in seinen Briefen und Erlassen*. Ebenhausen bei München: Langewiesche-Brandt, 1912.

Meyer, Ulrich. *Biblical Quotation and Allusion in the Cantata Libretti of Johann Sebastian Bach*. Lanham: Scarecrow Press, 1997.

Neubrand, Maria. "Das Johannesevangelium und 'die Juden.'" *Theologie und Glaube* 99 (2009): 205–217.

Nirenberg, David. *Anti-Judaism: The Western Tradition*. New York: W. W. Norton, 2012.

Nirenberg, David. *Neighboring Faiths: Christianity, Islam, and Judaism in the Middle Ages and Today*. Chicago: University of Chicago Press, 2014.

Oberman, Heiko A. *The Roots of Anti-Semitism in the Age of Renaissance and Reformation*, translated by James I. Porter. Philadelphia: Fortress Press, 1984.

Oehler, K. Eberhard. "Die Historie von der Zerstörung Jerusalems." *Jahrbuch für Liturgik und Hymnologie* 38 (1999): 88–98.

Oleskiewicz, Mary. "The Trio in Bach's Musical Offering: A Salute to Frederick's Tastes and Quantz's Flutes?" *Bach Perspectives* 4 (1999): 79–110.

Pelikan, Jaroslav. *Bach among the Theologians*. Philadelphia: Fortress Press, 1986.

Petzoldt, Martin. *Bach-Kommentar*, vol. 1, *Die Geistlichen Kantaten des 1. bis 27. Trinitatis-Sonntages*. Kassel: Bärenreiter, 2004.

Petzoldt, Martin. "Bachs Prüfung vor dem Kurfürstlichen Konsistorium zu Leipzig." *Bach-Jahrbuch* 84 (1998): 19–30.

Petzoldt, Martin. *"Texte zur Leipziger Kirchen-Musik": Zum Verständnis der Kantatentexte Johann Sebastian Bachs*. Wiesbaden: Breitkopf & Härtel, 1993.

Petzoldt, Martin. "Zur Theologie der Kantate BWV 46 'Schauet doch und sehet, ob irgendein Schmerz sei': Entwurf zum Vortrag in Arolsen, 5./6. Juni 1998." Unpublished paper. *Tagung der*

Internationalen Arbeitsgemeinschaft für theologische Bachforschung, Bad Arolsen, Germany, June 6–8, 1998.

Pseudo-Hegesippus. *Vom Jüdischen Krieg*. Tübingen, 1735.

Reinhartz, Adele. *Befriending the Beloved Disciple: A Jewish Reading of the Gospel of John*. New York: Continuum, 2001.

Reinhartz, Adele. "Introduction and Annotations: The Gospel According to John." In *The Jewish Annotated New Testament*, edited by Amy-Jill Levine and Marc Zvi Brettler, 152–196. New York: Oxford University Press, 2011.

Reinhartz, Adele. "'Jews' and Jews in the Fourth Gospel." In *Anti-Judaism and the Fourth Gospel*, edited by Reimund Bieringer, Didier Pollefeyt, and Frederique Vandecasteele-Vanneuville, 213–227. Louisville: Westminster John Knox Press, 2001.

Reinhold, Josef. "Jüdischer Messebesuch und Wiederansiedlung von Juden in Leipzig im 18. und frühen 19. Jahrhundert." In *Judaica Lipsiensia: Zur Geschichte der Juden in Leipzig*, edited by Manfred Unger, 12–27. Leipzig: Edition Leipzig, 1994.

Rolf, Ares. "Die Besetzung des sechsten Brandenburgischen Konzerts." *Bach-Jahrbuch* 84 (1998): 171–181.

Rolf, Ares. *J. S. Bach, Das sechste Brandenburgische Konzert: Besetzung, Analyse, Entstehung*. Dortmund: Klangfarben Musikverlag, 2002.

Saisselin, Rémy Gilbert. *The Enlightenment against the Baroque: Economics and Aesthetics in the Eighteenth Century*. Berkeley and Los Angeles: University of California Press, 1992.

Saldarini, Anthony J. *Matthew's Christian-Jewish Community*. Chicago: University of Chicago Press, 1994.

Sandmel, Samuel. *A Jewish Understanding of the New Testament*. New York: KTAV Publishing House, 1974.

Schade, Günter, ed. *Kunst der Reformationszeit*. Berlin: Henschelverlag Kunst und Gesellschaft, 1983.

Schleuning, Peter. *Geschichte der Musik in Deutschland—Das 18. Jahrhundert*. Reinbek: Rohwolt, 1984.

Schmidt, Johann Michael. *Die Matthäus-Passion von Johann Sebastian Bach: Zur Geschichte ihrer religiösen und politischen Wahrnehmung und Wirkung*. Stuttgart: Kohlhammer, 2013.

Schmidt, Ph. *Die Illustrationen der Lutherbibel 1522–1700*. Basel: Reinhardt, 1962.

Schneider, Wolfgang. *Leipzig: Streifzüge durch die Kulturgeschichte*. Leipzig: Gustav Kiepenhauer, 1995.

Schöne, Albrecht. *Emblematik und Drama im Zeitalter des Barock.* Munich: C. H. Beck, 1993.

Schulenberg, David. "'Musical Allegory' Reconsidered: Representation and Imagination in the Baroque." *Journal of Musicology* 12 (1995): 203–239.

Schulze, Hans-Joachim. "Bach in the Early Twenty-first Century." In *The Worlds of Johann Sebastian Bach,* edited by Raymond Erickson, 291–305. Milwaukee: Amadeus Press, 2009.

Schulze, Hans-Joachim. "Johann Sebastian Bachs 'Musikalisches Opfer'—Bemerkungen zu seiner Geschichte und Aufführungspraxis." In *Zur Aufführungspraxis und Interpretation der Musik von Johann Sebastian Bach und Georg Friedrich Händel,* edited by Eitelfriedrich Thom, 11–15. Blankenburg/Michaelstein: Kultur- und Forschungsstätte Michaelstein, 1985.

Schürer, Emil. *The History of the Jewish People in the Age of Jesus Christ (175 B.C.–A.D. 135),* revised and edited by Geza Vermes and Fergus Millar. Edinburgh: T. & T. Clark, 1973–1987.

Schütz, Adalbert. "Zur Deutung des Musikalischen Opfers (Joh. Seb. Bach und Friedrich der Große)." *Wort und Dienst: Jahrbuch der Theologischen Schule Bethel* 6 (1959): 170–179.

Schweitzer, Albert. *J. S. Bach.* Leipzig: Breitkopf & Härtel, 1908.

Schweitzer, Albert. *The Mysticism of Paul the Apostle.* New York: Seabury, 1968; German orig. 1930.

Scribner, Robert W. *For the Sake of Simple Folk: Popular Propaganda for the German Reformation.* Oxford: Clarendon Press, 1994.

Segal, Alan F. *Paul the Convert.* New Haven: Yale University Press, 1990.

Sheridan, Ruth. "Issues in the Translation of οἱ Ἰουδαῖοι in the Fourth Gospel." *Journal of Biblical Literature* 132 (2013): 671–695.

Sheveloff, Joel. *J. S. Bach's Musical Offering: An Eighteenth-Century Conundrum.* Lewiston: Edwin Mellen Press, 2014.

Smend, Friedrich. *Johann Sebastian Bach: Kirchen-Kantaten.* Berlin: Christlicher Zeitschriftenverlag, 1947–1949.

Smend, Friedrich. "Was bleibt? Zu Friedrich Blumes Bach-Bild." *Der Kirchenmusiker* 13 (1962): 178–188.

Sommer, Michael S. *Battles between Windmills: "Heresy" and "Orthodoxy" in Johannine Interpretation.* Oxford: Michael S. Sommer, 2011.

Spalding, Keith. *An Historical Dictionary of German Figurative Usage.* Oxford: Basil Blackwell, 1952–2000.

Spitta, Philipp. *Johann Sebastian Bach.* Leipzig, 1873–1880.

Stapert, Calvin R. *J. S. Bach*. Oxford: Lion Hudson, 2009.

Steiger, Lothar. "Affekt und Leidenschaft in biblischer Streitkultur oder daß unsere Unfähigkeit zu streiten, z.b. dies über 'Antijudaismus' zu tun, nicht zuletzt darin seinen Grund hat, daß wir nicht mehr von der Hermeneutica sacra der Frühen Neuzeit wissen, weshalb die folgende Erörterung hier zu orten ist—Eine freundliche Entgegnung auf Michael Marissen, 'Blood, People, and Crowds in Matthew's Gospel, Luther's New Testament, and Bach's St. Matthew Passion Libretto.'" In *Passion, Affekt und Leidenschaft in der Frühen Neuzeit*, edited by Johann Anselm Steiger, 2:585–590. Wiesbaden: Harrassowitz Verlag, 2005.

Steiger, Renate. "Bach und Israel." *Musik und Kirche* 50 (1980): 15–22.

Steiger, Renate. *Gnadengegenwart: Johann Sebastian Bach im Kontext lutherischer Orthodoxie und Frommigkeit*. Stuttgart-Bad Cannstatt: Frommann-Holzboog, 2002.

Steiger, Renate. "Johann Sebastian Bachs Kantaten zum 10. Sonntag nach Trinitatis und die Frage nach dem Antijudaismus." In *Festschrift Georg Christian Macholz zum 70. Geburtstag*, edited by Angelika Berlejung and Arndt Meinhold, 283–323. Neukirchen-Vluyn: Neukirchener-Verlag, 2004.

Steiger, Renate. "Methode und Ziel einer musikalischen Hermeneutik im Werke Bachs." *Musik und Kirche* 47 (1977): 209–224.

Steiger, Renate, ed. *Theologische Bachforschung heute: Dokumentation und Bibliographie der Internationalen Arbeitsgemeinschaft für theologische Bachforschung 1976–96*. Glienicke and Berlin: Galda and Walch, 1998.

Steiger, Renate. "'Die Welt ist euch ein Himmelreich': Zu J. S. Bachs Deutung des Pastoralen." *Musik und Kirche* 41 (1971): 1–8, 69–79.

Steiger, Renate. "'Wo soll ich fliehen hin?': Das Lied und Bachs Kantate BWV 5—Theologische und musikalische Akzente in J. S. Bachs Passionen." In *"Wie freudig ist mein Herz, da Gott versöhnet ist": Die Lehre von der Versöhnung in Kantaten und Orgelchorälen von Johann Sebastian Bach*, edited by Renate Steiger, 37–104. Heidelberg: [no publisher], 1995.

Stendahl, Krister. *Final Account: Paul's Letter to the Romans*. Philadelphia: Fortress Press, 1976.

Stiehl, Herbert. "Das Innere der Thomaskirche zur Amtszeit Johann Sebastian Bachs." *Beiträge zur Bachforschung* 3 (1984): 5–96.

Stokes, Richard, trans. *Johann Sebastian Bach: The Complete Church and Secular Cantatas*. Ebrington: Long Barn Books, 1999.

Strathmann, Hermann. *Das Evangelium nach Johannes*. Göttingen: Vandenhoeck und Ruprecht, 1968.

Strecker, Georg. "Das Geschichtsverständnis des Matthäus." In *Das Matthäus-Evangelium*, edited by Joachim Lange, 326–349. Darmstadt: Wissenschaftliche Buchgesellschaft, 1980.

Strecker, Georg. *Der Weg der Gerechtigkeit: Untersuchung zur Theologie des Matthäus*. Göttingen: Vandenhoeck & Ruprecht, 1971.

Swack, Jeanne. "On the Origins of the *Sonate auf Concertenart*." *Journal of the American Musicological Society* 46 (1993): 369–414.

Terry, Charles Sanford. *Joh. Seb. Bach: Cantata Texts, Sacred and Secular; with a Reconstruction of the Leipzig Liturgy of His Period*. London: Constable, 1926.

Thouret, Georg. *Friedrich der Große als Musikfreund und Musiker*. Leipzig, 1898.

Thouret, Georg. "Die Musik am preußischen Hofe im 18. Jahrhundert." *Hohenzollern-Jarhbuch* 1 (1897): 49–70.

Trebilco, Paul. *Self-Designations and Group Identity in the New Testament*. Cambridge: Cambridge University Press, 2012.

Unger, Melvin P. *Handbook to Bach's Sacred Cantata Texts*. Lanham: Scarecrow Press, 1996.

Van Leeuwen, Raymond C. "Proverbs 30:21–23 and the Biblical World Upside Down." *Journal of Biblical Literature* 105 (1986): 599–610.

Vermes, Geza. *The Religion of Jesus the Jew*. Minneapolis: Fortress Press, 1993.

Wallman, Johannes. "Johann Sebastian Bach und die 'Geistlichen Bücher' seiner Bibliothek." *Pietismus und Neuzeit* 12 (1986): 162–181.

Walter, Meinrad. *Musik—Sprache des Glaubens: Studien zum geistlichen Vokalwerk Johann Sebastian Bachs*. Frankfurt: Verlag Josef Knecht, 1994.

Wengert, Timothy J. *Human Freedom, Christian Righteousness: Philip Melanchthon's Exegetical Dispute with Erasmus of Rotterdam*. New York: Oxford University Press, 1998.

Wiemer, Wolfgang. *Die wiederhergestellte Ordnung in Johann Sebastian Bachs Kunst der Fuge*. Wiesbaden: Breitkopf & Härtel, 1977.

Wolff, Christoph. *Bach: Essays on His Life and Music*. Cambridge: Harvard University Press, 1991.

Wolff, Christoph. *Kritischer Bericht* for Johann Sebastian Bach, *Neue Ausgabe sämtlicher Werke*, series VIII, vol. 1, *Kanons/Musikalisches Opfer*. Kassel: Bärenreiter, 1976.

Wolff, Christoph. *The New Grove Bach Family.* New York: W. W. Norton, 1983.

Wolff, Christoph. "New Research on Bach's *Musical Offering.*" *Musical Quarterly* 57 (1971): 379–408.

Wolff, Christoph. "Der Terminus 'Ricercar' in Bachs Musikalischem Opfer." *Bach-Jahrbuch* 53 (1967): 70–81.

Wolff, Christoph. "Überlegungen zum 'Thema Regium.'" *Bach-Jahrbuch* 59 (1973): 33–38.

Wright, N. T. *Christian Origins and the Question of God*, vol. 2, *Jesus and the Victory of God*. Minneapolis: Fortress Press, 1996.

Yearsley, David. *Bach and the Meanings of Counterpoint.* Cambridge: Cambridge University Press, 2002.

INDEX OF BACH'S WORKS

INDEX OF BIBLICAL AND OTHER ANCIENT SOURCES

Hebrew Scriptures / Old Testament

1 Chronicles 6:39 156n9
2 Chronicles 5:12 156n9
Daniel 9:26 118n116
Deuteronomy 13:6–10 140
Ecclesiastes 7:7 54
Ecclesiastes 10:12a 91n64
Exodus 12:48 162n7
Exodus 24:8 184
Exodus 29:37 219
Exodus 34:6 120n122
Ezekiel 16:36–37 54
Ezekiel 26:4–5 57
Ezekiel 26:14 57
Genesis 4 182
Genesis 19:24–28 117n115
Genesis 25:23 184
Genesis 27:13 182–184
Genesis 29:11 18
Genesis 32:26 42
Genesis 32:31 177
Genesis 43:30 18
Genesis 46:29 18
Hosea 2:5 85

Hosea 5:1 57
Isaiah 1:9 117n115
Isaiah 10:22–23 90
Isaiah 11:9 105
Isaiah 21:9 105
Isaiah 23:13 105
Isaiah 24–25 105n89
Isaiah 25:2–3 104–106, 120n121
Isaiah 30:1 88n57
Isaiah 49:8 92n66
Isaiah 52:13 153
Isaiah 56:7 93n72
Jeremiah 2:19 117n113
Jeremiah 18:2–6 174
Jeremiah 19:1–11 174
Jeremiah 21:8 16n17
Jeremiah 23:3 120n121
Jeremiah 23:6 120n121
Jeremiah 30:23 100
Jeremiah 31:3 33
Jeremiah 32:6–15 174
Job 30:11 57
Jonah 3:3 116n112

Deuterocanonical Books / Apocrypha

New Testament

Lost Gospels

Mishnah and Talmud

Josephus

INDEX OF NAMES AND SUBJECTS